TRIALBOOK

THIRD EDITION

TRIALBOOK

THIRD EDITION

John Sonsteng

and

Roger Haydock

NATIONAL INSTITUTE FOR TRIAL ADVOCACY

Address inquiries to:

Reproduction Permission
National Institute for Trial Advocacy
361 Centennial Parkway, Suite 220
Louisville, CO 80027
(800) 225-6482 Fax (720) 890-4860
permission@nita.org

ISBN 978-1-60156-104-6
FBA1104

Printed in the United States.

To

All those who toil in the courtrooms pursuing justice
and our NITA colleagues who have inspired and taught us

R.H.

J.S.

INTRODUCTION

Trialbook consists of five chapters:

Chapter One—Planning to Win: Effective Preparation

Chapter Two—Motion Practice, Opening Statements, and Final Arguments

Chapter Three—Examining Witnesses: Direct, Cross, and Expert Examination

Chapter Four—Objections and Exhibits

Chapter Five—Jury Trials

The *Trialbook* provides a systematic approach to the preparation and presentation of a case. This book is designed to be a primer, an advocacy refresher, and a resource manual.

This book can be used in all dispute resolution forums, including courts, arbitrations, and administrative hearings. The materials apply to all types of cases, including civil and criminal cases.

The format of this notebook has been designed to be flexible. You can create your own Trialbook by using a binder or laptop files and electronic forms. The *Trialbook* allows you to incorporate copies of rules, statutes, cases, and other materials and create one source for all your advocacy information. Forms have been provided that act as a guide to the planning and organization of a case. You may create one general trial notebook or specific notebooks for individual cases, or a combination of notebooks.

Advocates at all levels of experience will find this *Trialbook* useful. Novice advocates have, in one readily available source, the information they need to prepare and present a case. Experienced advocates can use this book to refresh their approaches and augment what they already know. We encourage you to adapt it to your own use and make it a part of your everyday practice. You may revise, add, or delete sections and develop your own approach.

Chapter One explains how to efficiently and economically prepare and plan a case. Chapter Two describes how to conduct effective opening presentations and closing summations. Chapter Three explains how to conduct successful direct and cross-examination of witnesses, including experts. Chapter Four summarizes and analyzes evidentiary objections and exhibits. Chapter Five explains jury selection and jury instruction.

Advocacy is an exciting, challenging, anxious, and often frustrating experience. The *Trialbook* will assist you in becoming the best advocate you can be. We wish you the best.

JOHN SONSTENG

ROGER HAYDOCK

ACKNOWLEDGMENTS

This *Trialbook* represents a joint effort by many individuals who suggested ideas, made revisions, encouraged us, and assisted us in a variety of ways.

The students, staff, and faculty at William Mitchell College of Law deserve special acknowledgement. They have provided us with support and invaluable assistance.

We also acknowledge those individuals who assisted us in earlier editions of the *Trialbook*. Our publisher and editors at NITA also deserve our thanks. We owe much to our colleagues, clients, students, friends, and families. Without them the *Trialbook* would not be.

Caldene Bonde provided invaluable assistance in layout, design, format, and word processing. Her humor and advice kept us going.

CONTENTS

Section 2: Planning Before the Case

Chapter Two. Motion Practice, Opening Statements, and Final Arguments

Section 1: Motion Practice

Chapter Three. Examining Witnesses: Direct, Cross, and Expert Examination

Section 1: Direct Examination

Chapter Four. Objections and Exhibits

Section 1: Objection Procedures

Chapter Five. Jury Trials

Section 1: Selecting the Jury

Section 2: Instructing the Jury

Disk Contents

CHAPTER ONE

PLANNING TO WIN: EFFECTIVE PREPARATION

SECTION 1: ADVOCATING A CASE

A. SCOPE

Trialbook provides an efficient and useful system to review the advocacy theories, strategies, tactics, procedures, and techniques involved in judicial, administrative, and arbitration forums. The *Trialbook* contains suggestions, ideas, and approaches that work for many advocates. It provides a structure and system to add new approaches to develop and maintain a trial book on a laptop, in a desktop computer, or on printed or written pages in a binder.

B. THE PROFESSIONAL ADVOCATE

1.01 Why Be an Advocate?

The goal is to win. This goal, however, must be kept in perspective, for the end does not justify all means. Successful advocates use all reasonable tactics and techniques to present a case while being governed by and balancing the best interests of clients, rules, ethics, common sense, and the public interest.

1.02 How to Be an Advocate

An effective advocate is a counselor, investigator, facilitator, negotiator, dreamer, artist, psychologist, historian, and theater director. Creativity, imagination, intuition, reasoning, logic, discipline, and the ability to predict what may happen are critical skills.

1.03 Characterizing the Advocate

Character and personality influence the approach to advocacy. Integrity, honesty, fairness, sensitivity, and respect for others are essential. An advocate who can be trusted will be effective.

1.04 Enjoying Advocacy

Live a balanced life and enjoy the work of being an advocate. Reflect on the reasons for taking a case and expectations. Maintain a proper relationship with the client, don't worry about matters that can't be altered, expect personal disruptions, discuss feelings with family members, monitor workload, exercise, avoid alcohol and drugs, discuss the case with a colleague, and celebrate the end of the case regardless of the outcome.

C. HOW TO BE PERSUASIVE

1.05 Primacy and Recency

People generally remember best that which they hear first and last. The doctrine of primacy and recency applies to all stages of a case. Begin and end strong with the best evidence and strongest arguments.

1.06 Reasonable Repetition

The more times individuals perceive something, the more likely they will remember and believe it. Evidence and arguments that are repeated a reasonable number of times increase the chances of recall and belief. What constitutes reasonable depends on the circumstances.

1.07 The Rule of Three

Trials and arbitration allow three opportunities to tell the story—outline what happened (opening statement), explain what happened (evidence), and summarize what happened (final argument). Tell them what you're going to tell them, tell them, and tell them what you told them.

1.08 Expanding the Senses

Studies demonstrate that individuals remember a much larger percent of what they both see and hear compared to what they just hear. People remember more if they participate in the decision-making process. People need to be actively engaged in order to understand and make a decision. Mixing images from exhibits and words from testimony help decision makers understand and remember key facts and points.

1.09 Requiring Thought and Analysis

Judges, arbitrators, and jurors think about the case presentations and analyze the facts. They should conclude that favorable witnesses are telling the truth and that the arguments presented reach the right conclusion. If they reach these conclusions on their own—helped by the advocate—they will adopt them as their own.

1.10 Using Emotion Effectively

The emotions inherent in a case should be used effectively. Advocates need to create an atmosphere in which the fact finders are affected by the appropriate emotions at the right time. Every case involves human interactions. The more the decision makers feel the human dimensions involved the more they will remember and the more likely they will understand what happened.

1.11 Impact Words

Descriptive words (e.g., "mashed," "huge," "shrieked") are more persuasive and memorable than less graphic words. Impact words should be selected carefully and should not exaggerate a position.

1.12 Visual Information

There are a variety of ways information can be visually presented during a trial or arbitration. A case may have real evidence that establishes facts in support of or in opposition to oral testimony. Facts may be presented with the aid of demonstrative evidence methods. Modern electronic devices provide alternative ways to introduce, explain, and highlight facts. These methods should be used to present a case efficiently and effectively. Their over use or misuse may overly complicate or unduly lengthen a presentation.

D. HOW TO TELL A STORY

1.13 Storytelling Techniques

Techniques employed in literature may be adapted to a case. Creating an attention-getting image, setting the scene, and providing a clear structure are important techniques in getting and keeping the fact finder's attention.

Techniques should also reflect effective storytelling approaches. The use of the spoken word and exhibits that display images can both be effective. The availability of modern technology and electronic methods can bring to life an event.

1.14 Images

Use words and descriptions that create images that accurately and vividly describe the story. The fact finder should understand the story in a positive way based on the effective use of images. People understand events through the pictures they form in their minds. Computerized displays can be very helpful in displaying images and re-creating events.

1.15 Imagination

Images must be presented to enable the fact finder to imagine aspects of a case not presented in detail. There is never enough time to present all the facts. Some details will need to be filled in (imagined) by the fact finder. These imagined facts should reflect a winning story.

1.16 Understandable Language

Clarity of expression is critical. Understandable language is preferable to legalese. Do not talk down, or talk up, to the listener. Select words that can be easily understood.

1.17 Simple Explanations

The more straightforward and simple an explanation, the more likely it will be accepted as true. The challenge is to take confusing or complicated events and present them simply so that the fact finder can understand them with minimal effort.

1.18 Avoiding Contradictions

The theory of a case must be explained in a cohesive and integrated manner. The advocate must avoid presenting contradictory positions. Alternative explanations may be appropriate as long as they are not inconsistent.

1.19 Developing Interest

Every case involves relationships, transactions, and events. It is important that these events be presented in an interesting manner through testimony, arguments, exhibits, electronic devices, and visual aids. The structure of the presentation, the use of effective communication techniques, word choice, and the use of images are important considerations.

1.20 Active Involvement of the Fact Finder

Fact finders who become mentally and emotionally engaged in a case are more likely to be interested and more likely to remember evidence. The advocate must involve the fact finder—have them ponder, react to, and sometimes wonder about the presentations.

E. HOW TO BE CONVINCING

1.21 Attention Span

Audiences have limited attention spans. A case must be presented in such a way as to make use of that limited attention. The presentation should be interesting, reasonably paced, concise, and well presented. Observe the listeners to make sure they are paying attention to the presentation. Adapt when necessary to keep their attention.

1.22 Crafting a Realistic Story

An imperfect story is more likely to be believed than one that is perfectly remembered and artificially told. It is natural and normal for people not to recall everything that happened or was said. Fact finders will more likely conclude a story is real if the witness is real and does not have a rehearsed presentation and perfect recall.

1.23 Presenting an Almost Complete Story

It may seem more effective to leave out the weak points and tell only the good parts of a story that supports the case. Witnesses may believe they should only relate helpful events and ignore or forget unhelpful circumstances. However, an honest, candid complete story is more likely to be credible.

1.24 Establishing Realism

The role of the advocate parallels that of the playwright and director. The fact finders should believe they are observers at a real event unfolding before them. Involve their minds, feelings, and emotions. Effective use of electronic hardware and computer software can help create a realistic atmosphere.

1.25 Avoiding Confusion and Weariness

It can be quite difficult to select and present the best issues and facts. There is often so much information that the challenge is to winnow it down to the essential facts and issues that support the best opportunity to win. This can become a problem for advocates who prefer complicated and lengthy presentations that cover everything. Usually short and simple presentations are better than those that are complex, lengthy, and result in confusion.

1.26 Balancing the Presentation

The advent of computerized programs and electronic documents can be both a presentation boon or bust. If improperly used, technology can make presentations long and confusing. If underused, the advocate may lose an excellent opportunity to tell a compelling and complete story. The key is to have a balanced presentation based on the applicable issues, available information, and effective use of technology.

1.27 Identification with Fact Finder

Fact finders are more likely to believe witnesses or favor parties if they can identify with them. Similarities between fact finders and witnesses or parties help form this identification. Select factual and other similarities and present and explain them to the decision makers.

F. HOW TO APPROACH ADVOCACY

1.28 Focusing on the Decision Maker

It may seem obvious, but advocates must focus, focus, and focus on influencing the decision makers. In order for you to win the case, it is the decision makers who must be convinced. The facts and witnesses must be presented in a way that will influence the decision makers. Do not forget that the fact finders are the only audience.

1.29 Identify Values of Decision Maker

All decision makers have a set of principles and norms that guide their professional and personal lives. These values may be identified in the jury selection process or by studying and asking questions (research) about the judge/arbitrator. Decision makers are more likely to want you to win if the client's position is consistent with their values.

1.30 Match the Values of the Decision Maker to the Case

Case theories, factual conclusions, positions, and arguments should match, support, and promote the values that guide the decision maker. The facts, conclusions, positions, and arguments need to reflect the principles and norms that the decision maker believes in. To the extent possible, match the values inherent in or attendant to the case with those of the decision maker.

1.31 The "Right" Approach

Many advocates believe that they must convince the fact finder of the correctness and righteousness of their client's position by attempting to "sell" a position. Others believe that the advocate provides the fact finder with information that would lead reasonable people to come to but one conclusion. The first approach is persuasive, but may appear inappropriately biased or manipulative; the second approach allows the fact finders to reach their own conclusions based on the information the advocate presents but may appear uncertain and unsure. The approach that combines the benefits of both will be the most effective.

1.32 Being Personal

Some argue that advocates should not emphasize their professional beliefs during a case, while others argue that it is critical to establish these beliefs in a proper way. The common principle is that no matter what, the decision makers must understand that the advocate believes in the client and the case.

1.33 Being Objective

The advocate has a dual nature. An advocate is both a partisan and objective participant and should be an "objective partisan." The advocate must be perceived as being fair and presenting relevant facts and applicable law.

1.34 Being Trustworthy

The advocate who is sincere, honest, and trustworthy has a greater chance for success. Trust must be cultivated and nurtured through a case. The advocate does not have to be liked by everyone, but should be respected.

1.35 Making Mistakes

All advocates make mistakes. It is the reaction to the mistakes that increases or decreases the chances of winning. An advocate cannot let mistakes affect the presentation. Do not embarrass the client or witness when they make a mistake. Assume responsibility for mistakes.

1.36 Understanding the Fact Finder

Decision makers may have some biases and prejudices, and may be partial to one side or the other. Every fact finder develops an initial reaction to the case, and the degree to which these initial impressions develop into a firm opinion varies among fact finders. The lack of open-mindedness on the part of the fact finders affects the way an advocate presents a case. The more the advocate understands the fact finder, the more likely facts, structure, and delivery can be shaped to influence the fact finder.

1.37 Understanding Witnesses

Determine the credibility and motivation of witnesses. The range of recollections, perceptions, memory, and recall is infinite. When the advocate understands the witness, knows the witness's strengths and weaknesses, the witness can be presented in a realistic, believable way and not be called on to do too much or too little.

1.38 Understanding the Clients

Demonstrate a belief in the client and the client's case. The nature of the case and the kind of client dictate the relationship that may be displayed between an advocate and client. The advocate must understand the client and how the client will be perceived by others. The demonstrated relationship will impact how others think about the case.

G. HOW TO GET AN OVATION

1.39 Be a Good Person

An effective orator is a "good person who speaks well." An effective advocate must be a person who displays good sense, good will, and good character.

1.40 Exude Confidence

Appear confident and in control of the case. If the decision makers are unable to accept what is said or start having doubts about the case because the advocate appears uncertain, the client and the case will lose their support.

1.41 Speak Well

Effective speakers focus on the ideas and images they wish to express and evoke. A speech that is simply read from a prepared text is rarely interesting or convincing. The important points and themes may be repeated and explained as if the advocate is having a focused, sincere conversation with the fact finders.

1.42 Talk Well

The tone, volume, modulation, and pace of delivery affect the ability of the listener to pay attention. Sometimes the best thing an advocate can say is nothing. Silence is an effective way to highlight a point, gain attention, or create a transition.

1.43 Present Well

Exhibits should be selected or crafted to best present a case. The initial decision involves identifying the real and demonstrative evidence that can be used. Choices can be made regarding how that evidence can most efficiently and effectively be presented. There are a large variety of traditional and modern methods that can be employed, ranging from simple printed visual aids to dazzling computer-generated graphics. The methods used should enhance and not distract from the issues and facts.

1.44 Look . . . Well

Eye contact is critical to establishing credibility and persuasion. Speak to the audience and avoid the ineffective use of notes, which makes it difficult to make effective eye contact. Avoid using visual aids that require a fact finder to unnecessarily multi-task. It may be too confusing to force a judge, juror, or arbitrator to listen to oral testimony, observe the witness testifying, and watch the testimony highlighted on a computer screen, all while comparing it to other evidence. Maintain focus on the decision maker and make sure the decision maker understands the evidence.

1.45 Understand Body Language

Body language is a significant part of the communication process. Body language should match what is being said and communicated. Be constantly conscious of how to stand, sit, and move.

1.46 Use Gestures

Appropriate gestures make a presentation more effective. Keeping hands steady, controlling arm movements, and avoiding odd physical behavior demonstrates confidence and makes a presentation more interesting. Using visual and electronic aids can help focus attention on the facts and issues and away from distracting body language.

1.47 Look Good

Appearance is an important consideration throughout a case. A speaker's appearance often affects the listener's perceptions of that person. Comfortable, appropriate dress should conform to the customs or rules of decorum established in a jurisdiction. Clothing, hair style, and jewelry should not detract attention from the presentation.

H. BE BETTER THAN GOOD

1.48 Professional Rules of Conduct

The rules of professional conduct and state ethical rules provide a set of rules and guidelines for advocates that establish standards and impose restraints on behavior. The Model Rules of Professional Conduct, available at the ABA website, guide lawyer conduct and behavior: http://www.abanet.org/cpr/mrpc/mrpc_toc.html.

1.48.1 Abide by Client's Decisions

Model Rule 1.2(a) states that "a lawyer shall abide by a client's decisions concerning the objectives of representation and . . . shall consult with the client as to the means by which they are to be pursued." The U.S. Supreme Court has approved this rule and the following standard: "[A]n attorney's duty is to take professional responsibility for the conduct of the case after consulting with his client. . . . [S]trategic and tactical decisions are the exclusive providence of the lawyer after consulting with the client." *Jones v. Barnes*, 463 U.S. 745,753 n.6 (1983). Similar standards govern behavior in arbitrations and administrative hearings.

1.48.2 Competent Representation

The advocate must provide competent representation and act with reasonable promptness and diligence. Competency is reflected by community legal standards concerning what is acceptable and what is not acceptable representation.

1.48.3 Confidentiality

What a client tells a lawyer and the advice a lawyer gives to a client is confidential and may not be revealed unless the factual information is known by others, the client consents, or certain other situations permit or require disclosure. It is critical that a client understand that certain communications are absolutely confidential if the lawyer is to gain the trust of the client.

1.48.4 Conflict of Interest

A lawyer may not represent a client if that representation will compromise, or be compromised by the lawyer's responsibilities to another client or to a third person. If the lawyer's own interests conflict, the case should be referred elsewhere. Common sense, coupled with specific regulations explained in Model Rules 1.7 and 1.8, provide the standard for determining and dealing with conflicts.

1.48.5 Good Faith

Model Rule 3.1 states that: "A lawyer shall not bring or defend a proceeding, or assert or controvert an issue therein, unless there is a basis in law and fact for doing so that is not frivolous, which includes a good faith argument for an extension, modification or reversal of existing law." Federal Rule of Civil Procedure 11 and similar state rules contain a similar standard.

1.48.6 Expediting the Case

An advocate must make reasonable efforts, consistent with the legitimate interests of the client, to expedite a case and not delay proceedings for improper reasons. Most clients want their dispute resolved as quickly as possible, and lawyers should strive to be prompt and responsive.

1.48.7 Evidence

Model Rule 3.3(a)(3) states that: "A lawyer shall not knowingly . . . offer evidence that the lawyer knows to be false. If a lawyer . . . has offered material evidence and . . . comes to know of its falsity, the lawyer shall take reasonable remedial measures . . . ." Model Rule 3.4(a) further states that: "A lawyer shall not unlawfully obstruct another party's access to evidence or unlawfully alter, destroy or conceal a document or other material having potential evidentiary value."

1.48.8 Disclosing Controlling Authority

Model Rule 3.3(a)(2) states that: "A lawyer shall not knowingly fail to disclose to the tribunal legal authority in the controlling jurisdiction known to the lawyer to be directly adverse to the position of the client and not disclosed by opposing counsel."

1.48.9 Influencing an Official

An advocate may not seek to influence a judge, juror, or other judicial or administrative official by means prohibited by law and may not communicate ex parte with such persons unless permitted by law.

1.48.10 Do This

Model Rule 3.4(c) states that: "A lawyer shall not knowingly disobey an obligation under the rules of the tribunal except for an open refusal based on an assertion that no valid obligation exists."

1.48.11 Do Not Do This

The most egregious and outrageous misconduct by an advocate will be handled through a contempt citation. Misconduct may prompt a reprimand or other sanction from a professional responsibility board or office. It is critical for the advocate to develop and maintain a reputation as an honest, trustworthy, ethical, and professional advocate.

1.49 Constraints

Clients have limited resources. The lack of sufficient funds and time makes it impossible to do everything that could be done in a case. The client and the case will limit what should be done to prepare and present a case. The advocate and client must set priorities and must work within these limitations.

SECTION 2: PLANNING BEFORE THE CASE

A. HOW TO SELECT A CASE THEORY

A theory of the case consists of the legal theories and a summary of the essential facts. A theory of the case may be constructed by selecting the most effective legal positions and persuasive facts. The theory of the case provides the decision maker with the reasons why a client is entitled to a decision and why the decision maker will want to find in favor of a client. It should be a short, concise declarative statement.

2.01 What Is a Legal Claim or Defense?

A legal theory consists of the elements of a claim or defense supported by the facts of the case. The legal claims or defenses are based on existing law or a good-faith argument extending, modifying, or attempting to change existing law.

2.02 How to Select a Legal Theory

Select a legal theory by researching law, assessing the strengths and weaknesses of available legal theories, matching the legal theory with the facts, and selecting the best legal theory or theories that support the case.

2.03 What Is a Factual Summary?

A factual summary is a description of what happened; it is based on the evidence that is available and admissible in a case. The facts of a case will usually be susceptible to various interpretations. Factual summaries must be selected from reasonable interpretations and favorable inferences available from the evidence.

2.04 How to Compose a Factual Summary

The factual summary must contain sufficient information to survive a motion for summary judgment, judgment as a matter of law, or dismissal. It must be supported by the evidence and overcome problems of difficult proof.

2.05 How to Present Case Theories and Summaries

The selected legal theory and factual summary can be presented as a case statement. It can be enhanced with the addition of real or demonstrative evidence that helps explain it in a concise and understandable fashion.

2.06 Considerations That Apply to Legal Theories and Factual Summaries

The following factors apply to developing legal theories and factual summaries:

- Assert affirmative positions.
- Employ an approach based on common sense.
- Select a position with which the fact finder will identify.
- Use an approach that results in a fair and just decision.
- Avoid taking positions that require difficult choices.
- Use an approach that provides a basis for the admissibility of evidence adverse to the opposition.
- Select a theory and summary that contains the most persuasive and compelling legal issues and facts.
- Test the approach with colleagues.
- Use good judgment.

B. HOW TO DEVELOP A STRATEGY

2.07 Identifying the Issues

Determine what issues the fact finder must decide to reach a favorable decision. Effective advocates put themselves in the place of the fact finder.

Fact finders must decide:

- Which story to believe.
- Whether a witness is credible.
- What reasonable inferences may be drawn from the evidence.
- How to interpret and apply the law to the facts.

2.08 Determine the Evidence

Evidence must be relevant and have sufficient foundation to be admitted.

Evidence may be presented through:

- Witnesses
- Real evidence

- Demonstrative evidence
- Visual, electronic, and computer aids
- Stipulations
- Admissions
- Former testimony
- Judicial, arbitral, and administrative notice

2.09 Assess What the Fact Finder Knows

In every case, the advocates presume that fact finders understand certain information, and so refrain from introducing evidence that explains the obvious. There are certain elemental facts based on common life experiences that a fact finder will know. To prove them would be a waste of time and insulting to the fact finder. The advocate must make a common-sense determination about which facts must be explained and which can be assumed.

C. HOW TO PLAN FOR SETTLEMENT

2.10 How to Settle

Settlement requires compromise. The vast majority of civil cases settle, and criminal cases are settled by plea bargains instead of trial. The most common form of settlement is when the advocates and parties negotiate the resolution themselves. A settlement allows the parties to decide and control the outcome of the dispute.

2.11 Settlement Strategies

Effective settlement strategies, tactics, and techniques increase the opportunity for a successful resolution. Have an overall case plan and trial strategy to properly evaluate a case. Develop settlement approaches and positions to obtain the best settlement. The use and presentation of an opening statement, evidentiary summaries and exhibits, and a final argument may increase the chances of a favorable settlement. The opposing party may be impressed and persuaded by the preparations made to try a case and be more willing to settle. Specific settlement strategies and techniques can be found in a number of texts and sources on negotiations.

2.12 Mediation

Mediation is an effective way to resolve a dispute. If the parties are unable to settle it on their own, they can engage the services of an expert mediator, who uses her disinterested status to attempt to get the parties to agree to a settlement. The mediator has no power to coerce a settlement, but can use a variety of approaches to encourage and prod the parties to settle. Some courts mandate a mediation process and require the parties to talk to a mediator before proceeding with the case in court.

2.13 Fact Finding and Minitrials

Mediators can also assist the parties to settle by giving their own opinion as to the value of a case. They can conduct fact finding where they identify and evaluate the disputed facts. They can also conduct a minitrial, in which they serve as an advisory "judge" and render an opinion as to the outcome of a case. The parties can then use this information to discuss settlement.

2.14 Summary Jury Trial

A panel of prospective jurors can issue an advisory verdict in a case. The parties and their lawyers present a condensed version of the evidence to the jurors, who deliberate and render a decision that the parties can then use as a basis for settlement discussions. A summary of the evidence and arguments can be enhanced with the aid of electronic presentations and computerized programs.

2.15 Settlement Documents

In civil cases, settlement documents typically include a written settlement agreement and a stipulated dismissal with prejudice or a proposed order that requests a dismissal with prejudice. There are a variety of settlement forms the parties can obtain through online legal research. These forms can be used as a template for developing settlement documents.

D. HOW TO CHOOSE A FORUM

2.16 Available Forums

If the parties and their advocates are unable to settle a dispute on their own or through the services of a mediator, they will need to have someone else decide who will win. Some cases should not be settled because parties ought not compromise. It is these cases that will be decided in an adversarial proceeding.

There are three primary available forums:

- Courts where a judge or jury decides the case,
- Arbitrations where an arbitrator issues a final award, and
- Administrative proceedings where an administrative law judge determines an outcome.

2.17 Who Should Decide the Case?

One of the initial and critical decisions an advocate must determine is who can and who should decide the case. An advocate may be able to choose the forum and select whether the case will be decided by a judge, jury, arbitrator, or administrative judge.

There are several factors to consider in determining who is more desirable as the fact finder:

- *Nature of factual issues.* A case involving emotional or sympathy issues may be better tried before a jury than a judge/arbitrator.

- *Type of client.* The personality and nature of a client may be very appealing to a jury while a professional decision maker may not be affected by personal appeal.

- *Nature of legal theory.* If the case involves a legal issue that presents a legal technicality, a professional decision maker may be more inclined to provide a recovery.

- *Scope and methods of discovery.* The type of discoverable information may influence who should decide the case. Court rules typically allow broad discovery; arbitration rules usually allow for reasonable discovery; and administrative rules limit available discovery. Also, a case involving a lot of electronically stored information may be better handled in a federal court or by an expert arbitrator.

- *Complexity of the case.* A jury may be able to understand and decide complex cases as well as a professional decision maker. Extremely difficult issues may better be left to an expert.

- *Presentation of the case.* Trial procedures are lengthier in a jury trial and the rules of evidence are generally more strictly enforced than in other forums.

- *Effectiveness of advocate.* Whether the advocates on either side are more effective before an arbitrator, a judge, or a jury may influence the decision.

- *Preferences of client.* The client's wishes should also be considered. The client may prefer a decision reached by jurors or may prefer a judge/arbitrator.

- *Type of professional decision maker.* Some cases may be better decided by a neutral and independent private judge/arbitrator with a specific expertise.

- *Nature of potential appeal.* Appellate courts are much less likely to overturn the factual findings of a jury than those of a trial judge or administrative judge because the standards of review are higher in a jury case. The grounds for an appeal from an arbitrator's decision are limited.

- *Familiarity with counsel.* There may be situations where, either in a social or professional context, an advocate and judge/arbitrator are acquainted with one other. This may affect the choice of forum.

- *Timing of the decision.* A jury trial usually takes the longest amount of time to be completed, and an arbitration the shortest.

2.18 Who Could Decide the Case?

In criminal and most civil trial cases, the parties have a right to a trial by jury or may choose a judge to decide in a bench trial. In arbitration, parties have to agree to submit a claim or dispute to arbitration through a written predispute binding arbitration agreement or a post-dispute agreement. The case may be decided by an arbitrator or panel of arbitrators. In administrative cases, a statute or regulatory rules may require parties to proceed before an administrative judge or body.

2.19 A Jury

In federal court cases, the Seventh Amendment to the U.S. Constitution guarantees a jury trial. Similar state constitutional provisions or rules guarantee that same right in state cases. Jurisdictions vary on how a party may demand a jury trial. Federal Rule of Civil Procedure 38(b) states that a party may make a jury demand at any time after commencement of an action and within fourteen days after the close of the pleadings. In federal courts and state courts that impose a time limit for the jury demand, a party waives the right to a jury trial unless the party complies with the applicable rule.

2.20 Advisory Jury

A judge may empanel an advisory jury to render a verdict in cases in which there is no right to a jury. *See, e.g.,* FRCP 39(c). While an advisory jury is not often used, an advisory jury may be used when the judge believes that jurors will assist the court in finding the facts.

2.21 Role of Judge and Jury

In a jury trial, the judge administers the trial, manages the attorneys and the participants, rules on motions and the admissibility of evidence, instructs the jury regarding the law, issues orders, and enters judgments. In a jury trial, the jury is the fact finder. The jurors apply the law given by the judge to the facts.

2.22 Role of Arbitrator

The arbitrator is like a judge in a bench trial. A neutral and impartial arbitrator conducts the hearing, finds the facts, applies the substantive law, and issues an award based on the merits of the case.

2.23 Role of Administrative Judge

The power and authority of an administrative judge depends on the type of administrative hearing. Some administrative judges act similarly to judicial judges, others have a broader or a more restrictive role.

2.24 Role of Support Staff

Judicial personnel assist with and affect the progress of a court case. Court personnel include court administrators, court reporters, law clerks, assistants, and bailiffs. Court administrators are court clerks; court reporters record a case. A law clerk may research the law and help the judge draft memoranda and orders. An assistant to the judge performs clerical duties. The bailiff enforces order in the courtroom and is responsible for tending to the jury.

Arbitration providers commonly provide administrative support in an arbitration. They accept cases for filing, process the case, and appoint or provide clerical support to the arbitrator. They perform similar functions to court clerks. The American Arbitration Association (www.adr.org), the National Arbitration Forum (www.adrforum.com), and JAMS (www.jamsadr.com) are national arbitration organizations.

Clerks in administrative agencies typically help process an administrative law case. They also perform functions very similar to court clerks.

E. HOW TO SCHEDULE A CASE

Rules, orders, customs, and procedures govern the scheduling of a case.

2.25 Scheduling a Trial

The rules of civil procedure that apply in the jurisdiction govern how an attorney places a civil case on the trial calendar. Typically, a written demand for a jury or court trial is required, after which a case is placed on the trial calendar by the administrator or clerk of court. Criminal cases are also scheduled by the office of the administrator or clerk.

The assignment of a judge depends upon the type of calendar used by the court. There are three types of calendar systems: a master calendar system in which judges are assigned on a rotating basis; an individual calendar system with the entire case being assigned to an individual judge (also known as the block system); and a combination of these two systems.

2.26 Scheduling an Arbitration

The arbitration organization typically schedules the arbitration proceedings and hearings with a specific beginning and concluding time. The hearing occurs on a date and time certain, and the parties do not have to wait for other cases to be heard that day. Because there is no crowded court calendar, the hearing can be set promptly after discovery has been completed.

2.27 Scheduling an Administrative Hearing

Administrative hearings are typically scheduled for a specific, limited period of time by an administrator from the administrative agency. The extent of the docket depends on how soon and when a case is set for a hearing.

F. HOW TO DISQUALIFY THE DECISION MAKER

2.28 Removing a Trial Judge

Federal and state codes of judicial conduct and statutes determine when a judge must be disqualified. Personal bias, personal knowledge of disputed evidentiary facts, and personal interests are typical grounds of disqualification. A judge may also be disqualified due to illness or physical disability.

2.29 Removing a Judge for Cause

In cases where judges do not remove themselves, all jurisdictions allow attorneys to request that a judge be removed from a case for cause. An attorney must bring a motion and establish good cause for removal.

2.30 Removing a Judge without Cause

In cases where parties can remove the first judge assigned to a case without showing cause, attorneys do so in hopes that the second judge will be less biased or more favorable. In this procedure, the lawyer files a notice of removal or similar document, which must be filed promptly.

2.31 Removing an Administrative Judge

The procedures for challenging an administrative judge will be established by statute or administrative rules. These options are usually limited and available only for substantial cause.

2.32   Removing an Arbitrator

Parties may be able to mutually choose the arbitrator. An arbitration provider may also appoint a neutral, impartial arbitrator. Parties have an opportunity to refuse, remove, or challenge an appointed arbitrator. The arbitration organization appointing an arbitrator will provide the parties with information about the arbitrator or arbitrators. The parties may refuse to accept an arbitrator if a conflict of interest exists or the appointed arbitrator has objective prejudice or bias or insufficient expertise.

2.33   Removing a Juror

See Chapter Five, Section 1(J).

G.   DETERMINE THE BURDEN OF PRODUCTION, PROOF/PERSUASION, AND PRESUMPTIONS

2.34   What Is the Burden of Production?

The burden of production (also known as the burden of going forward) requires that a party produce sufficient evidence so that a reasonable fact finder could find on behalf of that party. An opposing party challenges the sufficiency of the evidence presented by bringing a motion for a directed verdict in a jury trial or a motion to dismiss in a bench, arbitration, or administrative trial. The opposing party may also challenge the sufficiency of the evidence through cross-examination, presenting evidence, and in final argument.

2.35   What Is the Burden of Proof/Persuasion?

The burden of persuasion (also known as the risk of nonpersuasion) requires a party to introduce evidence sufficient to win. There are three types of burdens:

Preponderance of the Evidence. In civil cases this burden requires a party, usually the plaintiff, to prove that it is more probable than not that the party's facts are true.

Clear and Convincing. This is a standard of proof that applies to some issues in some civil cases that involve a higher burden of proof. To satisfy this burden, a party must establish proof greater than the preponderance of evidence.

Proof Beyond a Reasonable Doubt. This is the highest of the three burdens of proof. It is the burden of proof in criminal cases. Specific instructions define this burden. All jurisdictions have jury instructions that define proof beyond a reasonable doubt.

2.36   Who Has What Burden?

The burden of production and the burden of proof for each issue in a case may be allocated between the plaintiff and defendant in four ways:

- The plaintiff has both burdens.

- The plaintiff has the burden of production, and the defense has the burden of persuasion.

- The defense has the burden of production, and the plaintiff has the burden of persuasion.

- The defendant has both burdens.

The law of a jurisdiction determines how the burdens are allocated.

2.37 Who Cares about Burdens?

The advocates care because the allocation of the burdens affects the order of the presentation of evidence and the amount of evidence necessary. The judge cares because burdens affect the instructions given to a jury. The fact finders care because the allocation of burdens affects how they view the evidence and how the law is applied to the evidence. The arbitrator or administrative law judge care because the application of the burdens may determine who wins and loses if the evidence is equally balanced.

2.38 What Are Presumptions?

A presumption is the conclusion a fact finder must reach unless contrary evidence of that conclusion has been presented. There are hundreds of legal presumptions established by statute or case law in each jurisdiction.

Presumptions have different meanings. A "trial" presumption is a rebuttable presumption. A "substantive" presumption is irrebuttable. A presumption is not the same as an inference. The difference in their effect is that an inference is permissive and a presumption is mandatory.

2.39 Effect of Burdens and Presumptions

Presumptions may have an effect on the burden of production and the burden of persuasion. The precise effect depends upon the law of the respective jurisdiction. The applicable law and proper jury instructions to be given in a case depend on the law of the jurisdiction regarding presumptions and burdens.

H. MANAGING COMPLEX CASES

2.40 What Is Complex?

Cases are complex because of complicated factual and legal issues, a lot of parties, many lawyers, collateral issues, satellite litigation, large amounts of money, huge numbers of documents, complex electronic discovery issues, or multiple jurisdictions.

2.41 Planning for Complex Cases

When planning for complex cases:

- Analyze and define issues
- Create a team
- Design a communication system for the team
- Have regular meetings and conference calls
- Establish a budget
- Have an operation headquarters
- Create an information management system
- Review the litigation hold communicated to clients for retaining all potentially relevant documents
- Develop an organization and computer system
- Develop an electronic documents filing and search system
- Determine the extent of electronically stored information
- Retain technology experts for advice and counsel
- Craft a discovery plan
- Develop a consistent team of deposition reporters
- Craft a motion practice plan
- Cooperate with insurance carriers and others outside the team
- Develop ways to deal with the media and public relations
- Maintain complete notes with up-to-date email addresses, phone numbers, and office addresses of everyone involved
- Make cost-effective and efficient preparations for travel and lodging
- Plan regular information and strategy meetings

2.42 Manual for Complex Cases

The Federal Manual for Complex Litigation may govern federal cases. It can be a guide in state actions. The manual provides procedures by which complex cases can be managed effectively and proceed efficiently.

2.43 Multi-District Litigation

The Federal Judicial Panel on Multi-District litigation considers and resolves motions to transfer cases pending in different federal judicial districts and related issues. *See* 28 U.S.C. Sec. 1407, et. seq. Once multidistrict cases are transferred, all pretrial matters including discovery and motion proceedings are conducted by the transferee court. If the cases are not resolved or settled, they are remanded to the original court for trial.

2.44 Coordinating Committees and Liaison Counsel

A coordinating committee with lead counsel administering the litigation and organizing work assignments helps organize complex litigation. Liaison counsel can coordinate communication among the court, opposing counsel, and co-counsel. Additional committees may be made up of both plaintiff and defendant lawyers to comply with "meet and confer" rules and to provide judges with proposed stipulated orders.

2.45 Joint Party Privilege Agreement

This agreement assures work that is shared among all the same parties (i.e., all defendants) remains privileged. No information that is exchanged among participants in the agreement can be disclosed outside the group without written waiver.

2.46 Document Management Systems

A document management system must effectively and efficiently provide ready access to relevant documents. Documents depositories are typically composed of electronically stored information and documents that have been scanned into or made part of a computer-based system. A search protocol makes it feasible for the advocates to locate and review relevant documents.

In creating a document management system:

- Issue a litigation hold to clients and client representatives to retain potentially relevant documents
- Monitor the litigation hold to make sure it has been communicated to the appropriate employees
- Review client document preservation policies to assure preservation
- Advise clients of the possible discovery of newly created documents
- Make sure documents are not being improperly destroyed or deleted
- Determine what paper documents exist and their location
- Determine what electronically stored information (ESI) exists
- Identify the native format of ESI and what metadata may exist
- Identify who has custody, copies of, or access to documents and ESI
- Select someone or a law firm to be in charge of gathering and preserving documents
- Select a company that creates and supports an electronic discovery depository
- Arrange for document security
- Review with in-house and outside counsel documents that may be privileged and determine status

- Determine what materials may or may not be trial-preparation materials
- Make sure proper logs are maintained for work product information

Documents must be identified by category as confidential, privileged, trial-preparation materials, or other applicable category. Documents should have a title and number and should be separated in different files or disks.

2.47 Depositories for Discovery Documents

Discovery documents must be kept in a secure depository administered by professionals. All parties and advocates can have access to this depository via password. These depositories include rooms with file cabinets or computer systems with electronically stored information and electronic documents.

2.48 Discovery Plans in Complex Cases

A specific, detailed plan based on factual and legal issues must be developed. The Manual for Complex Litigation or a discovery protocol from a previous case can be a guide. Plaintiff and defense lawyers typically work together and prepare a mutually acceptable plan offered to the judge as a stipulated order.

2.49 Confidential Discovery Responses

Federal Rule of Civil Procedure 26 and similar state rules protect against improper disclosure. The discovery information is commonly only available to the lawyers and parties who have a reason to have access to the information. A confidentiality order typically prohibits third parties from access to discovery responses.

2.50 Depositions in Complex Cases

A written protocol should address the following deposition issues:

- Scheduling
- Postponements
- Locations
- Simultaneous depositions
- Procedures for audio and video recording
- Who may be present
- Which lawyers take the deposition
- Which lawyers attend
- Duration
- Documents to be used
- Printed or electronic copies of documents

- Objections and instructions to answer
- Judicial supervision
- Reading, signing, and filing
- Indexing transcripts
- Location of deposition depository

2.51   Settlement of Complex Cases

Complex cases may be categorized as single situs or multiple situs. Single-situs cases involve many people at one place and time. Multiple-situs cases involve many people at a number of places over a period of time.

Single-situs cases may be more likely settled on a mass basis because resolution of a representative case may resolve many cases due to similar liability issues, similar damages, and other common factors. Multiple-situs cases involve more diverse liability and damage issues and more complex settlement approaches strategies based on liability and damage formulas.

The type of case will influence settlement approaches and techniques. Computer models and uniform settlement plans can assist in reaching settlement. Multi-district litigation procedures pursuant to 28 U.S.C. Sec. 1407, class procedures pursuant to FRCP 23, or similar state procedures will affect possible settlement.

2.52   Case Proceedings in Multi-Issue Cases

There are multiple issues that need to be resolved in complex case trials. Commonly, a representative case or series of representative cases are tried, and their resolutions determine the outcome of future proceedings and individual cases.

2.53   Special Masters and Judicial Adjuncts

A judge may appoint a special master in a case to serve a variety of functions. In complex cases, a special master may serve as a discovery master to resolve discovery disputes, or as a mediator to help settle a case, or as a judicial adjunct to chair committees of lawyers to reach agreement on stipulated orders, or as a technology expert regarding electronically stored information. FRCP 53 lists the types of special masters and the process used to appoint them. For an explanation of the use and availability of special masters and judicial adjuncts, see www.courtappointedmasters.org.

I. PROBLEMS, PROBLEMS, PROBLEMS

2.54 Problem Decision Makers

Occasionally, a decision maker creates problems for the advocates and parties. Any inappropriate behavior or comments should be noted in affidavits supporting a motion challenging the behavior or noted on the record of the hearing or trial when they occur.

2.55 Problem Advocates

And perhaps more often, opposing advocates create problems. Opponents may be controlled by objecting to improper conduct and seeking relief from the judge. It is best to avoid arguing with the opponent or getting drawn into similar inappropriate behavior.

2.56 Problem Witnesses

Advocates must be responsible for controlling their own witnesses. Proper witness preparation should eliminate or reduce the likelihood of a problem witness. If necessary during a hearing or trial, the examiner may admonish an uncooperative witness and seek assistance from the judge/arbitrator.

2.57 Problem Evidence

Evidence problems may arise regarding the storage and accessibility of paper and electronic documents. The native format of electronically stored information and its metadata may create preservation and introduction issues that need to be monitored or resolved.

SECTION 3: PREPARING THE CASE

A. EFFECTIVE PREPARATION

Experienced advocates share similar approaches and systems in preparing a case. This chapter summarizes commonly used effective approaches.

3.01 Develop a Trial Notebook

Preparation for a case includes the creation of a trial or hearing notebook, which may include:

- Summary of case theory
- Pleadings
- Discovery
- Motions
- Chambers discussions
- Trial brief

- Objections and applicable rules of evidence
- Jury selection
- Opening statement
- Witnesses
- Real and demonstrative exhibits
- Electronically stored information and documents
- Direct examination
- Cross-examination
- Jury instructions and verdict forms
- Final argument
- Expenses, including costs, bills, timesheets
- Trial or hearing errors

3.02 Begin with the Final Argument

The final argument occurs at the end of the case, but its composition is the first step in a thorough case preparation. The outline and content of the final argument provides a form and structure for the creation and presentation of the entire case. A final argument developed early in case preparation will undoubtedly undergo some change as the case progresses.

3.03 Be Objective

Facts and law must be assessed objectively. Advocates must put themselves in the place of the fact finder as they assess the facts, determine the credibility of witnesses, draw inferences, and prepare arguments.

3.04 Analyze the Opponent

The strong and weak points of an opponent affect the presentation of an attorney's case. Information about an opponent can be obtained from colleagues, lawyers from other firms, individuals who know the opponent, and online search engines.

Information includes:

- Degree of experience
- Skill level
- Overall demeanor
- Reputation
- Habits

- Experience with tribunal
- Nonlegal factors

3.05 Analyze the Decision Maker

Familiarity with the judge's/arbitrator's strengths and weaknesses helps an advocate present a case.

Factors that should be considered include:

- How does this judge/arbitrator usually handle proceedings?
- How does this judge/arbitrator make rulings?
- What demands or expectations does this judge/arbitrator have of advocates?
- How does this judge/arbitrator apply the rules of evidence?
- How has this judge/arbitrator tried similar cases?
- What is the educational and professional background of this judge/arbitrator?
- What is the judicial philosophy of this judge/arbitrator?

3.06 Analyze the Case

When planning a case, ask the following questions:

- What is the most effective theory?
- What are the elements of the claim or defense?
- What facts prove the elements in the case?
- What are the significant issues?
- How will the facts be proven?
- What is the most effective strategy?

B. STAGES OF THE CASE

3.07 Stages of a Civil Jury Trial

The sequence and stages of a civil jury trial:

- Pretrial conference
- Chambers discussion
- Jury selection
- Opening statement by the plaintiff

- Opening statement by the defense (the defense may reserve opening statement and present it just before the defense's case)

- Plaintiff's case

- Defendant's motion for directed verdict

- Defendant's case

- Plaintiff's rebuttal

- Motion for directed verdict or judgment as a matter of law

- Removal of alternate jurors (alternator jurors used in high-profile or lengthy trials)

- Final argument by plaintiff, followed by defendant's final argument, followed by plaintiff's rebuttal (in some jurisdictions the defense argues first, followed by the plaintiff, with no rebuttal by the defense)

- Charge/instructions to the jury

- Jury deliberations

- Verdict

- Post-trial motions

- Notice of appeal

3.08 Stages of a Criminal Jury Trial

The sequence and stages of a criminal trial:

- Pretrial conference

- Chambers discussion

- Jury selection

- Opening statement by the prosecutor

- Opening statement by the defense (the defense opening may be reserved and presented before the defense's case)

- Prosecution's case

- Defendant's case

- Defendant's motion to dismiss or for acquittal

- Prosecution rebuttal

- Renewal of defendant's motion for acquittal

- Removal of alternate jurors (alternate jurors are used in high profile or lengthy trials)

- Final argument by prosecution followed by the defense with prosecution rebuttal (in some jurisdictions, the defense proceeds first, followed by the prosecution with no defense rebuttal)
- Charge/instructions to the jury
- Jury deliberations
- Verdict
- Post-trial motions
- Notice of appeal

3.09   Stages of a Bench Trial

The stages of civil and criminal bench trials are the same as jury trials, except that there is no jury selection, jury instruction, jury deliberation, or verdict. Instead there are findings of fact, conclusions of law, and an order for judgment entered by the judge.

3.10   Stages of an Administrative Hearing

The type of administrative hearing determines the procedures and stages. Some administrative hearings are identical or similar to a bench trial. Some administrative hearing formats allow the administrative judge to act as an active participant in the presentation of the case by questioning witnesses. Another type of administrative hearing involves regulatory law, with the administrative body receiving evidence in a variety of ways.

3.11   Stages of an Arbitration

There are two types of arbitration hearings—document hearings and participatory hearings. In a document hearing, the parties submit their case in writing to the arbitrator who issues an award after a review of the written submissions. A participatory hearing resembles a bench trial. Parties attend the hearing and present their evidence through witnesses and exhibits and make arguments, with the arbitrator conducting the hearing and issuing an award after its conclusion.

C.   PRELIMINARY PROCEDURES

3.12   Pretrial/Prehearing Statements

Some judges and arbitrators require advocates to exchange written pretrial/prehearing statements that summarize aspects of the case.

Pretrial/prehearing statements typically include:

- Name and address of client
- Name and address of attorney/advocate
- Identity of any insurance carriers

- Summary of pleadings
- Issues
- Claims or defenses
- Description of discovery
- List of any pretrial/prehearing motions
- Names and addresses of witnesses
- Concise statement of the party's version of the facts
- List of all exhibits
- Issues regarding electronically stored information
- Stipulations the parties have agreed to regarding facts, procedures, or evidence
- Elements of law
- Citations to relevant statutes
- Itemized list of special damages
- Estimated length of trial or hearing
- Jury instructions

3.13 Pretrial Conference

Sometime prior to trial, the judge will order, or a party will request, a pretrial conference. *See* FRCP 16.

Conferences permit the judge to:

- Establish or clarify rules governing the trial
- Discuss settlement
- Determine issues
- Establish the order and sequence of opening and final arguments
- Estimate the time required for trial
- Inquire about exhibits
- Review electronic evidence and digital evidence presentations
- Resolve issues with electronically stored evidence
- Make arrangements for daily transcripts
- Review procedures
- Rule on any other motions or requests made by the advocates

3.14 Prehearing Administrative Conference

The existence and scope of a prehearing conference for an administrative proceeding depends on the type of the administrative process. Some administrative hearings do not use prehearing conference; others will have a conference similar to a conference before trial.

3.15 Prehearing Arbitration Conference

Arbitration parties may have an opportunity to participate in a prehearing conference with the arbitrator, similar to a pretrial hearing, often conducted through a telephone conference call.

3.16 Case Briefs

Many judges, arbitrators, and administrative agencies require advocates to submit briefs or memoranda in support of their case. The content of these briefs varies depending on the requirements of the jurisdiction. A trial or case brief may consist, in part, of short memoranda regarding various issues in the case. These submissions allow advocates to present their case theories and supporting facts and law.

D. HOW TO ACT AS AN ADVOCATE

3.17 Avoid Familiarity

The advocate should not display or take advantage of any familiarity with the judge, arbitrators, administrative hearing judges, jurors, parties, witnesses, or other counsel.

3.18 Use Appropriate Names

The judge should be addressed as "Judge," "Your Honor," or "the Court." An arbitrator may be addressed as "Arbitrator" or by surname. It is improper for advocates to address the attorneys, participants, or jurors by their first names during trial. Some witnesses, such as children, may be appropriately referred to by their first name, and some advocates may call witnesses by their first names for strategic reasons, if permitted by the rules of the jurisdiction.

3.19 Avoid Interruptions

Do not interrupt an argument, question, or response unless they are objectionable or unfairly prejudicial.

3.20 How to Approach the Witness/Bench

Do not wander around the court or hearing room, approach a witness, or approach the bench without first determining whether the judge/arbitrator requires the advocate to request permission to do so. Some do. Many do not.

3.21 Discussions Outside the Hearing of the Jury

Several events that occur during a jury trial should or must occur outside the hearing of the jury to prevent jurors from being influenced or prejudiced. *See* Federal Rule of Evidence (FRE) 103(c) and 104(c).

3.22 The Place for Bench/Sidebar Conferences

All matters to which the jurors should not be exposed should be resolved by the judge at a bench/sidebar conference. The attorneys approach the bench and talk quietly with the judge when a topic must not be heard by the jury. These bench/sidebar conferences are usually recorded by the court reporter.

3.23 Where Is Counsel Table?

In many forums, custom dictates which table is for plaintiff/prosecutor and which is for the defense. In other forums, the attorney to arrive first selects a table. In arbitrations, the arbitrator may assign places. In a jury trial, the advantage in having the table nearest the jury is that the attorney can more easily observe the jurors. The advantage of having the far table is counsel can observe the entire courtroom, including opposing counsel.

3.24 Arrange the Room

The arrangement of most courtrooms is fixed. Some judges may permit tables and lecterns to be arranged to meet the needs of the attorneys, the number of attorneys, and technology requests. Most arbitration and some administrative hearing venues are informal and may be arranged by the advocates to facilitate effective presentations. Requirements vary regarding whether an advocate should stand or sit during the various stages of a trial or hearing. At formal trials and hearings, advocates usually stand during opening and final argument and may stand or sit during witness examinations. The effective advocate considers the entire room and stands, sits, or moves as necessary to enhance the persuasiveness of the argument or witness examination.

3.25 Check Available Equipment

Court and hearing rooms typically include an easel with paper and white board and marking pens. Modern court and hearing rooms include monitors and computer access. Some rooms also have video equipment, projectors, screens, speakers, and other equipment. The advocate must determine what is available and if the equipment works. Many advocates bring the necessary equipment with them: laptops, electronically stored information devices, marking pens (permanent and dry erase), scissors, white-out, staples, staple puller, extension cords, etc.). In cases requiring more advanced technology, advocates should bring their own and set up and test the technology system in advance.

3.26 Bring Case Materials

Advocates commonly bring a variety of materials and books to the proceeding, including the case notebook, exhibits, laptop, deposition or preliminary hearing transcripts, parts of the case file, rules of evidence and procedure, and law books. They should be organized for easy access and not look cluttered so as to negatively affect the presentation.

3.27 Act Appropriately

Act with respect for the forum and all participants in the case at all times. Avoid exaggerated facial expressions, body language, head shaking, gesturing, shouting, or other inappropriate conduct that indicates disagreement or approval.

3.28 Making Requests

Any request, including requests to mark an exhibit, go "off the record," read something into the record, or take a recess, should be addressed to the judge and not to the reporter or clerk.

E. PRESENTING EVIDENCE

3.29 How to Schedule Witnesses

Witnesses should be scheduled in an efficient manner to avoid unnecessary delays. Advocates should share good-faith estimates concerning sequence, timing, and expected length of witness examinations. Witnesses should be scheduled to maximize the effectiveness of the presentation. The advocate should consider the relationship of witnesses to each other, the importance of their testimony, their ability to communicate effectively, and the most effective time of the day or week for each witness.

3.30 Subpoenaing Witnesses

Witnesses should be subpoenaed to make certain they appear to testify. Most jurisdictions require that a witness fee, established by statute, be tendered to the witness along with the subpoena. A witness who fails to abide by a subpoena may be subject to a contempt citation. *See* FRCP 45(e).

3.31 Sequestering Witnesses

The judge/arbitrator has the power to exclude or separate witnesses during a case in order to avoid witnesses influencing each other's testimony. The effectiveness of a sequestration order depends on how thoroughly the witnesses have been prepared, how familiar they are with the testimony of other witnesses, and whether the sequestration order prohibits contact with other witnesses during the trial or hearing.

3.32 Using Interpreters

A witness may need an interpreter in order to testify. Advance arrangements should be made with the tribunal.

3.33 Order of Witness Examinations

The advocate must determine the best order to examine witnesses. However, the mechanics of the proceeding and the method of interrogating witnesses are left to the discretion of the judge/arbitrator. *See* FRE 611(a).

3.34 Scope of Direct Examination

A competent witness may testify to any relevant matter unless excluded by a specific rule, statute, or case.

3.35 Scope of Cross-Examination

A witness can be cross-examined regarding any matter covered on direct examination, evidence related to credibility, or any relevant matter, even if the matter is not covered on direct examination.

3.36 Scope of Redirect, Recross, and Subsequent Examination

Redirect examination is confined to new matters brought out on cross-examination. Recross-examination is limited to matters brought out on redirect examination. Subsequent examinations are confined to the scope of matters covered during the previous examination. The judge/arbitrator has discretion to permit questions on matters not covered in previous examinations.

3.37 Scope of Rebuttal

After the defense has rested, the plaintiff/prosecutor may present additional evidence in rebuttal. The scope of this evidence is limited to those material areas covered during the defense case that were not covered during the plaintiff's case and which are not redundant. Rebuttal is limited to new and significant areas of evidence and cannot be used to repeat evidence. After the plaintiff has introduced rebuttal evidence, the defense may offer rebuttal evidence. Further rebuttal evidence may be allowed by the judge/arbitrator.

3.38 Stipulations

Stipulations present evidence in a case without calling witnesses. A stipulation is reduced to writing and signed by the advocates or made orally on the record.

3.39 Admissions

Statements made by an opposing party may be admitted as evidence against that party. The party seeking to introduce admissions must affirmatively offer them into evidence. In civil cases, admissions occur orally, in written documents, and discovery responses. In criminal cases, admissions made by the defendant may be contained in a statement or formal confession.

3.40 Former Testimony

Situations arise where witnesses are unavailable to testify during a trial or hearing. In civil cases, the previous testimony of a witness who is not available may be presented as substantive evidence. Testimony is often introduced by a video recording of a deposition or through the reading of a transcript of testimony given by unavailable witnesses, including expert witnesses. In criminal cases, former testimony is usually not admissible because of the constitutional right of the defendant to confront witnesses during the trial. *See, e.g.*, FRE 804(b)(1).

3.41 Judicial, Administrative, and Arbitral Notice

Facts that are indisputable or highly authoritative and widely accepted may be introduced through judicial, administrative, or arbitral notice. *See* FRE 201.

3.42 Evidence Summaries

Parties may stipulate to several types of summaries, including a summary of the testimony of the witness based on a deposition, a summary list of exhibits and their contents, summary outlines of information, or any other summary that makes the evidence more understandable.

3.43 Computer and Electronic Evidence

Many cases are commonly presented with the use of computer hardware and electronic software. The use of these devices and formats affects the flow of information in a case. Advocates need to prepare for their use in conjunction with the various stages of a trial, and make sure they will work as planned.

F. CAN THEY DO THIS?

3.43 Appoint Experts?

A judge may appoint an expert witness to testify in a case. Federal Rule of Evidence 706 and similar state rules govern the appointment of experts. This rule is rarely invoked because the parties commonly have experts testify.

3.45 Call Witnesses?

A judge may call a witness who has not been called by a party. Federal Rule of Evidence 614(a) and similar state rules authorize a judge to call any person as a witness, with the exception of a criminal defendant. This is rarely, if ever done, because it is not usually the role of the judge to introduce additional evidence.

3.46   Ask Questions?

A judge may question any witness. *See* FRE 614(b) and similar state rules. Advocates have a right to object to questions asked by the judge as well as to the court appointment an expert and calling a witness. *See* FRE 614(c). In jury trials, judges rarely ask questions because they leave questioning to the lawyers. In bench trials, many judges will ask questions as they are the finder of fact and may need specific information to decide a case.

3.47   Can Jurors Ask Questions?

In some courts, jurors are permitted to ask questions of witnesses. Usually the jurors submit written questions to the judge, who reviews the questions, determines if they may be asked, and reads the question. The attorneys may object to any questions asked by a juror.

3.48   What Can the Administrative Judge Do?

Administrative judges may be active or passive in a case. In some administrative hearings, it is the role of the judge to present evidence, call witnesses, and raise issues. In other hearings, the administrative judge acts in a manner similar to a trial judge or arbitrator.

3.49   What Can the Arbitrator Do?

Arbitrators may ask questions of witnesses to clarify evidence and may ask questions of parties regarding legal issues. Arbitrators typically do not raise new issues or call their own witnesses.

3.50   What about a Trial Master/Referee?

A judge may appoint a master or referee to assist with the factual or legal matters in a case. *See* FRCP 53. The judge may allocate the costs of appointing a master or referee to both parties. Special masters can be designated as trial masters, but are more often used in pretrial stages described in Chapter One, Sec. 2.53.

G.   HOW TO PRESENT A CASE TO A JUDGE/ARBITRATOR

This section discusses considerations applicable to making a presentation to a trial or administrative judge or an arbitrator.

3.51   Explain the Case

Opening statements should be made, unless the decision maker is very familiar with the issues and case. An opening statement can have a persuasive impact. It is usually helpful to present the issues that need to be resolved and a summary of the supporting facts.

Judges and arbitrators appreciate counsel explaining to them the factual and legal questions that need to be addressed and answered.

If a decision maker is familiar enough with the issues, facts, and the positions of the parties, an opening statement may not be needed. However, a brief opening may still be helpful in clarifying and emphasizing the theory of the case, important persuasive facts, and the ultimate issues.

3.52 Consider Evidentiary Rulings

The decision maker who must decide both the facts and the admissibility of evidence may have a difficult time avoiding the influence of inadmissible evidence. Fact finders are usually more inclined to admit evidence than to exclude it. When deciding whether to admit or deny the introduction of certain evidence, a decision maker must understand what the evidence is and its impact before ruling on admissibility.

3.53 Introduce Evidence

The presentation of evidence through witnesses and documents must be addressed to the fact finder as concisely and effectively as possible. Professional decision makers may not need as much background about a witness as jurors may need, but they need to hear and see all relevant facts.

The presentation of evidence involves a balanced use of witness testimony and exhibits. These exhibits may be real or demonstrative evidence. Computer software can be used to highlight these forms of evidence.

Care should be taken so that the use of visual aids does not detract from the focus of the judge/arbitrator and jurors. It can be helpful to have the decision maker follow along on a large screen with highlighted testimony. It can be confusing if the decision maker has to multitask and divide attention among the testimony, the demeanor of the witness, the visual aid, the highlighted evidence, and a trial book that contains the exhibits.

3.54 Summarize

A final argument should have a persuasive and informative impact on the decision makers and touch on their values and norms. A final argument must be presented in a way that restates the theory of the case, summarizes all important facts, applies the law to the facts, and assists and persuades the decision maker to decide in favor of the advocate's client. This information can be presented orally and with the aid of visual aids.

Be prepared for and invite the judge/arbitrator to ask questions during final argument. It's much better to know what the decision maker is thinking about the case and be able to respond directly to those concerns. Advocates can ask judges or arbitrators if they have any questions or if there are any issues they specifically want the advocate to address. Some arbitrators and administrative hearing judges prefer to have the final argument submitted in writing.

3.55   Findings of Fact and Conclusions of Law

In a bench trial, attorneys usually submit proposed findings of fact and conclusions of law to the judge after the case is ended. These submissions may also be made in administrative cases and in arbitrations. An order that includes the judgment of the judge will contain findings and conclusions, and often these statements reflect the proposed findings and conclusions submitted by the winning party.

H.   MOTIONS

In litigation, arbitrations, and administrative proceedings, motions, requests, and petitions seeking relief are submitted to the decision maker. These may be written or oral.

3.56   Motion Documents

Written motion and request documents include:

- *Notice of Motion.* The notice of motion advises all parties of the time and place of the motion hearing. An arbitration organization may schedule and give notice of a motion hearing. Anywhere from five to thirty days may be required to give timely notice of the hearing.

- *Motion.* This document explains the motion that is being brought, contains a reference to the applicable law, and states the relief sought. Some motions may also include a summary of the supportive facts.

- *Affidavits.* An affidavit is a sworn statement containing facts or opinions. An affidavit is necessary when no facts in the case have previously been submitted under oath that support the motion and the decision maker needs to review and rely on facts to grant, or deny, the motion.

- *Memorandum of Law.* Most forums require written legal authority supporting or opposing a motion/request. The submission of a persuasive memorandum of law increases the chances that the motion will be granted.

- *Proposed Order.* Most forums require submission of a proposed order by the moving party that makes clear the specific relief sought.

3.57   Opposing Motions

Generally, there is no need for the opposing advocate to bring a motion seeking to deny the relief sought in a moving party's motion. Whether the opposing party should submit any written documents depends on the rules, the timing of the motion, and strategy. Procedural rules ordinarily state whether any written opposition documents are required. It is common to provide an opposition memorandum or brief to the motion, and it may be advisable to submit opposing affidavits as well.

3.58 Trial and Hearing Motions

Many types of motions may be made before or during a trial or hearing, depending on events. For an explanation of available pretrial, trial, and post-trial motions, see David Herr, Roger Haydock, and Jeffrey Stempel, *Motion Practice, 5th Edition* (Aspen Publishing, Annual Supplements).

3.58.1 Motion to Amend Pleadings

The procedure to amend pleadings at the trial stage is commonly known as a motion to amend to conform the pleadings to the evidence. *See, e.g.,* FRCP 15(b). This amendment is ordinarily allowed if the parties expressly or impliedly consent to the evidence offered during the trial. The requirements of the motion to amend the pleadings ensure that one party does not surprise the other party at trial.

3.58.2 Motion in Limine

A motion "in limine" is usually brought to exclude from the trial the introduction of inadmissible evidence. An in limine motion may also be brought to include evidence. A motion in limine may also be brought to make sure that nothing is mentioned about a particular matter until there is further legal argument to the judge/arbitrator. An in limine motion requests an advance ruling from the judge concerning the admissibility of evidence to prevent the opposing party from offering objectionable evidence during the trial in the presence of the jury, or to avoid lengthy motions and arguments during trial. An in limine motion can be helpful in determining disputed issues relating to electronically stored information evidence.

3.58.3 Motion for Summary Judgment

A summary judgment motion is designed to resolve all or part of the issues in a case and is dispositive because the case, some of the claims, or some of the defenses are resolved by the judge because there are no disputed issues of material fact. *See* FRCP 56. Typically, a summary judgment motion is a pretrial motion and is brought before the case has been set for trial. In some instances a summary judgment motion is available when there are undisputed facts regarding one or more issues in a case. Ordinarily, summary judgment motions are written.

3.58.4 Motion to Strike

A motion to strike is a formal procedural device made during trial in reaction to some objectionable matter such as an improper question, an inadmissible answer from the witness, or some inappropriate behavior. The stricken evidence, however, remains in the record. In a jury trial, a curative instruction from the judge is often necessary and may be requested instead of, or in addition to, the motion to strike.

3.58.5 Motion for Involuntary Dismissal

In a bench trial, after the presentation of the plaintiff's evidence, the defendant may move for dismissal of the case on the ground that the plaintiff has not demonstrated a right to relief or has not proven the claims asserted. *See* FRCP 41(b). The motion for involuntary dismissal is seldom granted.

3.58.6 Motion for Directed Verdict, or Judgment as Matter of Law, or to Dismiss

In jury trials, a motion to challenge the legal sufficiency of the evidence may be brought at the close of a party's case or after the close of all the evidence. This motion may be called a motion for directed verdict, or a motion for judgment as a matter of law, or a motion to dismiss all or part of a claim. *See, e.g.,* FRCP 50. Any party may bring such a motion, which should only be made if the party has sufficient grounds to support such a motion or unless the rules of a jurisdiction require such a motion be made to preserve the opportunity to subsequently bring a motion for a judgment notwithstanding the verdict. Judges seldom grant these motions because the losing party is deprived of a jury determination on the merits and sufficient evidence has been introduced requiring the case to be decided by a jury.

3.58.7 Motion for Leave to Reopen a Case

If a motion to dismiss, or motion for judgment as matter of law, or a directed verdict motion is granted, the losing party may make a motion to reopen the case and present additional evidence. Judges usually grant this motion if the evidence is readily available and substantial.

3.58.8 Motion for Mistrial

Incidents involving significant unfairly prejudicial events may occur during trial and give rise to a motion for mistrial. The grounds for a mistrial must be so severe and uncorrectable that a party is denied a fair trial. Few cases result in a mistrial.

3.59 Additional Motions

Common motions include:

- To request a jury or court trial
- To remove or disqualify the decision maker
- To disqualify an advocate
- To strike jurors for cause

- For a court reporter to record proceedings
- To sequester witnesses
- For recess or adjournment
- To limit testimony
- To change order of witnesses
- To exclude testimony or exhibits
- To require electronic documents to be introduced in their native format or with metadata
- To make an offer of proof
- For judicial notice
- To instruct jurors
- To sequester jury
- To discharge jury
- To poll jury

Post-trial or hearing motions include:

- For judgment as a matter of law (a/k/a directed verdict)
- For judgment notwithstanding the verdict (J.N.O.V., abbreviation for the Latin term, judgment "non obstante veredicto")
- For a new trial or hearing
- For amended findings of fact or conclusions of law
- For remittiturs (decrease verdict amount)
- For additurs (increase verdict amount, not in federal court)
- For a stay of judgment
- To enforce a judgment
- For interest and costs
- For attorney's fees

I.   HOW TO MAKE A RECORD

3.60   Making the Record

The primary purpose of making a record is to establish and preserve grounds for appeal. It may also assist a fact finder in remembering facts accurately. Records are commonly made in trial and administrative hearings. Arbitration hearings often do not include a record because there is no appeal.

To preserve an error for appeal, typically the record must reflect an objection to an error in the case, a record of the ruling, an offer of proof showing what the evidence would have proved if an evidentiary objection had been sustained, a request for a curative instruction in a jury trial, and the submission of a post-trial or hearing motion to the judge.

Before an appellate court will review an error, the error must not have been cured, waived or abandoned. *See* Federal Rule of Appellate Procedure (FRAP) 10. The advocate must ensure that all rulings, orders, findings, verdicts, and judgments are entered on the record.

In judicial and administrative cases, the court supplies the reporter, who should be present for all trial and hearing proceedings, including everything that occurs in the court or hearing room and in chambers. If a judge refuses to honor the request that a reporter be made available, the advocate can ask that an independent reporter be obtained, to be paid by the client. In arbitration hearings, the parties usually provide the reporter, if there is one.

Because of recent budgetary cutbacks, some courts have reduced or eliminated the availability of court reporters for motion hearings and for some civil trials, including bench trials. Some courts use audio recorders for some civil proceedings.

3.61 Creating the Record

A losing advocate may not need or want to pay for the costs of an entire trial or hearing transcript. It is helpful to maintain a log of the transcribed proceedings to help determine what portions of the transcript should be ordered from the reporter. For proceedings that are audio recorded, those portions of the audio that are needed can be transcribed.

Exhibits are commonly part of the record and are maintained as introduced by the "custodian" of the evidence during the trial, often a court clerk. Not all exhibits will be needed for an appeal; only those referenced by the lawyers are included in the record that goes to the appellate court.

3.62 Making an Accurate Record

Advocates can assist the reporter by speaking clearly, proceeding at an appropriate pace, spelling difficult names, providing the reporter with any necessary information that helps the reporter understand the nature of the case and the identity of witnesses, not blocking the reporter's view of the witness, not speaking simultaneously with the witness, describing all conduct or events that may not appear on the record, avoiding superfluous comments, and properly referring to exhibits by number or letter. For proceedings that are audio recorded, all participants must be careful not to talk at the same time and to be sure their voices are identifiable.

SECTION 4: PLANNING AFTER THE CASE

A. SCOPE

This section covers the procedures that occur after all evidence has been introduced and the trial, arbitration, or hearing is completed.

4.01 Judicial Decisions

In a civil bench trial, the judge usually decides the case by making findings of fact and conclusions of law in writing or orally on the record. To withstand the challenge at the trial or appellate court level, findings and conclusions should accurately reflect the supporting evidence and the law. In a criminal bench trial, the judge will declare the defendant either guilty or not guilty.

4.02 Administrative Decisions

An administrative law judge issues a decision, often called an order, with an accompanying explanation of supporting reasons or findings of fact and conclusions of law. The applicable statutes or rules determine the type of decision made.

4.03 Arbitration Awards

An arbitrator issues an award after an arbitration proceeding or hearing. The award describes the relief the prevailing party has sought, which is typically money damages, but may be any form of relief, including injunctive relief. The award may be a short, summary decision or may include findings, conclusions, and reasons. The arbitrator has the power to issue an award within the scope of the agreement, the rules, and the law.

Arbitration awards can be confirmed to a judgment in either state or federal court by following the applicable statutory proceedings. After the arbitration is confirmed by a court, the award becomes a judgment and can be enforced like any other civil judgment.

B. HOW TO PRESENT POST-TRIAL AND POST-HEARING MOTIONS

After a decision, one or all parties may submit post-trial motions requesting the court to review the case.

4.04 Motion for a Judgment as a Matter of Law or a Directed Verdict

A motion for a judgment as a matter of law or as a directed verdict may be made during a trial at the close of the opponent's evidence, at the close of all the evidence, or on both occasions. This motion requests the judge to review the evidence in a light most favorable to the nonmoving party and rule that the evidence is insufficient to sustain a verdict for the opponent. *See* FRCP 50(a); FRCrimP 29(a)(b). This motion, made outside the hearing of the jury, is rarely granted because judges prefer to allow the case to go to the jury and because at this stage of the trial, sufficient evidence has been offered.

4.05 Motion for Judgment as a Matter of Law or Judgment Notwithstanding the Verdict

A motion to challenge a verdict may be brought after the jury has returned a verdict. The standard for determining whether to grant or deny this motion is identical to the previously brought motion for judgment as a matter of law or a motion for directed verdict. *See* FRCP 50(b).

4.06 Motion for New Trial or Rehearing

A party may seek a second trial if some error or misconduct regarding the law, facts, rules, or procedure occurred during the first trial. *See* FRCP 59 and FRCrimP 33. A new trial may be granted if a party was deprived of a fair trial, there was misconduct, the trial was prejudiced, material evidence has been newly discovered that could not have been discovered before, excessive or insufficient damages were awarded, errors of law occurred, the verdict is not justified, or the verdict is defective.

4.07 Rulings on Post-Trial Motions

Although they are available, post-trial motions are seldom granted because there was sufficient evidence to support the verdict or because error that occurred was harmless.

4.08 Motions to Reduce or Increase the Jury Award in Civil Cases

In some civil jury cases, the losing party or unhappy prevailing party may not want a new trial on the merits, but may want a different dollar award. Procedures known as additur (the judge increases the amount of the verdict) and remittitur (the verdict is decreased) govern the procedures. Only a remittitur is available in federal court.

4.09 Motion to Amend Court Findings and Conclusions

In a court trial, any party may move to amend the findings of fact, the conclusions of law, or an order a judge has entered. *See, e.g.,* FRCP 52. Such a motion must explain which findings are not supported by the evidence, which conclusions are not supported by the law, and why the order is improper.

4.10 Timing

When a post-trial motion must be made depends on rules of practice and procedure, which vary from jurisdiction to jurisdiction. The time available to submit post-trial motions is ordinarily limited to no more than fourteen or twenty-eight days after the verdict or after a party has been notified of the filing of the decision. *See, e.g.* FRCP 59; FRCrimP 29.

4.11 Supportive Memorandum

Submitting a supportive memorandum that explains the factual and legal grounds for the motion may be required and will increase the chances of obtaining a favorable ruling from the judge.

4.12 Stay of Entry of Judgment or Enforcement of Judgment

A losing party ordinarily needs to obtain an order from the court staying entry of judgment or the enforcement of a judgment until the post-trial motions have been decided and an appeal taken. If a stay is imposed, the court may attach appropriate conditions for the security of the winning party. *See* FRCP 58(b) and 62(a); FRCrimP 34.

4.13 Enforcing Administrative Decisions

The nature of the administrative decision determines how it is to be enforced. The statute or rules governing the administrative proceeding or other statutes control the enforceability of the administrative decision. An administrative order is usually enforceable in the same way that a judicial order is enforced.

4.14 Vacating an Arbitration Award

A losing party may seek to modify or vacate an arbitration if unusual circumstances exist. The Federal Arbitration Act, 9 U.S.C. §§ 1–15, allows an award to be challenged if the award was procured by fraud, if the arbitrator is corrupt, or if no law or facts support an award.

C. COSTS, INTEREST, AND ATTORNEY'S FEES

4.15 Costs and Expenses

A prevailing party in a case may be entitled to receive reimbursement for the costs incurred during the case. *See* FRCP 54. Recoverable expenses typically include witness fees, reasonable expert witness fees, service fees, filing fees, trial deposition expenses, the cost of transcripts used during the trial, and related expenses.

4.16 Interest

A victorious party is usually able to recover interest in a case. There are two forms of interest—prejudgment interest and post-judgment interest. The law of the jurisdiction determines what is available and the percentage of interest recoverable.

4.17 Attorney's Fees

The prevailing party is usually not entitled to recover attorney's fees. This rule, known as the American rule, prevents the winning party from recovering attorney's fees unless a statute, contractual agreement, or judicially created exception (e.g., bad faith) permits the recovery of attorney's fees.

D. CIVIL AND CRIMINAL JUDGMENTS

4.18 Entry of Civil Judgment

A judgment is not effective or enforceable until entered by the clerk or administrator. *See* FRCP 58. Entry of judgment is critical in order to permit the filing of a notice of appeal or to permit a party to execute on the judgment.

4.19 Satisfaction of Civil Judgment

A judgment is satisfied when it is paid by the losing party. A partial satisfaction of a judgment occurs when only part of the judgment has been paid.

4.20 Execution of Civil Judgment

If the losing party fails or refuses to voluntarily pay a judgment, the winning party may need to enforce the judgment to collect the amount of the award. The methods available to enforce a judgment and collect it are described in books and treatises explaining execution, levies, garnishment, attachment, replevin, and foreclosures.

4.21 Entry of Criminal Judgment

A verdict of not guilty will be entered as a final judgment. A verdict of guilty does not necessarily mean a judgment of guilty will be entered and reflected on a defendant's record. The method of entry of judgment depends upon local law and practice.

E. APPEALS

All trial advocates must make certain that a record of appealable issues has been properly preserved. *See* Chapter One, Sec. 3.60 (Making the Record). There are several appellate considerations that a trial lawyer must understand.

4.22 Should an Appeal Be Made?

The major factors that influence the decision whether a case ought to be appealed include the following: type and degree of the error, the economic resources of the client, and the chances of success on appeal. The chances of success depend on the nature of the issues to be appealed and the prior decisions of the appellate court.

4.23 Type and Degree of Error

A party is not entitled to a perfect trial, but is entitled to a fair trial.

There are three types of errors most jurisdictions recognize:

4.23.1 Prejudicial Error

The substantial rights of a party have been adversely affected.

4.23.2 Harmless Error

This is an error that is not prejudicial. Any matter short of depriving a party of substantial justice will usually be deemed harmless and insufficient to overturn the verdict. *See* FRCP 61 and FRCrimP 52.

4.23.3 Plain Error

The "plain error" doctrine allows an appellate court to review an unduly prejudicial error that caused an unfair trial even though the error was not properly preserved.

4.24 How Much Will It Cost?

Client's resources and the amount spent on a losing effort will affect an appeal decision. The expense of an appeal may not make the effort worthwhile. A negotiated settlement may be based on an agreement not to appeal.

4.25 What Are the Chances of Success?

Issues with little or no chance of success should seldom be a basis for an appeal. Legal research in a jurisdiction regarding results in similar appeals can determine the likelihood of success.

4.26 Finality of Judgment and Order

The general rule is that a case is not appealable until a final judgment has been entered. The entry of a final judgment permits an appeal to be taken from the judgment and from any order entered by the judge during the trial prior to the entry of judgment.

4.27 Intermediate Civil Appeals

Pretrial and trial orders entered by a judge are generally not appealable during the trial.

4.27.1 An Appeal from an Order that Determines Some of the Claims

A judge may make a final decision on some claims in a complex case that ought to be appealed prior to completion of the entire case. *See* FRCP 54(b).

4.27.2 Immediate Appeal Designated by Federal or State Statute

Orders immediately appealable vary among jurisdictions but generally include interlocutory orders involving preliminary injunctive relief and other equitable remedies.

4.27.3   The Collateral Order Doctrine

Many jurisdictions permit a limited number of collateral orders to be appealable, such as a joinder order. The scope varies significantly among jurisdictions.

4.27.4   Writs of Mandamus or Prohibition

All jurisdictions permit a losing party to request the appellate court to order a trial judge to do something (mandamus) or to restrain a judge from doing something (prohibition) in accord with the applicable law.

4.27.5   Petitions for Discretionary Review

Some jurisdictions permit a party to bring a petition for discretionary review for specific orders issued before a final judgment that have a dispositive effect on some issues. Examples include relief from orders regarding privileged or work product disclosures.

4.28   Intermediate Appeals in Criminal Cases

A defendant's constitutional right to a speedy trial determines procedural rules whether an intermediate appeal is available. The government and defendant may appeal a very limited number of adverse rulings if the rulings have a substantial and prejudicial effect on a case.

4.29   Certification of Issue

A party may request an issue of substantial public or legal importance be certified to an intermediate appellate court or higher (culminating with the U.S. Supreme Court) for consideration.

4.30   Standard of Review

The standard of review is the standard employed by the appellate court in determining whether to affirm or reverse the decision of the trial court.

The three common standards are:

- *Clearly erroneous standard for errors of fact.*

  The appellate court will not reverse the factual finding of a lower court unless a clear factual error exists.

- *De novo standard for errors of law.*

  The appellate court reviews anew the legal issue without regard to the decision by the lower court.

- *Abuse of discretion standard for mixed questions of law and fact.*

  This standard is often used in determining whether a trial judge properly issued a pretrial or trial order.

4.31   Initiating the Appeal

An appeal is initiated by filing a "notice of appeal" in the trial court and with the appellate court within a prescribed period of time—for example, thirty days in a civil appeal and ten days in a criminal appeal.

4.32   Appeal Bonds

In civil appeals, the appellant may need to post a cost bond or a supersedeas bond, or both, with the notice of appeal. A cost bond ordinarily covers the costs of printing and submitting the briefs. *See* FRCP 62; FRAP 7–8. A supersedeas bond ensures payment to the appellee if the appellee prevails on appeal; it usually is in the amount of the money judgment.

4.33   Stays

The filing of a notice of appeal does not ordinarily stay the enforcement of a judgment of order. A stay order must also be sought.

4.34   Record

The appellant usually must order the record from the court reporter for the appeal. The record typically consists of the pleadings, the written rulings and orders appealed from, the requested portions of the trial transcript, and trial exhibits.

4.35   Briefing and Argument Schedule

After or during the completion of these procedural steps, the appellate court provides the attorneys with a briefing schedule indicating the deadlines for submission of the briefs and oral argument.

4.36   Oral Argument

Litigants typically receive an opportunity for oral argument in an appeal before a three judge panel. In some cases, oral argument may not be available, and the appellate court decides the appeal on the briefs. The appellate lawyer needs to become thoroughly familiar with the record, compose an effective oral argument covering the major issues, and be prepared to answer questions from the panel.

4.37   Appellate Decision

A state court of appeals or a federal circuit court of appeals will decide the initial appeal from a trial court. The losing party to this appeal may be able to appeal to the state supreme court or the U.S. Supreme Court. The availability of these appeals is limited.

APPENDIX A. FORMS *(FORMS ALSO AVAILABLE ON DISK)*

PLANNING

File Number: _____
Client Name: _____
Contact Info: _____
_____
_____

Preliminary Case Summary

Date of Events	
What Happened	
Location	
How Event(s) Happened	
Claims/Defenses	
Damages/Relief Sought	
Documents	
Settlement Efforts	
Results of Settlement Efforts	
Possible Dispute Resolution Methods **What Kind?** **Likelihood of Success?**	

File Number: _____
Client Name: _____
Contact Info: _____
_____
_____

Detailed Case Information

PARTIES AND WITNESSES	
PLAINTIFF(S) Name: Address: Telephone: Fax: E-mail:	**PLAINTIFF'S LAWYER(S) / ADVOCATE(S)** Name: Address: Telephone: Fax: E-mail:
DEFENDANT(S) Name: Address: Telephone: Fax: E-mail:	**DEFENDANT'S LAWYER(S) / ADVOCATE(S)** Name: Address: Telephone: Fax: E-mail:
OTHER PARTIES Name: Address: Telephone: Fax: E-mail:	**OTHER PARTIES' LAWYER(S) / ADVOCATE(S)** Name: Address: Telephone: Fax: E-mail:
WITNESSES Name: Address: Telephone: Fax: E-mail:	**WITNESSES' LAWYER(S) / ADVOCATE(S)** Name: Address: Telephone: Fax: E-mail:

DETAILED INFORMATION

Claims

Defenses

DEADLINES

Statute of Limitations

Pleadings

Discovery

Motions

Pretrial / Arbitration Conference

Trial / Arbitration

Other

PLANNING
Form 1-C: Case Evaluation Worksheet

File Number: _____
Client Name: _____
Contact Info: _____
_____
_____

Case Evaluation Worksheet

Legal Theory of Case
Factual Theory
Important Facts
Major Witnesses
Minor Witnesses
Relief/Damages
Law

Strengths of Case
Weaknesses of Case
Additional Facts Needed
Legal Research Needed

PLANNING
Form 1-D: Litigation (Trial/Arbitration)
Budget Worksheet

File Number: _____
Client Name: _____
Contact Info: _____
_____
_____

Litigation Budget Worksheet

Amount of damages:

Other damages—nonfinancial:

Probable amount of damages recoverable by settlement:

Probable amount of damages recoverable at trial/arbitration:

Probability of success at trial/arbitration:

Settlement potential:

Maximum financial resources available from client:

Maximum financial resources of opposing parties:

Estimated Attorney/Advocate Cost

    Estimated Attorney Cost

- Research $_____ fee/hr _____ hours $_____ cost

- Pleadings $_____ fee/hr _____ hours $_____ cost

- Discovery $_____ fee/hr _____ hours $_____ cost

- Motions and memoranda $_____ fee/hr _____ hours $_____ cost

- Trial preparation $_____ fee/hr _____ hours $_____ cost

- Pretrial/arbitration hearings and conferences $_____ fee/hr _____ hours $_____ cost

- Trial/Arbitration $_____ fee/hr _____ hours $_____ cost

    Total Estimated Attorney Cost $_____

Estimated Assisting Attorney Cost

- Research $_____ fee/hr _____ hours $_____ cost

- Pleadings $_____ fee/hr _____ hours $_____ cost

- Discovery $_____ fee/hr _____ hours $_____ cost

- Motions and memoranda $_____ fee/hr _____ hours $_____ cost

- Trial preparation $_____ fee/hr _____ hours $_____ cost

- Pretrial/arbitration
  hearings and conferences $_____ fee/hr _____ hours $_____ cost

- Trial/Arbitration $_____ fee/hr _____ hours $_____ cost

Total Estimated Assisting Attorney Cost $_____

Estimated Associate Cost

- Research $_____ fee/hr _____ hours $_____ cost

- Pleadings $_____ fee/hr _____ hours $_____ cost

- Discovery $_____ fee/hr _____ hours $_____ cost

- Motions and memoranda $_____ fee/hr _____ hours $_____ cost

- Trial preparation $_____ fee/hr _____ hours $_____ cost

- Pretrial/arbitration
  hearings and conferences $_____ fee/hr _____ hours $_____ cost

- Trial/Arbitration $_____ fee/hr _____ hours $_____ cost

Total Estimated Associate Cost $_____

Estimated Paralegal Cost

- Research $_____ fee/hr _____ hours $_____ cost

- Pleadings $_____ fee/hr _____ hours $_____ cost

- Discovery $_____ fee/hr _____ hours $_____ cost

- Motions and memoranda $_____ fee/hr _____ hours $_____ cost

- Trial preparation $_____ fee/hr _____ hours $_____ cost

- Pretrial/arbitration
  hearings and conferences $_____ fee/hr _____ hours $_____ cost

- Trial/Arbitration $_____ fee/hr _____ hours $_____ cost

Total Estimated Paralegal Cost $_____

Staff Cost

- Research $_____ fee/hr _____ hours $_____ cost

- Pleadings $_____ fee/hr _____ hours $_____ cost

- Discovery $_____ fee/hr _____ hours $_____ cost

- Motions and memoranda $_____ fee/hr _____ hours $_____ cost

- Trial preparation $_____ fee/hr _____ hours $_____ cost

- Pretrial/arbitration
  hearings and conferences $_____ fee/hr _____ hours $_____ cost

- Trial/Arbitration $_____ fee/hr _____ hours $_____ cost

Total Estimated Staff Cost $_____

Other Lawyer/Legal Expenses $_____ fee/hr _____ hours $_____ cost

Estimated Expert Witnesses Costs $_____ fee/hr _____ hours $_____ cost

Costs

Service of Process Costs $_____ fee/hr _____ hours $_____ cost

Court Costs $_____ fee/hr _____ hours $_____ cost

Investigation Costs $_____ fee/hr _____ hours $_____ cost

Discovery Costs $_____ fee/hr _____ hours $_____ cost

Witness/Subpoena Fees $_____ fee/hr _____ hours $_____ cost

Other Costs (List) $_____ fee/hr _____ hours $_____ cost

TOTAL ESTIMATED COST TO LITIGATE $_____

File Number: _____
Client Name: _____
Contact Info: _____
_____
_____

Evidence Worksheet

Elements of Claim or Defenses

Witness(es)
    Name
    Contact Information
        Address
 	
        Telephone
        Fax
        E-mail

Testimony Outline
Exhibit/Documents to Be Offered through Witness
Discovery Responses Outline
Admissions
Stipulations
Other Sources of Proof

File Number: _____
Client Name: _____
Contact Info: _____
_____
_____

Case Preparation Checklist

Investigate Facts/Case   _____ Date Completed
   Progress

   Comments

Develop Theory of Case   _____ Date Completed
   Progress

   Comments

Outline Elements of Claims   _____ Date Completed
   Progress

   Comments

Outline Elements of Defenses   _____ Date Completed
   Progress

   Comments

Review Evidence   _____ Date Completed
   Progress

   Comments

Research Applicable Law _____ Date Completed
    Progress

    Comments

Prepare Draft of Summation _____ Date Completed
    Progress

    Comments

Visit Scene of Event _____ Date Completed
    Progress

    Comments

Interview Witnesses _____ Date Completed
    Progress

    Comments

Conduct Depositions _____ Date Completed
    Progress

    Comments

Complete Discovery _____ Date Completed
    Progress

    Comments

Select an Expert _____ Date Completed
  Progress

  Comments

Prepare Expert for Trial/Arbitration _____ Date Completed
  Progress

  Comments

Subpoena Witnesses for Trial/Aribtration _____ Date Completed
  Progress

  Comments

Develop Witness List _____ Date Completed
  Progress

  Comments

Prepare Witnesses for Trial/Arbitration _____ Date Completed
  Progress

  Comments

Prepare Exhibits _____ Date Completed
  Progress

  Comments

Prepare Visual Aids
Progress

_____ Date Completed

Comments

Select Technology for Trial/Arbitration
Progress

_____ Date Completed

Comments

Prepare Technology Presentations
Progress

_____ Date Completed

Comments

Prepare Pretrial Materials
Progress

_____ Date Completed

Comments

Prepare Stipulations
Progress

_____ Date Completed

Comments

Prepare Legal Memo
Progress

_____ Date Completed

Comments

Prepare Jury Instructions
    Progress

_____ Date Completed

    Comments

Prepare Jury Selection Questions
    Progress

_____ Date Completed

    Comments

Prepare Final Argument
    Progress

_____ Date Completed

    Comments

Prepare Opening Statement
    Progress

_____ Date Completed

    Comments

Prepare Direct Examination
    Progress

_____ Date Completed

    Comments

Prepare Cross-Examination
    Progress

_____ Date Completed

    Comments

Prepare Rebuttal   _____ Date Completed
    Progress

    Comments

Organize Case Notebook   _____ Date Completed
    Progress

    Comments

Organize Trial/Arbitration Notebook   _____ Date Completed
    Progress

    Comments

File Number: _____
Client Name: _____
Contact Info: _____
_____
_____

Litigation Timetable

Event

Statute of Limitations

Deadline

Comments

Complaint   _____ **Deadline**

    Comments   _____ Date Completed

Answer   _____ **Deadline**

    Comments   _____ Date Completed

Reply   _____ **Deadline**

    Comments   _____ Date Completed

Other Pleadings   _____ **Deadline**

    Comments   _____ Date Completed

Interrogatories   _____ **Deadline**

    Comments   _____ Date Completed

Depositions   _____ **Deadline**

    Comments   _____ Date Completed

Production Requests   _____ **Deadline**

    Comments   _____ Date Completed

Examinations _____ **Deadline**

    Comments _____ Date Completed

Witnesses: Trial/Arbitration Timing _____ **Deadline**

    Name _____ Date Completed
    Comments

Witnesses: Notification/Subpoena _____ **Deadline**

    Name _____ Date completed
    Comments

Expert Witnesses: Trial/Arbitration Timing _____ Date needed for testimony

    Name _____ Amount of time anticipated
    Comments

Expert Witnesses: Notification/Subpoena _____ **Deadline**

    Name _____ Date Completed
    Comments

Admission Requests _____ **Deadline**

    Comments _____ Date Completed

Motions _____ **Deadline**

    Comments _____ Date Completed

Memorandums _____ **Deadline**

    Comments _____ Date Completed

Pretrial Matters _____ **Deadline**

    Comments _____ Date Completed

Trial _____ **Deadline**

    Comments _____ Date Completed

Other: _____ **Deadline**

    Comments: _____ Date Completed

PLANNING
Form 1-H: Pretrial/Prehearing
             Summary Worksheet

File Number: _____
Client Name: _____
Contact Info: _____
              _____
              _____

Pretrial/Prehearing Summary Worksheet

Summary description of pretrial or prehearing issues

Description of discovery that remains to be completed

Reasons why case has not been settled

List of pretrial or prehearing motions or requests

Description of motions in limine or prospective evidentiary problems

List of witnesses, including experts

List of exhibits

Concise statement of party's version of facts

Concise summary of party's claims/defenses

Concise statement of opponent's version of facts

Concise statement of opponent's claims/defenses

Stipulations of fact or undisputed facts

Elements of law that need to be proved for client

Elements of law that need to be provided for opposing party

Citations to specific statutes or case law

Case to tried by _____ Judge _____ Jury _____ Administrative Judge
_____ Arbitrator

If jury, number of jurors _____ Number of alternate jurors _____

Number of peremptory challenges _____

Estimated time for trial/hearing

Other matters

PLANNING
Form 1-I: Case Brief Worksheet

File Number: _____
Client Name: _____
Contact Info: _____
_____
_____

Case Brief Worksheet

Statement of Case

    a.   Type of case

    b.   Parties

    c.   Procedural history

    d.   Prior motions and rulings

Summary of Claims or Defenses

List of Witnesses Who Will Testify and Substance of Their Testimony

    Witness

    Substance of Testimony

    Witness

    Substance of Testimony

Stipulations

(Caption of case as required by court/arbitrator)

[Party] and [Party] agree that the following facts are true and require no further

proof at trial:

[state facts or testimony and describe exhibits and evidence]

_____

Attorney for plaintiff

Date _____

_____

Attorney for defendant

Date _____

CHAPTER TWO

MOTION PRACTICE, OPENING STATEMENTS, AND FINAL ARGUMENTS

SECTION 1: MOTION PRACTICE

A. HOW TO PREPARE FOR A MOTION ARGUMENT

1.01 Will There Be an Oral Argument?

In many administrative proceedings, arbitrations, and some court cases, a decision on a motion is based on the written submissions of the parties without oral argument. Parties may request an opportunity for oral argument. In litigation, parties typically have a right to an oral argument before a final decision is made. In some jurisdictions, a judge may advise the parties of a tentative ruling based on the written submissions and permit the parties an opportunity to present arguments relating to the tentative ruling and its reasoning. In other jurisdictions—with crowded dockets—no oral argument may be available.

1.02 How Much Time Will Be Available?

Whether a specific time limit will be set for an argument depends upon the decision maker. A reasonable amount of time is typically allowed. When the motion is scheduled with the calendar clerk, a specific amount of time may be requested. The advocate needs to decide how much time is necessary and how the available time should be used. If more time for argument is needed than is allocated, a request may be made for additional time.

1.03 How Prepared Is the Decision Maker?

An advocate must ascertain whether the judge has read or is familiar with the motion, the case, and the applicable law. The extent of the judge's familiarity with the motion determines the content of the motion argument. The extent of the preparation may be learned by contacting the clerk or law clerk and asking about the judge's usual preparation practice, by asking other advocates, or by previous experience before the judge.

1.04 Supporting Memorandum

Most forums require that a memorandum with a citation of authorities be submitted in support of a motion. A memorandum should contain a summary of the important facts and the legal authorities supporting the position asserted by the attorney. The memo need not cover in detail the commonly applied procedural rules, as the judge will know those. The memo should focus on the precedential law that supports the motion and how the relevant facts support the relief sought.

1.05 Opposition Memorandum

A written memorandum in opposition to a motion is required in many forums and expected in many others. An opposing memorandum should explain why the motion should be denied, what rebuttal facts the judge needs to know, and what law requires the motion to be denied.

1.06 Location

Motions may be argued in a judge's chambers, in a courtroom, or hearing room. Some judges may prefer to discuss the merits of the motion on an informal basis in chambers, but the majority prefer the formality of a court or hearing room.

1.07 Sequence

The moving party usually argues first followed by the opposing party or parties. Rebuttal arguments by the lawyers are usually permitted as long as they are not repetitive and respond to the oral argument made by the opponent.

1.08 Recording

The practice of recording the oral arguments varies among forums. Federal courts typically have a court reporter present, and many state courts will as well. A growing number of state courts use audio recording equipment or do not record unless there is evidence offered at the motion hearing. The making of a record usually influences the tenor and content of statements made and reduces the likelihood of injudicious or extraneous statements.

B. HOW TO PRESENT A MOTION EFFECTIVELY

An effective, efficient, and economical presentation in support of or in opposition to a motion must address the following question: What information does the decision maker need to decide the motion in favor of the client?

1.09 Be Brief

Be brief! Concise! Succinct! Explain the relevant law, grounds, and facts the judge needs to grant the motion.

1.10 Communicate

A formal approach may not be as effective as an approach in which the advocate converses with the decision maker. Rather than present an appellate-type argument, it may be better to present the relevant information as if asserting positions during a conversation. Try to engage the judge in a dialogue. To be an effective conversationalist, an advocate must adopt a persuasive style, display familiarity with the facts and the law, and demonstrate confidence.

1.11 Be Orderly

An advocate should preface the substance of an argument with a brief outline of what will be covered. The moving party who speaks first may also want to include a short preface that contains a description of the motion, its grounds, and the relief sought.

The argument must be structured in an effective, persuasive manner. The most effective structure depends on the type of motion. The motion, memorandum, proposed order, affidavits, or other moving papers may provide a structure for the argument.

1.12 Have Substance

The presentation should contain an explanation of the facts and the law mixed with reason, logic, emotion, and equity. The mix and balance of these factors depends on their availability and influence. If the substantial weight of the law supports the motion, the law should be emphasized. If other factors are stronger, they should be the focus.

1.13 Explain the Law

Legal explanations should be accurate, understandable, and concise. Leading cases, supporting statutes, and succinct persuasive quotations should be referred to as necessary. Avoid lengthy quotations—they can be included in the memorandum.

1.14 Describe the Facts, Accurately

Facts in a motion hearing are often presented through affidavits, which contain the relevant and necessary information. A description of the facts during the argument should include a concise recitation of the relevant evidence and how the facts support the relief sought. This description should be accurate and not incomplete or exaggerated. If the description is not objective and complete or unfavorable facts are not addressed, the advocate will lose credibility and the judge will lose faith in the argument.

1.15 Be Descriptive

The advocate must describe facts in as descriptive a way as possible so that they are memorable and persuasive. This presentation should be structured so that the facts are easy to follow. Rambling, disorderly presentations are neither descriptive nor persuasive and demonstrate weakness.

1.16 Use Notes

Arguments should not be read. Notes outlining the essential points of an argument may be used as a guide during a presentation. Maintain eye contact and present positions in a conversational, persuasive style. Visual aids can be used in a PowerPoint presentation providing an outline for the advocate to follow.

1.17 Use Exhibits

Exhibits—including real and demonstrative evidence; electronic and DVD presentations; or visual aids such as computer-generated documents, diagrams, charts, graphs, and summaries—may assist the presentation and help the decision maker understand an argument. Appropriately crafted visual aids can be useful in presenting positions that are difficult to explain.

1.18 Avoid Interruptions

An advocate should avoid interrupting an opponent or the decision maker. All statements should be directed to the decision maker, and advocates should avoid arguing directly with the opponent. It is unprofessional and discourteous to interrupt. Incorrect statements that are unfairly prejudicial, bear no relation to the motion, or mischaracterize a position can be addressed in argument on rebuttal. An advocate who interrupts unnecessarily will often be admonished.

1.19 Explore Weakness

An argument should contain references to the weaknesses of the opponent's case or to the inappropriateness of a position taken by the other side. An argument to expose the opponent's weakness should be directed in a positive, constructive manner. A defensive argument that merely attacks the opposition may appear weak. The advocate should also candidly deal with weaknesses of their own case. Weakness should not be ignored.

1.20 Be Candid

Be candid and flexible. An advocate may also have to compromise during a motion hearing. There may be other options beyond either granting or denying the motion. There may be other types of relief that would satisfy the needs of the client. The decision maker may view the hearing as an opportunity for the parties to agree to a resolution of the problem.

1.21 Answer Questions

Questions asked by the judge or arbitrator (decision maker) should be invited and answered as completely as possible at the time they are asked. Advocates want to know what the decision maker is thinking about the motion. The questions will explain what the decision maker is thinking. A motion presentation will be ineffective unless it responds to the issues that concern the decision maker. Asking decision makers if they have any questions or if any part of the presentation is unclear is a way to learn what they are thinking. Even if a decision maker has tough questions, it is better to try to answer them than to never know about them. Answer the questions when asked. Putting off an answer may meet the advocate's needs, but not the needs of the decision maker.

1.22 Involve the Decision Maker

The advocate should prepare to present an argument in such a way as to involve the decision maker in the motion. An effective presentation often develops an interchange between the advocate and the decision maker. The best way to develop this interchange is to invite questions from the decision maker. This may be done periodically throughout the argument as this also helps focus the decision maker on the relevant issues.

1.23 The Ruling

After hearing arguments on a motion, the decision maker may make the ruling orally on the record or may defer a ruling and issue it later in a written order. A few rulings or orders that involve significant issues dispositive of a case may be appealed immediately.

SECTION 2: OPENING STATEMENTS

A. SCOPE

2.01 Why Open?

The opening statement provides an opportunity to explain the evidence to the fact finder and to describe the issues to be presented. An opening statement has a significant impact on the initial understanding and impression of the case.

The purposes are to:
- Explain the evidence
- Tell an interesting story
- Explain to the fact finder what the case is about
- Persuade the fact finder of the merits of the case
- Motivate the fact finder to want to render a favorable decision

2.02 What to Say

The facts that can be described include direct and circumstantial evidence. The opinions that can be described include admissible lay and expert opinions. The advocate should state the legal and factual theory of the case.

2.03 What Not to Say

If a witness, document, or some other form of evidence will provide some information during the case, that information can be included in opening statements. Otherwise, it cannot be included.

2.04 Include Theories and Issues

During the opening statement the advocate should use the issues and theories developed in case preparation to establish a basis and structure for the presentation. Review the final argument and determine what from it should be included in the opening. Review the evidence to be introduced and decide what needs to be summarized in the opening and what the fact finder should first hear during the trial.

2.05 Explain the Appropriate Law

The advocate can explain the law to a trial judge, an administrative judge, or an arbitrator. How detailed an explanation depends upon what they know. They may already know the law, or may only know the basics, or may know very little. Determine what they need to know and explain the law to them at the level they can best understand. In a jury trial, the judge determines the law and explains the law to the jury. The legal elements are important components of an opening statement.

2.06 Why Argue?

Tell a story about the facts and law and present the most persuasive opening as possible without engaging in debate or argument. The opening presentation is generally called "opening statement," and it is not appropriate to argue. There is a fine line between being persuasive and arguing. Strong, powerful, persuasive opening statements can be presented within the limitations established by the judge or arbitrator and by rules governing a particular forum.

B. HOW TO PREPARE

To prepare an opening statement, select the evidence to be explained, the theories to be described, the law to be explained, the most effective way to present the information, and other planning considerations.

2.07 What About Preliminary Evidentiary Rulings?

Opening statements may not refer to inadmissible evidence. Evidentiary rulings made before the opening permit the advocate to know exactly what evidence will be admissible. A ruling on a summary judgment motion or in limine motion may determine what evidence will be admitted.

2.08 What Has Happened?

In a bench trial, what the judge knows and does not know about the case will determine the content of the opening. Remarks made during discussions with a judge, arbitrator, or hearing officer will affect what should be said and how it should be said during opening. In a jury trial, what the jury hears or sees during jury selection will affect what is presented in an opening.

2.09 What Will Be Presented in the Final Argument?

The final argument must be planned before the trial or hearing begins, and the opening statement must be consistent with what will be presented in final argument. The structure and content of the final argument can provide the structure and content of the opening statement. It is critical to review the final argument and determine what should be included in the opening and repeated in the final argument.

2.10 What Will the Opponent Say?

The advocate must anticipate and attempt to diffuse the other side's opening statement, theories, evidence, and case. Be the devil's advocate and predict what the other side will say—and be prepared to rebut it in your opening. Weaknesses should be addressed in the opening.

2.11 Select Visual Aids and Exhibits

Appropriate visual aids and exhibits will help the fact finder better understand the case theory and evidence, engage the fact finders interest, and add more to the persuasive impact of the opening. The fact finder is more likely to remember and understand an opening that has helpful exhibits. Real and demonstrative evidence that will be introduced during the case can also be used in the opening. A variety of computer-generated and paper-based visual aids can be created and used in the opening, as well as the final argument, to simplify issues and present information that can be difficult to explain orally.

2.12 Who Opens When?

Generally, the party with the burden of proof gives the first opening statement. In cases with multiple parties, the order of the opening statements is based on who has the more substantial burden of proof, the chronology of the factual events, which party has a counterclaim or an affirmative defense, or which party has the more substantial defense.

2.13 How Long Is Enough?

The opening statement should be long enough to explain what needs to be explained, yet short enough to maintain the attention of the fact finder. Common sense and an understanding of the listener's ability to pay attention is a good gauge of the proper length. All important facts, issues, and positions should be addressed. However, everything need not be included in the opening. Some matters should first be disclosed during the presentation of evidence and fully explained in the final argument.

2.14 Should the Opening Statement Be Waived or Delayed?

An opening statement should never be waived because of the advantage an effective opening statement provides. It is usually best for the defense to give an opening immediately after the plaintiff. The fact finder will then hear evidence with an understanding of both sides' positions. In some cases the defense may delay giving an opening until after the plaintiff's case for tactical reasons or if the defense is truly uncertain whether some evidence will be included or excluded.

2.15 Compose It

The material for the opening statement should be organized in an outline format, which includes the introduction, body, and conclusion. Distill the opening into a short, concise document that outlines the key points and words and use that for the presentation. Some advocates fully write out the opening, while others prepare an outline and practice from it.

2.16 Rehearse

Practice out loud. Learning the content is better than memorizing an exact script. Opening statements should not be read aloud from a written script, nor should they be memorized. The advocate should not try to remember the exact words used during the practice sessions (unless the exact words are significant), but rather express the ideas that have been prepared.

C. HOW TO ORGANIZE

2.17 The Structure

The structure should allow the entire case to be framed in the opening.

2.17.1 Time

Events are described in the order they occurred.

2.17.2 Flashback

The opening can start with the end of the story, and the remaining story can be told in flashbacks.

2.17.3 Parallel Events

The actions of the two parties can be told separately, culminating at the point when their stories mesh.

2.17.4 Claims, Defenses, Topics

The opening can be structured around the claims, defenses, or related topics that will be proved during the trial.

2.17.5 Order of Evidence

The opening can reflect the order in which the evidence is presented.

2.17.6 Liability and Damages

In civil cases, liability can be first discussed in the opening, and then damages; or damages can be the introduction to the liability presentation.

2.17.7 Mixture of Substructures

A number of these approaches can be mixed.

2.18 Parts of the Opening Statement

An opening statement has at least three major parts:

- Introduction
- Body
- Conclusion

2.19 Introduction

An interesting and dramatic introduction may be the most effective way to begin an opening. Explanations of the purposes of an opening, the names of the advocate, and general introductory remarks do not have much to do with winning the case and are not particularly effective. The introductory presentation should contain the theory of the case stated in a positive manner with impact words and conviction.

A description of the purpose of an opening before a judge, arbitrator, or hearing officer is not necessary. While it may help jurors understand their role, it may not have a persuasive impact.

The theory of the case should be explained in a concise and persuasive way. The overall themes of the case provide the basis for the entire case. Well-stated theories and themes provide focus and structure, but they should not be overstated. An explanation that blends the themes, theories, important facts, legal conclusion, and positions will make a strong beginning to the opening statement

2.20 The Body

The presentation should be designed to explain the material facts and elements of the case that the fact finder needs to understand. This is an opportunity to tell the story: what happened and why, the critical and helpful facts, the supportive witnesses, the useful exhibits, what decision a judge or arbitrator should make, or what verdict the jury should render.

2.21 The Conclusion

A strong conclusion may be achieved with a concise summary of the vital facts and a compelling statement that would justify a decision in favor of your client. At the very end of the opening, the fact finders should say: "If they prove that case, I want them to win."

2.22 Opening Statement Critique

Questions that may help determine whether an opening statement has been properly constructed include:

- Does the opening statement tell what happened?
- Does the opening statement tell the fact finder why to find for the client?
- Does the opening statement make the fact finder want to find for the client?
- Does the opening statement tell how to find for the client?
- Does the opening statement have a structure that is clear and simple?
- Is the opening statement consistent with what will be proved and with what will be argued in final argument?

D. TELL A STORY

The content of an opening statement depends on the facts and circumstances of the case and the strategic and tactical decisions of the advocate. The following factors should be considered when preparing the opening statement.

2.23 An Effective Story

The opening statement should be told in simple language in as dramatic a fashion as is appropriate, and in an interesting way. Don't talk down, or up, to the fact finder.

2.24 Details

The facts should be as detailed as necessary to provide a clear and complete story. There will be facts that should not be included because of available time and importance. Some facts may first be introduced during the trial. If necessary, the final argument can explain why the facts were saved for the trial and not described during the opening. There may be some details that should be left to the imagination of the fact finder. The details can be presented in testimony and explained in final argument.

2.25 Parties/Witnesses

Witnesses should be described in a way that will make their story understandable and their testimony credible. Emphasize why the witness is important to the case and the critical nature of the evidence they will introduce.

2.26 The Event

The description of the incident, occurrence, or event should be accurate and complete and should enable the fact finder to create a clear picture. The image created needs to be consistent with the evidence that is introduced during the trial.

2.27 Circumstances

Explanations about the time, date, participants, and other information should be provided to the extent necessary. Explaining the what, how, and why of circumstances is critical.

2.28 What Happened

The facts of a case dictate the parameters of the presentation. Usually there is not enough time to present all the facts. Select the facts that are essential to a favorable impression and to an overall understanding of the events and circumstances.

2.29 How It Happened

Usually an issue in a case will revolve around how something happened. An explanation of how something occurred needs to be part of the opening. The reason something happened or why someone did something will help the fact finder understand and remember these events.

2.30 Why It Happened

The fact finder may be curious about why something happened, and although the why may not be critical to the case, it should be explained if a good reason exists. Why something happened, or did not happen, or why someone said or heard something important will help the fact finder understand the importance of these circumstances.

E. TELL MORE OF THE STORY

2.31 Prefatory Phrases

Some common prefaces include "I will prove" and "the evidence will show." The usefulness of prefatory phrases is a matter of debate among advocates. Some prefer using these prefaces; others will simply tell a compelling story without referring to what they or the evidence will show.

2.32   Visual Aids and Exhibits

Effective visual aids significantly increase the persuasive impact of an opening and help the fact finder understand the facts and details of the case. Care must be taken that the visual aids are not confusing, contain too much information, or are poorly prepared and presented. Electronic, DVD, and computer devices are readily available to create compelling visual aids. A variety of computer software programs make it relatively easy to create effective visual aids. Even a simple printed outline of the opening can improve the presentation.

2.33   Claims and Defenses

References to the specific claims or defenses should be made. A civil case is about the claims asserted by the plaintiff and the defenses interposed by the defense. The opening presents a story with legal issues framed by these claims and defenses.

2.34   Disputed Issues

A reference to the conflict in the evidence or testimony may help the fact finders understand what they have to decide. The case is going to trial because there are at least two sides of the story, and it may be helpful to focus on these differences. On the other hand, some advocates prefer to tell the client's story without referring to the other side's version, making it appear that the client's version is the only believable and correct version.

2.35   The Law

The advocate may discuss the law in a bench trial, administrative hearing, and arbitration. The extent of this explanation depends upon the level of understanding the judge or arbitrator has. In a jury trial, the attorney may make a brief reference to the law and blend legal explanations with the facts.

2.36   Burden of Proof

It may be appropriate to mention the burden of proof in the opening statement if doing so is tactically advantageous. If there are factual disputes that can be interpreted one way or the other, it may be advantageous for the plaintiff in a civil action to mention that a preponderance of the evidence is sufficient for the plaintiff to win. If there is reasonable doubt surrounding some facts, a reference to this doubt by a criminal defendant will be helpful.

2.37 Damages in a Civil Case

The plaintiff or claimant needs to explain the types of damages, injuries, expenses, and other relief sought. The fact finder should understand what it is the plaintiff wants and why. The extent of the detail provided in the opening depends on what the fact finder needs to know at the beginning, what can be deferred until the trial, and what needs to be explained in final argument.

2.38 Amount of Damages

Advocates who prefer to present a detailed description of damages want the fact finder to know from the outset the extent of the damages sought. Mentioning a dollar amount creates this frame of reference. Other advocates do not state a specific amount sought because they prefer to wait until after the evidence is introduced and explain the amount sought in final argument.

2.39 Request for Verdict or Award

An opening statement should contain an explanation of the decision that the facts will support. This explanation should be clear and succinct so the fact finder understands what the party wants, who should win, and what conclusion must be reached for this to happen.

F. USE OF PERSUASIVE TECHNIQUES

The following sections involve techniques that apply to the presentation of an opening statement.

2.40 Offensive/Defensive Approaches

An opening statement should lead the fact finder to a conclusion that the client is entitled to a favorable decision. The plaintiff will naturally take the "offensive." Defendants may take a defensive or offensive approach or a combined approach, which may be more effective. Plaintiffs can easily present positive reasons why they should win. And defendants, even though negating the plaintiff case, should use positive reasons why they should win.

2.41 Anticipating Defenses

The plaintiff should anticipate defenses and deal with them in a positive way in the opening because there is no opportunity for rebuttal after the defense opening. All possible defenses need not be rebutted in an opening. Ignore weak or irrelevant defenses.

2.42 Making Promises

A "promise" that certain evidence will prove a certain fact can be effective as long as the promise can be fulfilled. If it cannot, credibility will be lost and the opposing advocate will remind the fact finder of the failure in final argument.

The advocate may promise that evidence and facts will not be misstated or exaggerated. This does not need to be said explicitly if the opening is well presented. Make certain to keep the promise.

2.43 Employing Understatement

Understatement can be a useful credibility-building tool when the advocate understates the case, sets an expectation, and then exceeds that expectation during the case. This can occur with supporting evidence. For example, if there are two sources of evidence, mention only one in the opening and introduce the other during trial.

2.44 Avoiding Overstatement

Avoid overstatement during an opening statement. If something is described that cannot be proved, the client's cause is damaged. The opponent may comment during final argument about the absence of exaggerated evidence.

2.45 Asserting Difficult Positions

The facts and issues in some cases will be more difficult for the fact finder to accept. This point can be acknowledged. For example, the client may have done or said something stupid or wrong, but that does not mean the client should lose the case. It is easier to win a case if the client is likeable and nice, but not everyone can be portrayed this way. Remind the fact finders that justice is for everyone—not just for nice people.

2.46 Describing Case Weaknesses

Weaknesses that will be brought out in testimony should be addressed in a candid and forthright manner to reduce the impact of the weakness. An honest disclosure may increase the credibility and appearance of sincerity of the advocate. Most cases have significant weaknesses, and they should be addressed in the opening. For example, damaging evidence, mistaken witnesses, or the criminal record of a client or witness should be addressed up front so that it does not comes as a shock to hear about it later.

2.47 Explaining the Absence of Evidence

During the opening, the advocate can describe critical facts that will not be proved, documents that will not be introduced, and evidence that will not be presented, and explain their absence. If there is significant information that does not exist or no longer exists, it should be addressed in the opening.

2.48 Qualifying Remarks

Statements to a jury explaining that the advocate's statements are not evidence and should be ignored are seldom necessary and diminish the impact of the opening. Make a presentation without qualifications that can reduce its persuasiveness.

G. HOW TO DELIVER THE OPENING

A number of considerations affect the quality of the opening presentation.

2.49 Stand

The advocate is usually more effective standing in front of the fact finder and not hidden behind a lectern or table, unless required by rule to do so.

2.50 Move

Movement and stance should be orchestrated so as not to be distracting. Appropriate movement can be very useful to maintain interest, develop transitions, and, when done well, to demonstrate confidence and authority.

2.51 Close or Distant?

The distance between the advocate and the fact finder should be neither so far away that personal contact is lost nor so close that the fact finder feels uncomfortable.

2.52 Gesture

Gestures must be consistent with the content of the opening statement and should appear natural.

2.53 Look

One of the most effective ways to establish credibility, sincerity, and attention is to look directly at the fact finder during opening statement.

2.54 Use Transitions

A clear structure, change of pace, silence, a louder voice, a softer voice, visual aids, movement, and gestures are all devices that can signal a transition. A properly signaled transition helps keep the fact finder's interest.

2.55 Observe the Reactions of the Fact Finder

Observe the reactions of the fact finder during the opening statement and adjust your presentation accordingly. If the fact finder appears not to understand or accept something, rephrase it to make it clearer.

2.56 Notes and Outlines

Overuse of notes or a script is distracting. When notes are used, the advocate should avoid pretending not to use them. An obvious, nondistracting use of an outline can be effective. Avoid using detailed scripts that distract the advocate or the fact finder.

2.57 Exhibits and Visual Aids

Real and demonstrative evidence that will be introduced as exhibits may be used during the opening, and visual aids can be created to help make the opening easy to follow and effective.

H. COMPLEX CASES

2.58 Opening Statements in Complex Cases

Complex issues must be simplified and explained in a straightforward manner. The fact finder must believe the issues are manageable. Resources such as creative visual aids, computer graphics, and communication consultants may help the advocate explain complex matters.

I. WHAT YOU CANNOT DO

2.59 What is Improper?

Certain statements and comments made during an opening are objectionable.

2.59.1 Referring to Inadmissible or Unprovable Evidence

Referring to inadmissible or unprovable evidence is prohibited, as is referring to real and demonstrative evidence that will not be introduced or used.

2.59.2 Referring to the Law

The law may be addressed in bench and administrative trials or arbitrations. The attorney in a jury trial may make brief references to the law, but should not explain details of the law or give instructions concerning the law to the jury.

2.59.3 Making Argumentative Statements

Making argumentative statements is not appropriate.

2.59.4 Stating Beliefs and Opinions

Stating personal and professional beliefs and opinions is inappropriate.

2.59.5 Putting Fact Finders in the Place of the Party

Putting fact finders in the place of the party is not appropriate. Fact finders are to base their decision on the evidence and not substitute their personal experiences.

2.59.6 Speculating about the Other Party's Case

Speculating about the opponent's evidence is improper.

2.59.7 Making Disparaging Remarks

Making disparaging remarks is improper, unfairly prejudicial, and often unethical.

2.59.8 Additional Prohibitions

Comments about insurance in civil cases, the failure of a defendant to testify in a criminal case, and pleas to passion or prejudice are prohibited.

2.60 Making Objections

Objections are usually not made during an opening and are appropriate only when the speaker violates one of the above prohibitions or goes beyond common-sense boundaries. If an objection is sustained, the mistake should be corrected and the opening continued. If the objection is overruled, the advocate should continue with the opening and may repeat or emphasize the statement.

2.61 Asking for Curative Instructions

After an objection has been sustained in a jury trial, the attorney making the objection should consider asking the judge to instruct the jurors to disregard the improper comment.

2.62 Opening Statement Motions

An opposing party may bring a motion to dismiss or a motion for a judgment as a matter of law or directed verdict on an issue in the case based on admissions made during opening statement, based on the ground that the opposing party has failed to establish a prima facie case during the opening, or based on the entire content of the opponent's opening statement. Other possible motions include a motion to have the court set restraints on the opponent's opening time and scope and a motion by plaintiff to present additional facts in rebuttal to defendant's opening.

SECTION 3: FINAL ARGUMENTS

A. SCOPE

3.01 Be an Advocate

Final argument is the final opportunity the advocate has to make an oral presentation to the fact finder. Final argument usually occurs after the close of all the evidence. Final argument is also called closing argument or final summation; however, the term *argue* is a misnomer. It is not merely an argument, but also an *advocation* of the case in a reasonable, persuasive manner.

3.02 What Is the Purpose?

The purposes of final argument are:

- To summarize the factual theories
- To explain the significance of the evidence
- To emphasize supportive evidence
- To highlight real and demonstrative evidence
- To draw reasonable inferences
- To explain the legal theories
- To highlight the rational and emotional dimensions of the case
- To integrate the theories, evidence, and law into a cohesive and comprehensive presentation
- To convince the decision maker the client deserves to win

3.03 What Is the Final Argument Story?

The story of the case that began with the opening statements is the story to be summarized in final argument. A final argument should focus on the theory of the case, explaining how the facts apply to the law, explaining the reasons why the case is a winning case, and containing a proper balance of appeals to reason and appeals to emotion.

B. WHAT CAN BE PRESENTED?

3.04 Facts and Opinions

All facts and opinions that are a part of the record, even those in dispute, may be described during final argument.

3.05 Inferences

Inferences are reasonable conclusions drawn from the evidence presented. The inference ought to be obvious from the direct evidence or at least reasonable based on the overall evidence.

3.06 The Story

Summarize in the words and phrases that have been used throughout the case. Being consistent with the opening statement, with what the witness said, and with the exhibits helps makes for a cohesive, credible, consistent final argument.

3.07 The Law and the Legal Theories

Explain how the law applies to the facts to support the result sought and how the evidence supports the legal theories. These explanations need to follow from the opening presentation, reflect the evidence introduced, and be consistent with the law.

3.08 Anecdotes

The advocate has the opportunity during final argument to use anecdotes, analogies, and metaphors involving common life experiences as well as a variety of other persuasive techniques. These techniques help explain what happened, why it happened, and why the parties and witnesses said and heard what they did. Literature is full of stories that reflect real life situations.

3.09 Urging a Result

The final argument is the last opportunity to explain the specific result the advocate wants. The decision maker must understand the precise relief sought.

3.10 What Not to Present

The advocate is not required to summarize everything; however, a failure to refute a credible position may be a mistake. Some advocates believe that ignoring a weakness is better than trying to explain it because explaining gives too much attention and credence to the weakness. Others believe that it is necessary to explain away weaknesses in order to maintain credibility and to avoid the perception there is something to hide. Each weakness needs to be analyzed to determine which approach is best.

C. HOW TO PREPARE

3.11 Do It Early and Often

Outlining a final argument ought to be one of the first things done in the presentation of a case. The planning of a case begins with the preparation of the final argument.

The final argument provides the focus for the entire case. The factual summary and legal theories of the case provide a framework for the final argument.

3.12   Rely on Jury Instructions

In jury trials, the judge informs the attorneys of the exact instructions of law to be provided to the jury. In most jurisdictions, the charge to the jury takes place after final argument. All statements of law made by the attorney must be accurate. The instructions provide a useful legal framework for the final argument. Jury instructions may also serve as a guide in preparing a final argument in a bench trial or arbitration.

3.13   Identify Central, Pivotal Issues

Identify, simplify, and address the important issues. A review of the factual summaries and legal theories will determine which facts and what legal elements are undisputed and the important, controversial, disputed issues that remain.

3.14   Anticipate the Opponent's Position

Anticipate the theories and positions of the opponent. The more accurate the prediction, the better the chances that the final argument can be constructed to rebut or reduce the impact of the opposing argument.

3.15   Select Exhibits and Visual Aids

Decide which exhibits and visual aids will be used during final argument. Any exhibit that has been introduced during the case may be used during final argument. Additional visual aids may be created and used in final argument to help the decision maker understand and recall the significant parts of the story and trial. A visual aid used during the opening statement may be used during the final argument.

3.16   How Long Is Enough?

Final argument should be long enough to cover the essential elements of the case, yet short enough to maintain the attention of the decision maker. There is no precise rule. However, a reasonable time period and common sense are guides. A complex lengthy trial may require a long final argument.

3.17   Who Closes When?

The general rule is that the party who has the burden of proof (plaintiff) closes last. In order to prepare effectively, the advocate must know the jurisdictional rules governing the order of argument. This occurs two ways: the plaintiff presents first, followed by the defense with a rebuttal by the plaintiff; or the defense argues first, followed by the plaintiff. However, in a few jurisdictions the plaintiff argues first and has no rebuttal.

3.17.1 The "Opening" Argument by Plaintiff/Prosecutor

In jurisdictions that permit rebuttal, the plaintiff must decide what to include in the initial final argument and what to save for rebuttal. A plaintiff may prefer to save some important points for rebuttal to deprive the defense of the opportunity to counter such arguments.

3.17.2 Rebuttal Argument

Rebuttal arguments should emphasize pivotal issues not addressed during the closing argument and should counter points made by the defense. Strong positions with impact may be saved for the rebuttal argument.

3.18 Write It Out

Key-word outlines are effective and usually sufficient. Many advocates prefer to prepare a written or printed "script" of their final argument; however, it is inadvisable to actually read from the prepared script. It diminishes the persuasive power of the presentation and the advocate.

3.19 Rehearse

The final argument must be rehearsed before presentation. Oral practice permits the advocate to improve both the substance and the style of delivery, increases familiarity with the content, and reduces reliance on the prepared notes. It is difficult to memorize a script. Practicing permits the advocate to learn the argument, experiment with language and structure, and present the argument persuasively.

3.20 Final Argument Critique

Does the final argument:

- Explain why to find for a party?
- Make the decision maker want to find for the party?
- Describe how to find for a party?
- Cover all factors that should be considered?

D. HOW TO ORGANIZE

The order of the final argument should be structured in a persuasive way.

The following structure is one way to organize a final argument:

- Introductory statement
- Explanation of pivotal issues in the case
- Summary of important facts, opinions, and inferences

- Description of who, what, when, where, how, and why
- Application of facts to support legal elements
- Summary of strengths of the case
- Responses to weaknesses of case
- Explanation of weaknesses of opponent's case
- Reference to burden of proof
- Explanation of key jury instructions or verdict form
- Explanation of reasons why jury should return favorable verdict
- Description of the result sought
- Conclusion

3.21   Use a Structure

The structure must be easy to follow. It depends on the theories, facts, law, circumstances and case strategies.

3.21.1   Time

Chronological presentations are easy to follow.

3.21.2   Flashback

The final argument can begin with the conclusion and flashback to earlier events.

3.21.3   Undisputed and Disputed Facts

The evidence can be explained first by describing the undisputed facts and then highlighting the disputed facts with an explanation.

3.21.4   Order of Key Witnesses

Structure can be based on the order of witness testimony.

3.21.5   Issues, Positions, Topics

Final argument can be structured to reflect the order in which the issues, positions, or topics were presented.

3.21.6   Claims or Defenses

The structure of a final argument can be based on the claims the plaintiff asserts or on the defenses the defendant raises.

3.21.7 Liability and Damages

In civil cases, the final argument could begin with an explanation of liability followed by damage issues, or vice versa.

3.21.8 Jury Instructions, Verdict Form

In a jury trial, final argument can be based on the order of the jury instructions and the verdict form.

E. INTRODUCING THE FINAL ARGUMENT

3.22 Introduction

The introduction sets the tone for the final argument and should be designed to have a persuasive impact.

The following examples demonstrate alternative introductory statements.

3.23 Case Theory Introduction

A few sentences can summarize the legal theories and apply them to facts.

3.24 Dramatic Introduction

An introduction should establish an atmosphere, set a tone, and grab attention.

3.25 Outline of Introduction

Final argument may begin with an explanation that outlines the content of the presentation.

3.26 Explanation of Final Argument for Jurors

While final argument may begin with an explanation of the purposes of final argument, this introduction has less persuasive impact than other introductions.

3.27 Expressing Gratitude

It may be appropriate during final argument to thank the decision makers for their attention and time—if done sincerely—but a "thank you" need not be presented at the very beginning.

3.28 Defense Introductions

The defense counsel can use any of the opening techniques where the defense argues first. The advocate who argues second need not provide a lengthy introduction, but may begin boldly and address the contradictory evidence or begin with a reference to a statement made by the opponent.

3.29 Rebuttal Introductions

The advocate who has a rebuttal argument can begin with a prepared introduction or with remarks that contradict the defendant's argument.

3.30 Alternative Introductions

Anticipate that there will be changes in expected testimony. Alternative introductions can be prepared in advance of the trial or arbitration. Prepare introductory remarks that most effectively meet the primary goal to be achieved during the beginning of the final argument.

3.31 Conclusion

Final argument should conclude with a strong ending. The conclusion of the argument should be well thought out and designed to tie the argument together in a clear and obvious ending. At its end, the decision maker should be thinking: that party deserves to win.

F. TELL A STORY

3.32 Examples of Arguments

The final argument allows an advocate to say most anything that falls within the broad definition of a persuasive presentation.

An advocate may:

- Draw reasonable inferences from direct or circumstantial evidence
- Suggest that certain evidence implies a reasonable conclusion
- Present conclusions based on the facts and circumstances of the case
- Suggest that the decision maker apply common sense in deciding a case
- Suggest that the decision maker apply life experiences in determining a fact
- Explain why the party deserves to win based on the facts, law, and merits of the case

3.33 Summarize the Story

The explanation of the facts may be told in a story form, which includes descriptions of the scene, the characters, and the event. The goal should be to summarize facts in a way that is reasonable and consistent with the evidence and the recollection of the fact finder.

3.34 Explain Why Something Happened

Whys are just as important as *whats* and *hows*. Final argument provides the opportunity to explain why something happened the way it did, what motivated someone to say or do something, or why something that should have happened did not.

3.35 Describe the Evidence

The description of evidence should be consistent both with the facts described in the opening statement and with the evidence produced during the case. Refer to the testimony of witnesses and the contents of documents to support these descriptions.

3.36 Present Witnesses

The advocate may summarize the evidence by identifying the witnesses who testified to certain facts and opinions. Refer to especially persuasive or credible witness by name.

3.37 Explain the Credibility of Witnesses

Statements can be made that explain the credibility of witnesses and why some witnesses are more believable than others. The advocate should present objective factors that result in a conclusion that a supporting witness is credible and that an opposing witness ought not to be believed. Use impeachment techniques during the case to establish facts that reduce the witness's credibility. The advocate can restate the facts developed on cross-examination that establish why a witness should not be believed or that a witness's perceptions are improbable or implausible.

3.38 Describe Circumstantial Evidence

The differences and importance of direct and circumstantial evidence should be explained, and the value of circumstantial evidence should be made clear. If direct evidence favors one party, that should be emphasized. If circumstantial evidence favors a party, explanations on how circumstantial evidence supports conclusions should be emphasized.

3.39 Detail and Corroboration

A detailed factual explanation has the advantage of explaining the relationship between various types of evidence that may not have been obvious or made clear during the case. Evidence may have been introduced in bits and pieces, and final argument provides the opportunity to present all the evidence in an ordered, comprehensive way.

3.40 Refer to Actual Evidence

The factual explanation may employ words used by the witness or words that appear in documents. Quoting the testimony of a witness and mixing that quote with a factual summary can be an effective approach. Evidence that appears in electronic or paper exhibits can be highlighted and shown for emphasis.

3.41   Explain the Law in Jury Trials

The judge will explain the law during final jury instructions. An attorney must summarize and explain pivotal instructions while being sure to accurately state the content of the instructions.

3.42   Describe Special Interrogatories

Local rules and case law will determine whether an attorney can inform the jury that the answers to any one of the interrogatories may determine the outcome of the case.

3.43   Explain the Jury System

One or both attorneys may explain the purpose the jury serves in our judicial system.

3.44   Request a Verdict

A final argument must include an explanation of the specific verdict the advocate wants for the client. The decision makers need to know what decisions need to be made in order for a party to win and an opposing party to lose.

H.   USE OF PERSUASIVE TECHNIQUES

3.45   Use Analogies, Metaphors, Anecdotes

The images described through an analogy, a metaphor, or anecdote may help the decision maker understand the point of law or application of fact to law.

3.46   Be Creative

One of the primary tasks is to be creative and innovative and explain the significance of inferences. An advocate can make a big difference in the outcome of a case by explaining something that no juror or judge or arbitrator has been able to perceive or understand. A creative, reasonable explanation of an event or circumstance may prove to be the reason why a party wins or loses.

3.47   Use Exhibits and Visual Aids

Exhibits and visual aids can add a great deal to final argument. They help maintain the fact finders' interest and may explain complex theories and facts. The design, placement, and use of exhibits in the argument are as important as the visual aid or exhibit itself. As with opening statements, electronic, DVD, computer devices, and a variety of computer software programs are readily available to help create compelling visual aids.

Advocates need to craft understandable and persuasive exhibits (or hire someone to do so) and practice introducing and using them for maximum effect.

3.48 Personalize Experiences

It can be helpful during final argument to mention situations the fact finder might have experienced that resemble what happened in the case. The advocate cannot ask the fact finder to consider evidence outside the trial or arbitration, but she can ask the fact finder to use common sense and life experiences to determine credibility or which party should win and why.

3.49 Appeal to Reason and Emotion

An approach that blends these two factors increases the chances of a successful result. Some cases have more logical supporting reasons; other cases have more emotive factors. Every case has some of both. The challenge is to identify and balance reason and emotion.

3.50 Ask Rhetorical Questions

Rhetorical questions can be an effective tool of persuasion because they directly involve the decision maker in the presentation. Ask a rhetorical question the decision maker will answer favorably. Do not create confusion by asking poorly phrased questions. Provide the answer to the rhetorical question so the fact finder gets it right.

I. BE POSITIVE ABOUT NEGATIVES

3.51 Explain Contradictions

Highlight the inconsistencies between witnesses to point out the contradictions in testimony. Summarize the major differences between witnesses, and explain the contradictions to show the witness is more credible or believable.

3.52 Comment on Case Weaknesses

If an advocate can think of a reasonable interpretation that reduces an obvious weakness, that explanation should be provided. If the advocate cannot think of a mitigating explanation, the weakness should be recognized and, if important, conceded in a candid and forthright manner.

3.53 Attack the Opposition's Positions

An effective technique may be to attack the logic and reasonableness of the opponent's contentions. Arguments that attack the opponent's case must be balanced with arguments that support the advocate's case.

3.54 Address Negative Suggestions

It may be viewed as inappropriate to raise insignificant weaknesses of an opponent in final argument; however, a tactful presentation that suggests the cumulative impact of these minor weaknesses creates a major weakness can help demonstrate the flawed nature of the opponent's case.

3.55 Identify Broken Promises

An advocate should address unfulfilled statements, promises, or references to evidence made by the opposing counsel in opening statement or final argument.

3.56 Explain Absent Evidence/Witnesses

An advocate may comment on the significance of facts not introduced by the opponent. If an opponent chooses not to introduce certain evidence that is or may be available, that failing may be proof that the facts are different than what the opponent suggests.

3.57 Explain Lies vs. Mistakes

It is a better tactic to describe a conflicting witness as mistaken about the facts rather than as a liar—unless, of course, the facts actually establish the lies. Most witnesses do not deserve to be called liars. However, there are some types of witnesses who are easily disliked and who, if caught in a lie, may be called a liar in final argument.

3.58 Anticipate Rebuttal Argument

In a jurisdiction where the party with the burden has an opportunity for rebuttal, the defense may need to explain that there will be no opportunity to counter what the plaintiff will say during the rebuttal argument.

J. FINAL ARGUMENT IN A CRIMINAL CASE

3.59 Describe the Criminal Burden of Proof

Both the prosecution and the defense should explain the "beyond a reasonable doubt" burden of proof.

3.60 Comment on Lesser Included Criminal Offenses

It can be difficult to deliver an argument that seeks conviction on two charges (one being less severe), because alternative arguments are hard to follow and the important issues may become confused. It may be useful to begin with the lesser crime and argue the facts support the greater.

3.61   The Defendant's Constitutional Right

The state and federal constitutions protect the defendant and place limits on what the prosecutor can say in final argument.

K.   FINAL ARGUMENT IN A CIVIL CASE

3.62   Describe the Civil Burden of Proof

Advocates for both sides must decide whether to discuss or describe the burden of proof. If it is advantageous to do so, the burdens of proof should be explained. If not, they can be left for jury instructions.

3.63   Address Liability and Damages

Liability and damages should be addressed. There is no "right" order. An advocate in a civil case may prefer to argue damages after explaining the basis for liability, or vice versa.

3.64   Describe an Award of Damages

The plaintiff needs to explain why damages should be awarded to reimburse the plaintiff for the injuries suffered or expenses incurred. The defense should explain why damages should be less or not appropriate.

3.65   Explain the Amount of Damages

The final argument should contain not only a request for a specific amount of damages to be awarded, but also an explanation of the why that specific amount is sought and how the damage amount was calculated. It is risky not to mention a specific amount, especially in a jury trial. because the jury may be uncertain or confused about how to calculate damages and what to award.

3.66   Making a "Per Diem" Argument

A plaintiff may use a "per diem" argument, which divides a period of time into small units and assesses a dollar value for each of these units. Some jurisdictions place restrictions on the use of this technique or prohibit it.

3.67   Do Not Comment on the Financial Status of Party

The general rule is that the financial status of a party is irrelevant and cannot be referred to during final argument. However, in some cases, such as a claim for punitive damages, this information is appropriate.

3.68   Explaining the Impact of Tax Laws

The general rule is that tax law or the tax impact on money damages cannot be mentioned during final argument. The amount of a damage award may or may not be taxable income.

3.69   Do Not Refer to Insurance

The general rule is that neither party may refer to the existence or nonexistence of insurance during a case, and this rule includes final argument. Insurance issues may be raised if offered to prove agency, ownership, control, bias, or some impeachment issues.

L.   HOW TO DELIVER THE FINAL ARGUMENT

The more effective and persuasive an advocate is in presenting a final argument, the greater the chance a favorable determination will be reached. Many of the factors that influence the presentation of an opening statement also affect final argument.

3.70   Stand

The advocate needs to present the final argument from a position that enhances its presentation. In general, the more effective location to stand is in front of the decision maker, not hidden behind a lectern.

3.71   Move

Movement is essential during final argument. The advocate's stance and movement should be consistent with what is being said and orchestrated so as not to be distracting.

3.72   Maintain Appropriate Distance

The advocate must maintain an appropriate distance from the decision maker. The layout of the courtroom or hearing room may determine what is available or optimum. Three to eight feet is a general guide; however, it may be effective at times to be closer or further away.

3.73   Gesture

Gestures must be consistent with the content of the final argument and should appear natural.

3.74   Make Eye Contact

Effective eye contact makes the advocate more persuasive and compelling. It also holds the attention of the decision maker.

3.75   Use Transitions

The final argument is more effective if the advocate employs transitions during the presentation. They give the listener a break, indicate new topics, and help maintain the fact finder's interest. Movement, gestures, eye contact, voice inflection, and exhibits can be used as transitions.

3.76   Develop Personal Style

An advocate should reflect personal abilities without copying and mimicking another advocate's style. Through practice, the advocate can learn to use the effective techniques of others. Practice the techniques when telling an interesting and persuasive story to friends and family. Be the same person in final argument.

3.77   Observe the Decision Makers Reaction

Watch the facial expressions, body language, and eye contact of the decision maker during final argument for signs of restlessness or confusion and adjust your presentation accordingly. If the fact finder appears not to understand or accept something, rephrase it to make it clearer.

3.78   Notes and Outlines

It will be necessary in many cases for an advocate to rely on notes or an outline during final argument to ensure all important points have been covered. An outline or list will ensure that important points are not missed. Do not read the argument. Practice so that the argument is learned, not memorized. Most advocates do not write like they speak, and a written script will appear stilted and unnatural. An outline will permit the advocate to experiment and practice with words, delivery, and structure.

3.79   Exhibits and Visual Aids

An outline or portions of a final argument can be shown in a PowerPoint presentation or printed displays. The facts finder may expect that computer-generated information and other forms of visual aids will be used. The fact finder may not be used sitting through an oral presentation that does not include the use of some exhibits or visual aids. The fact finder may be more likely to pay attention, to follow along, and to remember important parts of a final argument that are presented visually as well as orally.

M. COMPLEX CASES

3.80   Final Argument in Complex Cases

The challenge is to present and summarize massive amounts of information in an understandable and persuasive way. Time limitations, the factual and legal issues involved, and available resources will affect the presentation. The organizational structure of the final argument must be easy to understand. Creative use of exhibits, visual aids, computers, video presentations, and other technology can make complex final argument interesting and understandable.

N. WHAT CANNOT BE DONE

The advocate is generally allowed wide latitude in discussing the evidence and presenting theories during final argument. Objections may be asserted during final argument to prevent improper statements and conclusions.

3.81 Argue New Matters

An advocate may not introduce or argue new matters during final argument beyond the scope of admitted evidence. Final argument is limited to what happened in the trial.

3.82 Misstate the Evidence

Misstating evidence is improper. It is okay to present differing explanations of evidence since differing stories have been presented by the opposing side; however, an objection can be made if an opponent mischaracterizes testimonial or documentary evidence.

3.83 Improper Legal Argument

It is improper to misstate the law. Do not argue an incorrect interpretation of the law applicable to the case.

3.84 Improper Personal Argument

Do not state a personal viewpoint or make personal remarks about the facts, credibility of witnesses, expert opinions, or other evidence.

3.85 Improper "Golden Rule" Argument

The "Golden Rule" argument is a statement asking the decision makers to put themselves in the place of a party or witness and is improper.

3.86 Appeal to Passion

Statements are improper if they serve only to inflame passion.

3.87 Appeal to Prejudice

It is a violation of the fundamental precepts of our system to appeal to the prejudices or biases of the fact finder regarding race, gender, religion or other protected classifications, as the basis of a decision.

3.88 Other Improper Comments

Comments regarding the financial situation, insurance, or litigation history of a party are usually improper.

3.89 Improper References to the Invocation of a Privilege or Unavailable Evidence

All jurisdictions recognize evidentiary privileges, but they differ regarding whether the opponent may suggest that the decision maker draw adverse inferences from the invocation of such a privilege. In criminal cases, no adverse inference may be made from a defendant's assertion of the privilege against compelled self-incrimination.

3.90 The Scope of Rebuttal Argument

During rebuttal, the advocate may only make statements rebutting new matter introduced by the opponent. Arguments should not be repeated in rebuttal.

3.91 What Prosecutors Cannot Do

In criminal cases, the prosecutor must be careful not to overstep the bounds of fair argument and constitutional limitations. Prosecutors may be bound by a higher standard than defense counsel. While acting vigorously for the state, the prosecutor must be fair both to the system and the defendant.

3.92 Can There Be Interruptions?

Objections must have a legal basis and may not be made merely to interrupt or bother the opposing advocate.

3.93 Admonishing the Advocate

If the advocate continues making improper comments after an objection has been sustained, consider asking that the opponent be admonished.

3.94 No Whining

It is improper for the advocate to whine, grovel, or throw a tantrum during final argument.

APPENDIX B. FORMS *(FORMS ALSO AVAILABLE ON DISK)*

MOTION PRACTICE
Form 2-A   Motion Worksheet

OPENING STATEMENT
Form 2-B   Opening Statement Worksheet

FINAL ARGUMENT
Form 2-C   Closing Argument Worksheet

MOTION PRACTICE
Form 2-A: Motion Worksheet

File Number: _____
Client Name: _____
Contact Info: _____
_____
_____

Motion Worksheet

Case	Court File Number
Judge/Arbitrator	Date of Motion
Location	Time

Service Required	Date _____	
Service Accomplished	Date _____	Continue to (date): _____
Filing Required	Date _____	
Filing Accomplished	Date _____	Continue to (date): _____
Response Required	Date _____	
Response Accomplished	Date _____	Continue to (date): _____

Purpose of Motion

Supporting facts/discovery responses/affidavits/evidence

Legal memorandum issues

Proposed order issues

Served Date   **To be Filed Date**

File Number: _____
Client Name: _____
Contact Info: _____
_____
_____

Opening Statement Worksheet

Introduction

Theory of Case

Story

Witnesses

Exhibits/Visual Aids

Explanation of Law

Request for Relief

Conclusion

File Number: _____
Client Name: _____
Contact Info: _____
_____
_____

Closing Argument Worksheet

Theory of Case

Introduction

Facts

Inferences/Conclusions

Exhibits/Visual Aids

Case Weaknesses

Anticipated Opposing Argument

Emotional Aspects of Case

Relief/Damages

Witnesses and Their Credibility

Analogies/Anecdotes

Analogies/Anecdotes

Request for Relief/Verdict

Conclusion

Rebuttal

CHAPTER THREE

Examining Witnesses: Direct, Cross, and Expert Examination

SECTION 1: DIRECT EXAMINATION

A. SCOPE

1.01 Why Be Direct?

The purpose of direct examination is to allow the witnesses to tell their stories. Direct examination should present evidence that is legally sufficient to survive a motion for judgment as a matter of law, easily understood and readily remembered, convincing, strong enough to survive cross-examination, and able to anticipate, counter, or contradict evidence submitted by the opposition. A party's case cannot be won without effective direct examination and, in that sense, it is the most critical part of a case—and so must be done well.

1.02 What Is the Evidence?

Four primary evidentiary considerations apply to direct examinations: competency, relevancy, foundation, and form.

1.03 Who Is Competent?

A witness must satisfy four requirements to be competent to testify:

- *Oath or Affirmation.* The witness must understand the meaning of an oath or affirmation and agree to tell the truth.

- *Perception.* The witness must have personally perceived something that is relevant. *See* FRE 602.

- *Recollection.* The witness must be able to remember what he or she perceived.

- *Communication.* The witnesses must be able to communicate through her own words or through an interpreter.

1.04 What Is Relevant?

Relevant testimony has a tendency to make more or less probable any facts of consequence to the case. FRE 401. If the testimony is relevant, it has probative value, it is admissible. FRE 402.

However, relevant evidence may be excluded in the following circumstances:

- Prejudicial value outweighs probative value, confuses issues, causes undue delay, or is needlessly cumulative (FRE 403)

- Improper character evidence (FRE 404 and 405)

- Improper habit evidence (FRE 406)

- Subsequent remedial measures (FRE 407)

- Offers of compromise (FRE 408)

- Payment of medical expenses (FRE 409)

- Plea bargains (FRE 410)

- Liability insurance (FRE 411)

1.05   What Is Foundation?

Foundation consists of the sufficient facts that establish the reliable source of the evidence. Evidence based on unknown or unreliable sources is not admissible.

1.06   What Is Reliable?

The evidence introduced through direct examination must be assessed to determine its reliability.

The following analysis is a method of assessing the admissibility of evidence:

- Does the witness have personal knowledge of the matter? (FRE 602)

- Has sufficient information been provided to establish the source of the information? (FRE 901–903)

- Is the opinion testimony rationally based on the perception of the witness? (FRE 701)

- Is the out-of-court statement not defined as hearsay? (FRE 801)

- Is the testimony admissible based on an exception to the hearsay rule? (FRE 803, 804)

B.   HOW TO PREPARE

1.07   The Plan

Preparation begins with a review of the legal theories, facts, and significant issues of the case.

1.08 The Legal Theories

The legal elements of a claim or defense provide a basis for the testimony and facts necessary to prove them.

1.09 The Factual Story

The direct examination must let the witnesses describe from their own knowledge the facts and opinions that provide part of the whole story supporting the legal theory.

1.10 The Significant Issues

Identify the witnesses who can testify about the important issues. Know how the witness will provide basic facts or supporting information. Plan the case and individual witness examinations around the witness's ability to provide this information.

1.11 Prepare the Right Questions

The presentation of an effective direct examination requires the preparation of effective questions. The questions may be a topic outline, a list of questions, or a combination of topics and questions.

1.12 Practice and Rehearsal

An effective way to prepare a direct examination is to practice asking the questions out loud, following the prepared outline. Practicing the examination does not require a witness and can be an effective way to work on content as well as form.

C. HOW TO PREPARE THE WITNESS

Consider which witnesses can make the most effective presentation and then determine the order of the witnesses. The information that has been obtained before a witness testifies will help shape the content and structure of the direct examination.

Review what the witness knows that is relevant to the case. Review exhibits to determine which ones need to be introduced through this witness. Consider using demonstrative evidence to help the witness tell a story—exhibits often can bolster the testimony.

Develop a system to ensure that all witnesses who will testify on direct examination have been contacted and subpoenaed to ensure attendance in the most effective order. The advocate is responsible to make witnesses appear on time and as scheduled.

1.13 What Information to Obtain

Determine:

- The ability of the witness to observe, remember, and communicate

- What facts the witness knows
- What opinions the witness has
- What exhibits the witness can identify
- What exhibits can be created to help the witness testify
- What prior statements the witness has made
- What weaknesses may be established by the cross-examiner
- How important the witness is
- What prior testimonial experience a witness has

1.14   Method of Preparation

Meet with the witness in order to prepare properly. The more critical the witness, the more thorough the preparation must be. The goal of witness preparation is to assist the witness to testify credibly and truthfully. Preparation methods will vary and will be shaped by the circumstances, availability, personality, style, and intelligence of both witness and advocate. It is important to carefully prepare the introduction and use of exhibits with witnesses.

1.15   Here Is the Direct

Witnesses must know what is expected and what will happen.

Areas to be covered include:

- Explanations about the stages of the proceedings
- The role of the participants
- Objection procedures
- Practical trial matters
- How real evidence is to be introduced
- How demonstrative evidence is to be used
- What the attorney may do if the witness forgets
- The need to testify only to what the witness knows
- The importance of not speculating or guessing
- The avoidance of the appearance of memorized answers

Directions for a witness include:

- Walk confidently to the witness stand
- Tell the truth
- Speak clearly and loudly

- Recreate the details of specific events
- Avoid trying to remember what it is you're supposed to recall
- Relive the experience in your mind and tell that story
- Listen carefully to questions
- If you do not understand a question ask for clarification
- Answer with positive, definite answers
- Use your own words and language
- Imagine you are having a conversation with the fact finder
- Make eye contact with the fact finder
- Answer the question asked without questioning the purpose of the question
- Use any exhibits to help tell your story
- Be aware of body posture
- Dress neatly
- Do not bring notes unless they are appropriate
- Stop immediately when an advocate objects
- Be courteous
- Do not make distracting gestures or facial expressions
- Ask for a break if you feel ill, are thirsty, or need a restroom

1.16 Here Comes the Cross

Directions the advocate should give before a witness testifies include:

- Listen carefully to questions
- Answer directly
- Do not ramble
- Testify only to personal knowledge
- Testify only to your best recollection
- Do not exaggerate
- Take your time
- If information is contained in a document and you are uncertain of an answer, ask to see the document, or say you are uncertain
- If a question is repeated from a deposition or prior statement, and you are uncertain about the answer, ask to seek the statement, or if uncertain say you do not recall

- Do not allow the cross-examiner to put words in your mouth

- Correct misstatements

- Expect the cross-examiner to obtain some information that may weaken your story

1.17 What to Do

A client who is present throughout the proceeding may need to be advised about specific procedures. The client should be aware that she will be observed by the fact finder while sitting at counsel table and that she must pay attention, not visibly overreact to testimony, and not interrupt or otherwise misbehave.

1.18 Whom to Call When

The order in which witnesses testify is a critical aspect of how a case is presented. There are a number of factors that must be considered in determining the most effective sequence of witnesses. The primacy/recency effect suggests that a strong witness is most effective when called first or last. Alternatively, a strong witness will be called immediately before a recess or after a weak witness to bolster the testimony of the weak witness. Witnesses will often be called in an order that supports a chronological presentation of the case.

D. PRESENTING THE DIRECT

1.19 What to Do

Many judges and arbitrators have established rules that restrict the advocate's location and movement during direct examination. An advocate in such a jurisdiction may ask permission to ask questions while standing or sitting, and the direct examiner should select a place that permits effective communication.

1.20 How to Approach the Witness

Judges and arbitrators permit advocates to approach the witness to show the witness an exhibit. Some judges require advocates to ask permission to approach the witness.

1.21 What Is Appropriate?

The formal procedures of conducting direct examination are established by the applicable rules of evidence. However, informal rules and preferences by the judge or arbitrator may affect how direct examination proceeds.

E. HOW TO COMPOSE DIRECT EXAMINATION

Every direct examination must be organized in a manner that most effectively achieves its purpose.

1.22 The Beginning

There are many ways to begin a direct examination. A common way to begin is to establish the background of the witness. However, when too much time is spent on the background of the witness at the beginning stages of the direct examination, the fact finders may become bored because they are not hearing evidence about what happened. Extensive background that does not relate to the case is often ineffective.

Background questions do accomplish a number of direct examination goals: they relieve some of the witness's initial anxiety, build confidence, help establish a witness's personality, develop credibility, identify similarities between the witness and the fact finder, and establish a foundation for later statements or opinions.

However, it may be more effective to start with the important events and introduce the witness's background in context with these events. The beginning must be interesting and get the attention of the fact finders when they are most alert and prepared to listen.

1.23 Structure

Direct examinations must be structured. The presentation must be simple, clear, easy to understand, and informative. Structures include:

- Chronological order
- Elements of claim or defense
- Flashback
- Combinations of the preceeding

F. LEADING QUESTIONS

A witness will not be permitted to answer direct examination questions that are phrased improperly. The advocate should assess whether the question falls into the following categories of improper questioning.

1.24 Permissible Leading Questions

A leading question is a question that suggests an answer. Leading questions may interrupt the flow of testimony because they may draw an objection. They do not give the witness an opportunity to testify and may prevent the witness from appearing credible. FRE 611.

Rule 611(c) and similar state rules permit leading questions when they are necessary to develop testimony.

Leading questions are permitted if they:

- Bring out preliminary matters
- Establish noncontroversial or inconsequential facts
- Suggest new topics
- Act as transitions
- Bring out negative facts
- Are asked of an adverse witness
- Are asked of a hostile witness
- Help a witness who has communication difficulties
- Refresh a witness's recollection
- Use specific words to lay an exhibit foundation
- Lay a foundation for past recollections
- Are asked of a witness to contradict a statement made by another

A careful use of permissible leading questions may achieve positive results. They can help by:

- Suggesting familiar and appropriate topics to a witness
- Speeding up presentation of information
- Introducing variety into the examination
- Demonstrating the advocate's honesty when used to elicit negative facts
- Demonstrating the advocate's knowledge of the facts
- Making the testimony more interesting, persuasive, and compelling

G. ASSORTED QUESTIONS

1.25 Refreshing a Witness's Recollection

A witness may have a memory lapse. A previous statement, some other evidence, or a leading question may help the witness recall the information. The direct examiner may show a document to the witness to refresh the witness's memory.

1.26 Narrative Questions

A narrative question may be improper depending upon the scope and timing of the question and the capability of the witness to answer. A narrative question is improper if the witness responds with a long, uncontrolled story. The narrative response denies the opponent the opportunity to anticipate and react to objectionable evidence. The narrative question reduces the ability of the direct examiner to control the direction or the scope of the answer.

1.27　Vague or Ambiguous Questions

Vague or ambiguous questions are improper because they confuse the witness, the opponent, and the other side, and make the testimony more difficult for the fact finder to understand.

1.28　Repetitious Questions

Repetitious questions are improper because they waste time. The question form need not be identical to be repetitious.

1.29　Multiple Questions

Multiple questions or compound questions are difficult to understand and create confusing responses. These questions should be withdrawn and rephrased.

H.　HOW TO ENHANCE PERSUASIVENESS

This section presents a variety of questioning techniques that can be employed to conduct an effective direct examination.

1.30　Use Background Questions

Background questions are usually allowed for a number of reasons. The extent and number of permissible background questions depends on the significance of the witness and the time available.

Questions regarding a witness's background accomplish the following:

- Puts the witness at ease
- Establishes a witness's personality
- Demonstrates credibility
- Displays the sincerity of the witness
- Identifies similarities between the witness and fact finder

1.30.1　Putting Witness at Ease

The witness may be more comfortable testifying about themselves than about the facts of the case. Background testimony concerning familiar matters permits the witness to develop a "rhythm" and get over initial nervousness.

1.30.2 Establishing a Witness's Personality

A witness's personality and believability can be demonstrated through background questions and by the way the questions are asked. The witnesses must be given the opportunity to talk/communicate so that the fact finder can become familiar with the witness's personality, characteristics, and individuality.

1.30.3 Demonstrating Credibility

Experiences, realism, and a common-sense connection between the facts and the witness's perceptions help demonstrate credibility.

1.30.4 Displaying the Sincerity of the Witness

The witnesses can use their own words to talk about themselves to help demonstrate sincerity.

1.30.5 Identifying Similarities between the Witness and the Fact Finder

Questions can be asked that reveal similarities between the backgrounds or interests of the witness and the fact finder.

I. HOW TO LAY A FOUNDATION

1.31 Establish Perception

Facts must be established that show the witness actually saw, heard, felt, or sensed what they are about to testify about.

1.32 Enhance Foundation

Foundation questions should be asked in such a way as to add details and enhance the reliability and accuracy of the story told by the witness.

1.33 Establish Foundation to Support an Opinion

Before a witness can render an opinion, she needs to be asked questions that establish the witness perceived events and has sufficient information to support the opinion or conclusion.

1.34 Set the Scene

The scene can be initially established before details are explained. The fact finder must be able to visualize the following:

> *Location*—including the view of the witness and an overview perspective.

Picture—a witness who describes an event in vivid detail will be more persuasive and credible than a witness who testifies in general terms.

1.35 Describe Details

Details are important because they set the scene and describe the action. The amount of detail that is presented must be appropriate to the situation. Excessive detail given repeatedly on minor issues can bore and confuse the fact finder, as well as draw the power of detail from the important issues.

1.36 Describe the Action

It is easiest for a witness to describe the events as they happened, and it is usually the easiest way for the fact finder to understand what happened. The action may first be described in broad terms to set the scene and provide context. Questions that then allow the witness to fill in the gaps are not repetitious, rather they provide the complete picture of an event.

1.37 Establish Conversations

Face-to-face conversations can be established by asking who said what to whom and when. Telephone conversations require the witness to identify the voice of the other person. Eliciting the exact words in conversations is more believable than a more generalized "what did you talk about?" The first method asks for detailed evidence of what occurred, the second asks for a summary.

1.38 Introduce and Use Exhibits

Exhibits can help bolster the story being told by the witness. There may be exhibits that are real evidence, which need to be introduced through a witness. Demonstrative exhibits such as lists or charts can be created to help illustrate the witness's testimony. Computer programs or electronic devices may be used to enhance the testimony of a witness. Parts of an exhibit can be highlighted and shown to the fact finder as a witness testifies about that exhibit. Parts of a story can be enhanced after a witness has testified orally about an event by introducing an exhibit that allows the witness to testify to additional facts and details.

J. HOW TO ASK QUESTIONS EFFECTIVELY

1.39 Ask Simple Questions

Simple, everyday conversational words are generally more effective because they are easy to understand.

1.40   Ask Short Questions

Short questions make it easier for a lawyer to control testimony and for a witness to be responsive. For example: "What was the first thing you did?"

1.41   Ask a Variety of Questions

A mix of short narrative and specific questions provide variety and help develop a complete story.

1.42   Complete a Sequence

Omitted information can be introduced at the end of a sequence to avoid interrupting the flow of the testimony.

1.43   Use Impact Words

Impact words are graphic words that vividly describe something in support of a perception. A careful choice of impact words can have a positive effect on how testimony is perceived.

1.44   Use Double Direct

"Double Direct" is a technique in which part of the previous answer is used as a preface to the next question. This format can be used to emphasize a previously significant answer.

1.45   Control the Answers and Correct Mistakes

The examiner must listen to every response carefully. When a witness makes a mistake or does not answer the question precisely, the examiner must correct the witness by asking a follow-up question.

1.46   Explain Terms

The direct examiner should make sure the witness explains terms that have specialized or multiple meanings.

1.47   Seek Responses That Witness Does Not Know

Witnesses do not have perfect recollection. There are some matters about which they will not know. They may actually lose credibility if they appear to recall every detail. If witnesses are asked about something they do not know, an honest admission of an inability to remember will help make the witness more human and may increase their believability. Some witnesses are concerned when they are not able to recall all vital facts when it would be normal for them not to have seen or heard or remember everything. Seeking a response they do not know allows them to be themselves and not a robot.

1.48 Volunteer Weaknesses

Weaknesses in the witness's background or testimony may be briefly presented during the direct examination to minimize the impact of its inevitable appearance during cross-examination and to enhance the credibility of the witness and the advocate.

1.49 Use Exhibits

When carefully planned and effectively used, real evidence, demonstrative evidence, and visual aids will enhance the testimony of a witness. The key to introducing and using exhibits effectively is to weave them seamlessly into the story being told by the witness. If exhibits break up the pace and flow of a story they can be counterproductive. To effectively use exhibits, the advocate and witness must practice together.

K. HOW TO CONDUCT A REDIRECT

1.50 What Can Be Asked?

The direct examiner has an opportunity to conduct a redirect examination after the completion of cross-examination. Redirect examination allows the witness to clarify or explain points raised on cross-examination and to cover new material raised by the cross-examination that was not covered on direct examination. The redirect examination may not be a repeat of the direct examination.

1.51 What Should Be Asked?

When considering whether to use redirect, consider what may go wrong: the witness may not be prepared to answer the question; the witness may misspeak; getting the last word may backfire; nothing useful may be added; final argument may be a more appropriate time to clarify and emphasize certain points; and cases may be damaged by too many questions. Redirect also gives the opponent the opportunity for a recross-examination.

1.52 How to Ask?

The same rules apply to both direct and redirect examination. However, there may be greater latitude with leading questions during redirect examination to permit the advocate to focus the examination. The leading question can refer to the question asked on cross to help the witness and fact finder understand the point of the redirect.

1.53 How to Correct Mistakes and Refresh Recollection

Redirect provides the opportunity to correct mistakes made by the witnesses on cross-examination and to explain testimony that was limited during cross-examination.

1.54   Should Introduction of Evidence Be Reserved for Redirect Examination?

Worthwhile information that could have been presented on direct examination should not be saved for a later redirect examination. It is potentially dangerous to save information for redirect examination. Many judges and arbitrators will not allow evidence not presented on direct examination to be raised on redirect examination if the cross examiner has not addressed the evidence in cross-examination.

There are occasions when the risk may justify reserving testimony. For example, damaging information could be omitted if it is likely the cross-examination will not cover it, or positive information could be reserved if it is certain the cross-examiner will go into the area.

L.   DIRECT EXAMINATION INFORMATION

1.55   Former Testimony

In civil trials, testimony of a witness may be introduced through former testimony given under oath at a deposition or another hearing. The introduction of deposition testimony is most common when a witness is unavailable. A deposition transcript may be read or a deposition video shown to the fact finder.

1.56   Past Recollection Recorded

The introduction of past recollections recorded may be presented if the witness has lost the capability to recollect. *See* FRE 803(5). The foundation includes the following:

- Witness has no present, independent recollection
- Witness once knew relevant information
- Witness accurately wrote down or recorded the information
- Information was created or adopted by the witness while still fresh in the witness's memory
- Witness authenticates written or recorded information

1.57   Witnesses with Communication Problems

A child or witness with communication difficulties requires special consideration. Leading questions are permissible; however, the more leading questions used, the less credible the witness.

1.58   Character Evidence

Character evidence is typically not admissible. It may be relevant, but the unfair prejudice and confusion of the issues resulting from the character evidence outweighs the probative value of such evidence. *See* FRE 803(5).

1.59   Character Evidence in Civil Matters

While character evidence is usually inadmissible in civil cases to prove a person acted in a particular way, it may be admissible if it:

- Proves motive, opportunity, intent, preparation, plan, knowledge, identity, or absence of mistake

- Is offered to show character for untruthfulness against a testifying witness.

- Counters evidence of untruthful character

- Relates to issue of liability or damages

1.60   Character Evidence in Criminal Cases

In criminal cases character may be admissible in limited situations:

- When offered by an accused as a relevant personal trait such as peacefulness in a self-defense case

- When offered by prosecution to rebut character offered by the defendant

- When offered by the defense in very limited cases with regard to a victim

- When offered by the prosecution to rebut a victim's character

- When offered to show character of untruthfulness of a testifying witness

- When offered to counter evidence of untruthful character

- When offered to prove motive, opportunity, intent, preparation, plan, knowledge, identity, or absence of mistake

1.61   How to Introduce Character Evidence

There are three ways in which character evidence may be introduced during direct examination of the witness:

- *Opinion testimony.* A witness may testify to a personal opinion about the character of a person if the foundation is first established concerning what the witness knows or has observed about the person over a period of time.

- *Reputation testimony.* A witness can testify to the reputation of a person in a community if the foundation is first established concerning what the witness has heard expressed about that person in a defined community. Reputation is the expressed community consensus about an individual.

- *Specific instances of conduct.* A witness may testify to firsthand knowledge about a person.

1.62 Habit Evidence

Evidence of a particular habit of a person or the routine practice of an organization is admissible in some cases to prove that a person or organization acted in conformity with that habit on a particular occasion. *See* FRE 406.

M. COMPLEX CASES

1.63 Direct Examination in Complex Cases

The same rules and techniques apply in complex cases as in simple ones. The order of witnesses is important to keep related evidence together in a reasonable sequence. Real and demonstrative evidence and visual aids help clarify and structure complex information. Complicated cases typically involve various types of evidence, including electronically stored information and other forms of exhibits. These techniques must be used to make a complex issue clear, interesting, and easy to understand.

N. WHAT CANNOT BE ASKED

1.64 Facilitating the Presentation of Perjured Testimony

The knowing use of fraudulent, false, or perjured testimony is prohibited. The Model Rules of Professional Conduct prohibit such use, as does ethical norms and common sense.

1.65 Soliciting Inadmissible Responses

The direct examiner must comply with the exclusionary rules of evidence and cannot prompt an inadmissible response, even with a question that is itself not objectionable.

1.66 Oops

Inadvertent blurting out of inadmissible evidence by the witness must be stopped by the direct examiner as soon as it becomes evident. The examiner bears responsibility for the testimony and must interrupt such testimony.

1.67 Allowing the Client or Witness to Disrupt a Proceeding

The advocate must control the witness and bears responsibility for disruptive behavior. The lawyer who does not control a witness may be sanctioned, and both the lawyer and witness may be cited for contempt.

1.68 Using Tricks to Confuse Identification

Deliberate substitution of someone other than a party to a proceeding to confuse identification is improper. However, a good-faith basis and prior disclosure to the court may permit this tactic.

SECTION 2: CROSS-EXAMINATION

A. SCOPE

2.01 Types of Cross-Examination

Cross-examination is the process of examining an opposing party or adverse witness. The purpose is to obtain necessary information for final argument. The goal is to reveal information that supports the cross-examiner's case and damages the opposing party's case. There are two types of cross-examinations—supportive cross and discrediting cross.

2.01.1 Supportive Cross-Examination

A supportive cross-examination seeks to develop information helpful to the cross-examiner's case. When cross-examining, the advocate should consider what statements need to be made in final argument that rely on the testimony of the witness, what admissible evidence the witness knows, what admissions the witness has already made, what information the witness has that corroborates favorable evidence, whether the witness can bolster the credibility of favorable witnesses, and what portions of the direct examination of the witness were helpful.

2.01.2 Discrediting Cross-Examination

The purpose of discrediting cross-examination is to show that the witness is not credible and testimony developed on direct examination and evidence introduced by the opposing party is inaccurate, incomplete, inconsistent, implausible, improbable, impossible, or unbelievable.

2.01.3 Supportive and Discrediting Evidence

Sometimes evidence can be both helpful to the case and harmful to the opposition. For example, if a witness has made a prior inconsistent statement, that statement could be introduced either to refresh recollection (because it helps the case), to impeach (because it makes the witness lose credibility), or both.

2.02 Risks of Cross-Examination

Cross-examination should be conducted with realistic expectations and with an assessment of the inherent risks. Most of the risks involved in cross-examination arise because the witness is adverse, hostile or uncooperative, or the examiner is not prepared or asks nonleading questions.

2.03 The Need for Good-Faith Basis

An advocate must have a good-faith basis for cross-examination questions. The advocate must have proof of the underlying facts and cannot fabricate or make false innuendoes or inferences on cross-examination.

2.04 Common Myths about Cross-Examination

The following is a list of cross-examination misconceptions which, if believed or followed, will often substantially reduce the effectiveness of a cross-examination:

- Only an experienced advocate can be an effective cross-examiner
- The cross-examiner need not be caring or sensitive
- Cross-examination should always be conducted aggressively
- The witness must be destroyed on cross-examination
- The witness should always be shown to be a liar
- Witnesses should not be cross-examined by using exhibits because it causes too much confusion
- Cross-examinations must produce immediate, dramatic results
- Cross-examination is an opportunity to debate with the witness
- Cross-examination often escalates into a shouting match between the witness and the advocate
- Cross-examination should result in the witness "confessing"
- Cross-examinations that appear on television or in the movies are usually realistic and appropriate
- Cross-examinations should always be short
- Cross-examination should cover only one point, and never more than a few points
- Cross-examination is the most difficult advocacy skill

With proper preparation and the avoidance of these myths, an advocate can conduct an effective cross.

B. HOW TO PREPARE

2.05 Planning

The preparation of a cross-examination begins early in the case and continues until the moment cross-examination begins. The cross-examiner listens carefully to the direct examination and adds, deletes, or modifies questions to be asked during cross. Adjustments may also be necessary during the cross-examination itself.

2.06 Should There Be a Cross-Examination?

The decision to cross-examine must be made both before and again during the case, immediately after a witness has testified. Witnesses usually merit cross-examination questioning. It is rare not to conduct some cross-examination of a witness.

Consider the following:

- Has the witness damaged the case?

- Is the witness important to the other side?

- Will the fact finder expect cross-examination?

- Did the witness omit important adverse information on direct examination?

- Will cross-examination unavoidably bring out information that is harmful to the case?

- Are questions being asked only for the sake of asking questions?

- Does this witness present any difficulties that may cause substantial problems?

2.07 Full and Fair Opportunity to Cross-Examine

An advocate has a right to cross-examine a witness fully and fairly. Unusual situations may arise that prevent cross-examination—when a privilege has been asserted, when illness makes a witness incapacitated, or when a witness refuses to answer. These problems may be resolved by a motion brought before a judge or arbitrator to allow a full or limited cross-examination.

2.08 What is the Scope of Cross-Examination?

Judges and arbitrators have broad discretion to permit inquiries into all relevant matters. The scope of cross-examination is usually limited to the subject matter of direct examination and matters affecting the witness's credibility. Beyond that, cross-examination may be restricted.

2.09 Preparing Topics and Written Questions in Advance

Cross-examination is most effective when topics and questions are prepared in advance. The extent to which specific written questions should be prepared depends on the nature of the question, the significance of the topic, the type of witness, and the abilities of the advocate.

2.10 Selecting Exhibits

Witnesses can be effectively cross-examined using exhibits the witness is familiar with. A piece of real evidence may have been introduced through another witness, and the cross-examined witness may be confronted with it. Or an exhibit can be introduced on cross-examination by having the witness—using leading questions—lay the foundation for the exhibit. An exhibit that provides supporting information can be introduced through an opposing witness.

2.11 How Should Cross Be Structured?

Cross-examination questions ought to be asked in an order that makes the cross-examination most effective, interesting, persuasive, and memorable.

Structuring techniques include:

- Listing all the points expected to be made
- Dividing the points into the two broad categories of cross-examination—supportive and discrediting
- Ranking each point from most to least important
- Reorganizing the order of the points into a final format

2.12 Order of Cross

If both categories of cross-examination questions—supportive and discrediting—are to be used, the supportive cross-examination questions ought to be asked first. There are a number of reasons for this approach—the witness is more likely to be more cooperative at the beginning of a cross-examination and the fact finder may be more likely to believe the supportive cross-examination responses. The advocate should begin and end the cross-examination with strong points. An alternative to a logical sequence of planned questions is to probe areas in a random fashion. However, this can confuse the fact finder and is difficult to conduct well.

If exhibits are used, they should be woven into the cross-examination. If only one or a few exhibits are to be used, they should be introduced when the relevant point or points are being made. If there are many exhibits, it may be best to structure their introduction so there are some breaks between the waves of exhibits to avoid confusion.

2.13 How Should Cross Be Concluded?

The concluding questions of a cross-examination should end on a high note, should not be objectionable, and should be the type the witness will respond to agreeably.

2.14 Recross Examination

The scope of recross-examination is limited to the subject matter of the redirect examination. The rules governing recross are the same as a cross-examination. There often is no need to conduct a recross-examination, and recross-examination should not be conducted merely because redirect questions were asked.

2.15 Where to Cross

The cross-examiner should be visible and conspicuous during the examination. The best location and movement strategy depends on several variables, including placement of witness, use of visual aids, position of fact finder, ability of the advocate, and rules and limitations placed on the examination by the judge or arbitrator.

2.16 "Uncross" Demeanor

Combative or angry cross-examination is usually ineffective. The focus of cross-examination is both on the advocate—because the advocate makes the substantive statement—and the witness—who gives the short responsive answer. Composure, persistence, confidence, and assertiveness make the examination effective and persuasive.

2.17 Tactical Considerations

Effective cross-examination requires the use of proper tactics and techniques. Many of these approaches are principles that should not be violated.

The advocate must consider:

- The form of the question
- The content of the question
- Seeking agreement with witness
- Controlling the witness's responses
- Emphasizing points
- Asking safe questions
- Preparing questions for specific witnesses

C. THE FORM OF THE QUESTIONS

2.18 Lead the Witness

Questions that suggest the answer and elicit "yes" or "no" answers should be asked on cross to control the testimony. An effectively phrased question contains the answer, which the witness must affirm or deny. It is best usually not to ask "why," "how," or "explain" questions.

2.19 Use Simple, Short Questions

Short, straightforward leading questions in simple understandable language are most effective. Lengthy, rambling, leading questions are confusing and often receive lengthy, rambling, and unwelcome answers.

2.20 Avoid Multiple Negative Questions

Questions that contain double or multiple negatives are confusing, misleading, and improper.

D. COMPOSING QUESTIONS

2.21 Ask Factual Questions

Questions that include specific facts prompt responsive answers, because the statement is true, because there is evidence to prove the fact, or because the witness previously made the statement. Questions that include words or phrases that are subjective or conclusory permit the witness to evade or explain an answer.

2.22 Properly Ask for Opinions

An effective way to compel a witness to provide an opinion is to first establish the factual basis that compels the witness's opinion to agree with the examiner's proposition. Once the foundation questions are established, the witness will feel compelled to agree with the reasonable conclusion or risk losing credibility.

2.23 Use Modifiers

The use of selective adjectives and adverbs as modifiers may help in obtaining favorable responses from a witness. If a witness agrees that she got a "good" look at someone, she may also agree she got a "very" good look.

2.24 Use Synonyms

If the cross-examination seeks to compel the witness to agree with a specific word or phrase, suggesting a synonym may be useful instead of trying to force the witness to admit the specific language. A witness may not agree that he was "exhausted," but will agree that he was "tired."

2.25 Be Courteous

Witnesses ordinarily deserve courteous treatment. Most witnesses do not deserve to be questioned in an obnoxiously aggressive manner. It is more effective to be polite, assertive, and persistent than very aggressive. Unless otherwise and obviously deserved, the judge, arbitrator, or fact finder expects the advocate to be respectful to the witness.

2.26 Enhance the Self-Interest of the Witness

Ask questions that make the witness look good. Witnesses are much more likely to agree with a position that serves their self-interest. If an employee is reluctant to admit she was tired at the end of a day of work, she will be more likely agree if that concession is softened by establishing that she worked a long day, was busy, and is a dedicated and hard-working employee.

2.27   Establish Concepts with the Witness

To provide the fact finder with a different perspective and explanation of a situation, ask questions that contain a concept with which the witness will agree, rather than trying to force an answer to a specific word. A witness may balk at saying it was very dark out, but will agree that there was not much light and the witness could only see about fifty feet ahead.

2.28   Employ Indirection

With indirect questions the witness does not perceive why a question is being asked or the purpose of the line of questioning until the point is made. The answers to indirect questions may obviously relate to issues in the case and be explained in final argument.

F.   CONTROLLING RESPONSES

2.29   Know the Answers

Ask only those questions to which the answer is already known by the cross-examiner and provide information that supports the final argument. Surprises in cross-examination are not fun. There will be situations where the cross-examiner will need to ask questions to which he can only predict how the witness will respond. Answers should be sought which are known or have a high degree of predictability.

It's also quite helpful to know where answers are preserved. The source typically is the deposition transcript of the witness or a document. Having those sources readily available and in plain view of witnesses will make them more likely to agree to factual assertions of what they know, what they said, or what they did.

2.30   Avoid the Prejudicial Unknown

Inquiry into uncharted areas on cross-examination can be especially dangerous because the witness may give answers that do not help the case. It can be difficult to rebound from such a response. It is best not to probe into unknown areas.

2.31   Listen and Observe

Listen to the answers and observe how the witness responds to follow-up questions. Listen carefully to the answers. Follow up on incomplete, nonresponsive, and inconsistent answers.

2.32 Control the Witness

The most effective way to control witnesses is to ask questions to which they must agree. Ask short, fact-based, simple questions. Compel the witness to answer. There is no reason not to agree with the leading question—it is understandable, it is based on the facts, and it is not confusing. If the witness does not answer the question the first time, repeat it.

Additional ways to control the witness include:

- Insist on an answer to the question
- Rephrase the question seeking the same answer
- Advise the witness to answer
- Seek an agreement from the witness to cooperate just like they did on direct
- Ask the judge for assistance

2.33 Close Loopholes

To increase the chances a witness will agree with an important question, it may be necessary to ask a witness a series of preliminary foundation questions that prompt responsive answers. Anticipate why a witness may try to evade answering and ask questions that eliminate the opportunity.

2.34 Avoid Asking One Question Too Many

Stop asking questions when the necessary information has been obtained. There may be no good reason to go further than planned. Get the answer and stop. Go on to the next point.

2.35 Avoid Explanations

Questions that ask "why" or "how" permit a narrative response and invite disaster. The witness should not be permitted to clarify or explain. Make the point and stop. The other side can clarify.

2.36 Expand Points

A single question on a topic can be broken into a series of questions that emphasize the point and have more impact. Instead of asking one question: "You had a few drinks that night." Ask three questions: "You had one drink? Then another? And one more?"

2.37 Save Point for Final Argument

While it can be effective to ask questions that only become clear in final argument, questions usually should be designed so that at the end of a series of questions the fact finder has an understanding of the point being made.

H. ASKING SAFE QUESTIONS

2.38 Repeat Supportive Direct Examination

Direct examination testimony that supports the cross-examiner's case should be repeated on cross-examination. Previous testimony that does not support the case should be avoided.

2.39 Ask "Neutral" Cross-Examination Questions

Safe, neutral questions can establish control and train the witness to answer "yes" or "no." They can establish a rhythm and an expectation. The witnesses will be inclined to answer questions the same way when the questioning becomes more difficult.

I. DESIGNING QUESTIONS FOR SPECIFIC WITNESSES

Children, experienced witnesses, experts, and witnesses with communication problems require special consideration with both the formulation and delivery of questions.

2.40 Cross-Examining the Evasive Witness

Efforts to control or correct the behavior of evasive witnesses often results in frustration. Continued questioning of an evasive witness using short, controlled leading questions demonstrates control, helps obtain the answer, and demonstrates the witness's evasiveness and lack of credibility. Final argument is the time to point out to the fact finder why the evasive witness should not be believed.

2.41 Cross-Examining Reputation Witnesses

This opportunity does not occur very often as few cases involve reputation witnesses. Questions can establish specific bad acts, prior misconduct, convictions, and other instances of misconduct that contradict the reputation established on direct examination.

J. DISCREDITING CROSS-EXAMINATION APPROACHES

Cross-examination can be structured to demonstrate how a story is implausible, improbable, or impossible.

2.42 The Implausible Story

The story does not comport with common sense or common life experience, making it appear incredible.

2.43 The Improbable Story

A witness's version of a story is hard to believe when it is unlikely the story could have happened that way.

2.44   The Impossible Story

Some witnesses may sincerely believe what they perceived and remember even if the story is completely impossible and wrong. Carefully crafted questions can get the witness to show the impossibility.

2.45   Establishing Inconsistencies Between Witnesses

Cross-examination can clarify and emphasize inconsistencies between witnesses' stories. Witnesses may be asked if they agree with answers given by another witness.

2.46   Employing Impeachment Strategies

Impeachment is a tactic designed to reduce the credibility of the witness, a story, or another witness. *See* FRE 106.

2.47   Using Material Issues to Impeach

Impeachment is most effective when important issues, significant facts, or opinions reduce the credibility of the witness or story. If an issue is collateral, immaterial, or insignificant the impeachment is usually ineffective or disallowed. Impeach on major points and not minor points, unless there are several minor points that amount to a major point.

2.48   Proving Impeachment through Extrinsic Evidence

A witness may occasionally deny the impeaching evidence, and the cross-examiner is usually permitted to introduce extrinsic evidence to establish the impeaching fact. An extrinsic source is any source of evidence (usually an exhibit or the testimony of another witness) other than the present witness.

2.49   Responding to Impeachment Evidence by the Direct Examiner

The direct examiner has a number of options when facing impeachment evidence. The direct examiner can:

- Object to the attempted impeachment
- Request related statements from a deposition or prior testimony be introduced immediately in an effort to reduce the impact of the impeachment
- Explain the impeaching evidence on direct or redirect examination
- Rehabilitate an impeached witness with a prior consistent statement if it rebuts a charge of fabrication or improper motive or statement

K.   AREAS OF IMPEACHMENT

There are eight established areas of impeachment.

2.50   Interest, Bias, or Prejudice

Witnesses may have an interest, bias, or prejudice in a case that motivates them to testify in a certain way.

2.51   Competency Deficiencies

Cross-examination may establish that a witness has deficiencies in the four competency requirements—oath, perception, recollection, and communication.

2.52   Inadequate Observation/Lack of Perception

To reduce the witness's credibility, the ability of the witness to observe an event or to perceive a situation may be challenged.

2.53   Poor Recollection/Lack of Memory

Cross-examination can reveal reasons why the witness's memory is lacking or unduly influenced.

2.54   Inconsistent Conduct

Cross-examination can show that the actions of the witness contradict the testimony.

2.55   Impeachment by Criminal Record

A witness may be impeached by introducing the witness's prior criminal conviction. *See* FRE 609.

2.56   Impeachment by Specific Instances of Untruthfulness

Evidence relating to the untruthfulness of a witness may be introduced against that witness during the cross-examination of that witness. *See* FRE 608(b).

L.   IMPEACHMENT STRATEGIES AND TACTICS

2.57   Impeachment by Prior Inconsistent Statements

The credibility of a witness may be diminished on cross-examination if prior statements made by the witness are inconsistent or contradictory. A witness can only be impeached with a prior statement that witness made, not with a statement made by another witness. *See* FRE 613.

2.58   Prior Inconsistent Statements

There are three major steps:

1.   Reaffirm the direct examination testimony

2. Describe the circumstances of the prior inconsistent statement

3. Introduce the prior inconsistent statement and obtain the witness's response to the inconsistent statement

2.59 Reaffirming Direct Examination Testimony

The witness is committed to the direct testimony by being asked questions that contain and repeat the earlier testimony. Precise questions prevent the witness from claiming confusion about the prior direct testimony when confronted with impeaching evidence.

2.60 Describing Circumstances

Although not required as a prerequisite to impeachment, the circumstances under which a prior statement was made help the fact finder understand the background and prevents a witness from explaining away the contrary evidence. For example, the procedures used (under oath) and persons present (their lawyer) when the witness testified at deposition can be established.

2.61 Introducing Statement

The impeaching statement is read by the advocate or shown to the witness, who reads the statement aloud.

2.62 Obtaining the Witness's Response

When the witness admits to making the prior statement, the impeachment is concluded. If the witness denies it, the statement can be introduced as an exhibit through the witness or extrinsic evidence (a person who heard and recorded the statement) may be offered to authenticate the statement. If a deposition is the source, that portion of the disposition transcript is introduced into evidence.

2.63 Significant Prior Inconsistent Statement

Only significant, material discrepancies should be the basis for impeachment, unless there is a pattern or a significant number of minor inaccuracies.

2.64 Introducing Contemporaneous Prior Statements

The direct examiner can request that additional portions of the prior statement be introduced contemporaneously with the impeaching part of the statement to prevent a cross-examiner from introducing selected facts out of context.

2.65 Types of Prior Inconsistent Statements

There are five major categories of inconsistent statements:

2.65.1   Prior Statements Under Oath (Oral Testimony)

These statements include testimony provided at depositions; administrative hearings; and previous trials, motion hearings, preliminary hearings, grand jury hearings, inquests, and other proceedings.

2.65.2   Prior Statements Under Oath (Documents)

Prior and consistent statements may appear in answers to interrogatories, the responses to requests for admissions, a verified complaint, or other documents signed by the witness under oath.

2.65.3   Written or Electronic Statements

Written statements include writings that have been signed, agreed to, or approved by a party. Examples include written statements given to a police officer or investigator, handwritten notes by the witness, typed statements that are signed by the witness, affidavits and court documents, business records, e-mails from the witness, electronic documents, and other printed documents.

2.65.4   Oral Statements

Any oral statement a witness has made to anyone may be used as a source during impeachment.

2.65.5   Omissions

A common method of impeachment involves a cross-examination of a witness regarding a matter testified to under direct examination that does not appear in a prior written statement. The omission is significant because there is no record of this material statement made in writing prior to the direct examination testimony, and it will appear to be unsupported or fabricated.

SECTION 3: EXPERT EXAMINATION

A.   EXPERTS

3.01   When to Use an Expert

An expert should be used when the scientific, technical, or other specialized knowledge of the expert will assist the fact finder in understanding the evidence or in determining a fact that is in issue. An expert is a person who has specialized knowledge gained by education, training, experience, or skill.

3.02   Purposes of Expert Testimony

Expert testimony may provide a fact finder with factual information, opinions based on expert knowledge, explanations regarding scientific principles and theories, testimony regarding test procedures and results, interpretations of the facts and real evidence, the amount of recoverable damages, and an opinion that contradicts the opposition's expert.

3.03   Who Is an Expert?

A person who has specialized knowledge gained by education, training, experience, or skill may be qualified as an expert.

3.04   Areas of Expertise

The general test that most jurisdictions apply to determine expertise is whether the area of expertise has gained general acceptance within the relevant scientific, technical, or other specialized expert community, or has been otherwise recognized as a subject of expert information.

3.05   Preparation for Expert Testimony

The advocate should know the subject on which the expert will testify as well or better than the expert. Without this specialized information, the advocate may miss critical information or be unprepared to conduct a direct or cross-examination.

B.   DIRECT EXAMINATION OF EXPERTS

3.06   Qualifying the Expert

The rules of evidence require that the expert must be qualified in the area about which the expert will testify. *See* FRE 702. The judge or arbitrator determines whether the expert is "competent" based on the expert's education, training, and experience. The expert may only testify in those areas in which she is qualified.

3.07   Establishing Qualifications

Qualifications may be presented in sequence at the beginning of the examination or may be mixed throughout. An effort should be made to "humanize" the expert. The qualifications should be presented in an interesting and nonbragging fashion. Common areas of qualifications are:

- Personal background
- How and when expert became involved in case
- Occupation
- Education and training

- Professional organizations
- Professional achievements
- Writings/scholarships
- Legal experience
- Specialized experience
- Firsthand knowledge about case
- Specific examination or tests involved
- Fee for time spent as an expert in case

3.08 Alternative Approaches to Qualifications

Alternative ways to qualify an expert include submission of the expert's resume or stipulations to the qualifications of the expert by opposing counsel.

3.09 Expert Opinions

An expert's testimony will usually include a number of opinions, and an expert needs to testify about the sources of information supporting an opinion, the opinion itself, and the bases of the opinion. The advocate in some jurisdictions may need to use specific words as a predicate to the introduction of an opinion such as: "Do you have an opinion to a reasonable degree of certainty?"

3.10 Outline of Expert Opinion

A summary outline includes:

- Subject matter of opinion
- Theories or supportive principles
- Sources of information
- Exhibits that support testimony
- Standard tests or procedures
- Specific tests or procedures used in case
- Opinion(s)
- Bases of opinion(s)
- Explanation of the opinion(s) and conclusion(s)

3.11 Sources of Information

Sources of information are critical to support the opinion. FRE 705 and similar state rules provide exceptions. Sources include:

- Firsthand information

- Information obtained from other experts, documents, records, files, and individuals (*see* FRE 703)

- Evidence, including testimony heard or told to the expert during the instant proceeding

- If necessary, hypothetical questions

3.11.1   Personal, Firsthand Information

The foundation for this knowledge requires the expert to testify about where, when, and how the observations were made; who was present; and then provide a description of the observations.

3.11.2   Information Obtained from Other Sources

An expert may rely on information from other sources as long as it is the type relied upon by other experts in the same area to reach conclusions. Commonly this information consists of discovered documents and deposition testimony. Documents include electronically stored information and paper materials.

3.11.3   Information Obtained at the Proceeding

The testimony of lay witnesses and other experts can provide the basis for an expert opinion.

3.11.4   Hypothetical Questions

Hypothetical questions are not required, but can be used if the expert has not been able to otherwise review the facts of a case. The direct examiner asks the witness the hypothetical question, which contains facts that have been or will be introduced during the proceeding. The expert is asked to form an opinion based on the hypothetical questions. Hypothetical questions should be prepared in advance with the assistance of the expert, and they should be read as written to avoid mistakes.

3.12   Narrative Questions and Responses

The direct examiner usually wants an expert to answer narrative questions with explanatory responses. More latitude is allowed to permit experts to provide narrative answers. A mix of short and long answers is helpful to maintain the fact finder's interest as well as effectively educate the fact finder. The expert acts like a teacher explaining circumstances and opinions to the fact finder.

3.13 Explaining Technical Terms

The direct examiner must understand and know how to pronounce all of the expert's technical terms and then explain those terms and concepts in plain language. The expert should testify in a way that is understandable to a lay person. If testing is involved, the expert must explain why the testing was done and why the result is valid.

3.14 Use of Treatises

A treatise, book, periodical, or pamphlet may be used on direct and cross-examination. The authenticity of a treatise may be established by a reliable authority, through the admission of a witness, through another verifying expert, or through judicial notice. The treatise information can be admitted as substantive evidence, or impeachment evidence, or both.

C. CROSS-EXAMINATION OF EXPERTS

3.15 Preparing to Cross-Examine the Expert

In cross-examining an expert, the advocate must gather information about the expert's identity, qualifications, opinions, bases for opinions, data and documents supporting opinions, information relied on in forming opinions, publications, previous trial or deposition experience as an expert, former times testifying on behalf of a plaintiff or defendant, and fees. The cross-examiner must become knowledgeable in the area by studying, using texts, taking classes, and consulting other experts.

Issues that need to be addressed include:

- What type of expert is involved in the case?
- Is the identity of the expert discoverable?
- What is discoverable?
- How can the expert help in preparing?
- How can the expert help during trial?
- What are the expert's qualifications?
- What are the sources of information?
- Are they ordinarily relied on?
- Is the information relied on admissible?
- Need it be?
- What are the expert's opinions?
- Are they consistent with others?
- Can differences be reconciled?

- What are bases for opinions?
- How will the expert be prepared?
- By whom?
- How will the expert testify most effectively?
- What exhibits are needed?
- What visual aids will be helpful?
- What writings has the expert authored that will be helpful?
- Harmful?
- Are there areas of impeachment?
- Will other experts be able to attack the opinion?

3.16 Cross-Examination Areas

The cross-examination approaches and techniques that apply to lay witnesses also apply to experts. Other tactics that can be used to cross-examine experts include the following supportive and discrediting approaches.

- *Obtaining Concessions.* An opposing expert may be used to establish, agree with, or corroborate positions and opinions of the supporting experts.

- *Criticizing the Other Side's Position.* The opposing expert may also be used to criticize the opposing party's position, statements, or conduct.

- *Expert Fees and Financial Interests.* If the expert receives an excessive amount of money for testimony, the amount of the fee can be established.

- *Bias or Prejudice.* An expert may have developed a bias because of an involvement in similar cases or because the expert is involved regularly with one side or has done previous work for the client or advocate.

- *Inadequate Sources of Information.* Questions may reveal that an expert relied on incomplete or inadequate sources.

- *Unreliable or Insufficient Information.* Some experts may base an opinion on subjective facts obtained from a party or other information that is not reliable because of its source or content.

- *Disputed Facts.* Some of the facts that form the basis for the expert opinion may be disputed. If the facts change, the opinion may change.

- *Using Exhibits.* Case exhibits may contain information that contradicts or differs from the expert's testimony. Sources include electronic and printed documents, e-mails, and paper materials.

- *Lack of Thoroughness.* Questions can be asked that show how little an expert has done and how much more an expert could have done.

- *Insufficient Testing.* An expert may not have conducted sufficient tests or followed adequate procedures to support an opinion.

- *Existence of Other Causes.* Often there are alternative explanations for something that happened other than that explained by the expert on direct examination. Cross-examination can demonstrate these other possible causes and diminish the credibility of the expert's opinion.

- *Inappropriate or Insufficient Expertise.* Some opposing experts may be vulnerable to attacks on the lack of education, training, experience, or skills in an area of expertise involved in the case.

- *Differences of Opinion Among Experts.* Opinions in some areas are subject to significant and legitimate differences of opinion among qualified experts. This is especially true in subjective or interpretive fields.

- *Subjective Opinions.* An expert may admit that the opinion the expert reached is a matter of judgment and not based on some immutable principles.

- *Inconsistent Prior Statements.* An expert witness can be cross-examined using any oral or written statement by that expert that is inconsistent with the opinion given at trial.

- *Hypothetical Questions.* If a hypothetical is used in direct examination, an effective way to cross-examine is to ask the expert concise hypothetical questions that contain facts different from the direct examination hypothetical and that result in differing opinions.

- *Safely Exposing Deficiencies.* If questions suggested in the previous subsections are too risky, "safe" questions can be asked that address the limited amount of time the expert spent reviewing the information, the fact that the information the expert relied on has been provided by the party who retained the expert, and the facts and information on which the expert relied are not the facts on which other testifying experts in the trial relied.

- *Lack of Reliability of the Field of Expertise.* If the cross-examiner does not present an expert in the so-called "field of expertise" presented by the opposing party's expert, the cross-examiner may use cross-examination to establish the unreliability of the "field of expertise" and the failure of experts in the broader area of study to accept the reliability of the posited field.

- *Treatises.* Treatises can be used to impeach the expert as well as for other purposes. *See* FRE 803(18).

APPENDIX C. FORMS *(FORMS ALSO AVAILABLE ON DISK)*

DIRECT EXAMINATION
Form 3-A   Witness Information Worksheet
Form 3-B   Direct Examination Outline

CROSS-EXAMINATION
Form 3-C   Cross-Examination Planning Worksheet
Form 3-D   Impeachment by Omission/Prior Inconsistent Statement Worksheet

EXPERTS
Form 3-E   Expert Witness Information Worksheet
Form 3-F   Expert Testimony Planning Worksheet

DIRECT EXAMINATION
Form 3-A: Witness Information
                    Worksheet

File Number: _____
Client Name: _____
Contact Info: _____
                    _____
                    _____

Witness Information Worksheet

Witness

Contact Info

Other Important Information

Witness Statement Made: Date _____ Signed _____ Copy Given Witness _____

Deposition: Date _____ Transcript _____ Read _____ Signed _____

Witness Prepared for Deposition: Date _____ Location _____

Deposition Transcript Read by Attorney _____ Summarized _____

Witness Prepared for Trial: By _____ Date _____ Location _____

Witness Subpoenaed: Date _____ Subpoena/Duces tecum Served: Date _____

Trial/Arbitration Appearance: Date _____ Time _____

Anticipated Purpose of Witness

Key Questions/Topics to Ask Witness

Exhibits to be Introduced or Used

File Number: _____
Client Name: _____
Contact Info: _____
                      _____
                      _____

Direct Examination Outline

Witness

Contact Info

Key Facts to be Proved by Witness

Key Phrases of Witness Testimony

Key Facts of Cross Examination

Exhibits to be Introduced through or Used by Witness

Key Points to be Covered in Redirect Examination

File Number: _____
Client Name: _____
Contact Info: _____
               _____
               _____

Cross-Examination Planning Worksheet

Witness

Contact Info

Key Facts of Anticipated Direct Examination

Key Areas for Cross-Examination

Source of Information

Supportive Cross—Facts that support case

Discrediting Cross

　　Poor Perception

　　Poor Memory

　　Poor Communication

　　Testimony inconsistent with common sense

　　Testimony inconsistent with other facts

Bias/Prejudice/Interest

Prior Criminal Record

Bad Reputation/Bad Acts

Character Evidence

Prior Inconsistent Statements

Other Areas for Cross

Prior Statement/Probable Testimony

Source of Information (statement, documents, other witnesses)

File Number: _____

Client Name: _____

Contact Info: _____

_____

_____

Impeachment by Omission/Prior
Inconsistent Statement Worksheet

Witness

Previous Statements Made

A. *Deposition Statements*   Date: _____   Signed: _____

    1.   Page _____ Line # _____
        Summary of Statement

    2.   Page _____ Line # _____
        Summary of Statement

    3.   Page _____ Line # _____
        Summary of Statement

    4.   Page _____ Line # _____
        Summary of Statement

    5.   Page _____ Line # _____
        Summary of Statement

    6.   Page _____ Line # _____
        Summary of Statement

B. *Interrogatories*   Date: _____   Signed: _____

   1. **Question # _____   Line # _____**
       Summary of Statement

   2. **Question # _____   Line # _____**
       Summary of Statement

   3. **Question # _____   Line # _____**
       Summary of Statement

C. *Request for Admissions*
   Date of Response

   Admission # _____

   Admission # _____

   Admission # _____

D. *Written/Signed Statements*

E. *Other Statements*

File Number: _____

Client Name: _____

Contact Info: _____

_____

_____

Expert Witness Information Worksheet

Expert Witness

Title, Degree

Personal Background

    Contact Info

    Family

    Length of residence

    Hobbies

    Clubs

    Social organizations

    Charitable organizations

How, When Expert Becomes Involved

    Treating physician

    Consultant

    Examination for trial (plaintiff or defense)

    Neutral expert

    Retained by plaintiff or defense

    Fees

Occupation

    Employer

    Position/description/responsibilities—how long

    Prior employers/positions/responsibilities

Education

    Undergraduate degree(s)

      Institution

      Graduation date

Advanced degree(s)

    Institution

    Graduation date

Advanced degree(s)

    Institution

    Graduate date

Training

What

Where

When

By whom

Certificates/licenses

Professional Organizations

    Name

    Purpose

    Length of membership

    Authority in organization

Professional Achievements

Books

Articles

Teaching

Lectures

Consultations with other professionals

Awards/honors

Legal Experience

As witness

    Plaintiff or defense

    Frequency of testifying

Consultant

    Organization or parties

    Frequency

Specialized Experience

    Type of experience

        Tests

        Examinations

        Study

        Consulting with others

        Personal interview

    Number of Tests

    Results

Specific Examination or Tests Involved in Case

    Why

    When

    Where

    How

Reports

    Date

    Summary

    Supplement

Exhibits

    Exhibits already prepared

    Exhibits to be prepared

Weaknesses

    Weakness of profession

    Weakness of expert

    Weakness of opinion

    Bias

    Prejudice

    Interest

    Lack of information

    Lack of testing

Opinions

Basis of Opinion

Sources of Opinion

Exhibits

File Number: _____
Client Name: _____
Contact Info: _____
_____
_____

Expert Testimony Planning Worksheet

Witness

Contact Info

How and When Did Expert Become Involved?

Qualifications

Options

Basis of Opinion

Sources of Opinion

Reports

Exhibits/Treatises

Probable Cross-Examination Areas

Redirect Examination

Fee Agreement

CHAPTER FOUR

OBJECTIONS AND EXHIBITS

SECTION 1: OBJECTION PROCEDURES

A. SCOPE

1.01 Why Object?

Decision makers base their decisions on relevant and reliable evidence, and evidentiary rules help determine what is relevant and reliable.

Objections are used to exclude evidence and to oppose improper questions, conduct, and procedures. An objection may emphasize an opponent's evidentiary problems, force the opponent to alter the introduction of evidence, alter the presentation of the case, or gain a tactical or strategic advantage.

All objections create a record and preserve an error as a ground for a new trial, new hearing, or an appeal. The failure to make an objection usually waives any right to an error as a ground for appeal.

1.02 The Type of Case

Rules of evidence govern the admissibility of evidence in trials. Evidentiary rules are not as rigidly or uniformly enforced in arbitrations and administrative hearings. However, evidentiary rules, applied flexibly, do guide arbitrators and administrative law judges.

1.03 Evidentiary Considerations

Objections should be planned around the following considerations.

- *Gaining a tactical or strategic advantage.* If making an objection will help win the case or gain a useful advantage, do it. If not, do not waste the time, energy, and effort.

- *Inadvertently helping the opponent.* If objecting helps the opponent by calling attention to things that need correcting, don't object.

- *The nature of the evidence.* Consider objecting to anything that lacks probative value, is unclear or confusing, is collateral to the issues in dispute, or breaches a rule of evidence. Even if an objection exists, don't object unless the improper evidence has an impact on the case.

- *The approach of the judge or arbitrator.* The knowledge and inclination of the judge, arbitrator, or administrative law judge to sustain or overrule an objection serves as a guide to the advocate when deciding whether to object.

- *The reaction of the fact finder.* Incessant objections may alienate and annoy the fact finder. The fact finder may perceive that the objecting advocate is attempting to hide evidence or is acting unfairly by making technical or too many objections.

- *Highlighting specific evidence.* Refrain from objecting, knowing that an objection might highlight the improper evidence and may unduly emphasize or increase its weight.

- *Making a clear and complete record.* Objections that are stated clearly and have a legal basis will create a good record and may hold participants accountable for offensive conduct.

- *Preservation of an error for post-trial motions and appeal.* Objections should be made to preserve an error for possible appeal.

- *The ability of an opponent.* Sustained objections may interrupt a poorly prepared or inexperienced opponent, while more experienced opponents won't be ruffled. Whether an advocate objects to take advantage of an opponent is a decision that must be made considering all the factors and whether the advocate is acting as an appropriate zealous advocate or an obstreperous meddler.

- *Strategic Impact.* By making appropriate objections, the advocate will appear alert, in control, and knowledgeable; the judge will be more likely to pay attention to subsequent objections; the opponent may be less inclined to offer inadmissible evidence; witnesses will be easier to control; and the fact finder may pay more attention to the argument of the more competent and skillful advocate.

B. PLANNING

1.04 Know the Rules of Evidence and the Judge, Arbitrator, or Administrative Judge

Objections are based on violations of the rules of evidence, local rules of practice, civil and criminal procedure, case law, common sense, and fairness. Not all judges recognize all objections. Even though the rules of evidence may not formally apply, administrative judges or arbitrators use them as guide.

1.05 Anticipating Evidentiary Problems

When preparing and presenting evidence, recognize and understand the potential objections that may be asserted—and structure questions to avoid evidentiary infirmities.

Anticipate potentially inadmissible evidence and prepare objections to that evidence. A motion in limine may be brought before the hearing begins or before a witness testifies to obtain a ruling on the admissibility of evidence before it is introduced. The judge, arbitrator, or administrative law judge may rule on evidentiary admissibility, which helps the advocates decide what evidence to offer.

1.06   What Is Admissible and Why?

The judge or arbitrator decides what is admissible and may make preliminary decisions regarding the admissibility of evidence (FRE 104). The fact finder decides the weight or probative value of evidence.

1.07   How to Make Evidentiary Objections

The process of making evidentiary objections includes two separate decisions:

- Is there a legitimate, good-faith available objection supported by the law and rules of evidence?
- Is there a valid strategic or tactical reason for making the objection?

An advocate must make split-second judgments whether to object even while concentrating on everything else happening in the trial or arbitration. This skill is learned and enhanced through practice and experience.

Suggestions to increase the ability to think quickly include:

- Become familiar with the types of common objections
- Ask whether evidence is relevant and reliable
- Learn to recognize patterns of evidence that create objectionable situations
- Prepare a list of objections to anticipated evidence
- Concentrate on the evidence as it is being introduced
- Listen and watch the examination attentively
- Rely on common sense
- Be willing to make mistakes and lose an objection
- Prepare to be surprised and anticipate the unexpected
- Watch the judge and see if an objection is encouraged
- Rehearse making objections to anticipated evidentiary problems

1.08   Deciding Whether to Make Objections

Whether an objection should be made depends on the value and impact of the evidence. The more critical the evidence is to winning or losing a case, the more likely the objection should be made. There are four basic guidelines to follow in determining whether to object to inadmissible evidence:

- If the evidence is clearly admissible, don't object
- If the offered evidence is clearly inadmissible and harmful, object
- If the evidence is probably inadmissible but not harmful, consider not objecting, or object but do not pursue the issue if the judge overrules the objection
- If the answer to the question will reveal favorable or neutral information, don't object

1.09 Making Alternative Objections

Objections that may be available to the same piece of evidence include:

- Improper form of the question
- Irrelevant
- Cumulative
- Unfairly prejudicial
- Lack of foundation
- Improper opinion
- Hearsay
- Original writing (best evidence) required

1.10 Explaining Why No Objection Is Made

In some circumstances, informing the fact finder why no objection is made may make the advocate appear more confident than merely saying, "We have no objection, Your Honor." The advocate may state: "We want the jurors to hear this testimony," or "We agree that the jurors should see this exhibit," or "We want you (the fact finder) to have the benefit of this evidence." Many judges or arbitrators do not allow speaking objections (or speaking nonobjections) and limit the objection to the legal grounds for the objection.

1.11 Accepting an Objection by Invitation

A judge may occasionally look at opposing counsel when evidence is being introduced and ask "Any objections?" This may be a routine practice by the judge or it may be a signal the judge will sustain an objection. An advocate should not object merely because the judge believes an objection ought to be made, but rather the advocate should reconsider and assert an objection if strategic reason exists for doing so.

C. HOW TO PRESENT OBJECTIONS

1.12 How to Object

Typically most jurisdictions and most judges require or expect an advocate to stand when objecting. The advocate may say "I object" while seated and then stand to state the reason for the objection. The extra time gained by standing may help in framing an objection. Typically, in arbitrations and administrative law cases objections may be made while seated.

1.13 When to Object

An objection must be timely made.

- If a question is improper, the objection must be made before the answer is given.

- If a question is proper but the response is inadmissible, an objection should be made as soon as the inadmissible nature of the evidence becomes apparent.

- If the examiner is asking questions too rapidly, or if the witness is answering questions quickly, the judge may be asked to instruct the questioner or witness to proceed at a reasonable pace, which provides an opportunity to object before the witness responds.

1.14 How to Phrase an Objection

The proper way to object in most jurisdictions is to say "objection" and state the specific ground or grounds with a few identifying words. Using the name or title of the rule involved is usually sufficient: "Objection, hearsay" or "We object, Your Honor, on the grounds of hearsay." More than one ground may support an objection, and all applicable grounds should be stated. It may be helpful to refer to an evidentiary rule number, especially if the judge relies on them.

1.15 Speaking Outside the Hearing of the Jury

Jurors should not be influenced by inadmissible evidence or the explanations of counsel. Speaking objections—arguments made in front of the jury—are rarely appropriate. If an advocate needs to explain an objection further, permission to approach the bench should be requested and arguments made at the bench so the jurors cannot hear.

1.16 The Applicable Law

Advocates often know before a trial or hearing that they will be opposing the introduction of particular evidence. Admissibility of the evidence may not be clear. A short memorandum of law can be prepared in advance and used at the time of the objection.

1.17 Demeanor

Objections and responses should always be directed to the judge or arbitrator and not the opponent. Speak with a firm tone of voice, appear calm, and display an air of professionalism and respect for the judge or arbitrator and the opponent.

1.18 Responding to the Judge

In order to be expeditious, some judges or arbitrators may pressure advocates to not make objections. If the judge or arbitrator interferes with the assertion of objections, the objecting party may put into the record that the interference is improper and adversely affecting the case.

1.19 Making Continuing Objections

If an objection is overruled, and similar questions are subsequently asked, the advocate may consider making a "continuing" objection to a series of related questions. The grounds for a continuing objection should be stated clearly. Continuing objections are not recognized in all jurisdictions.

1.20 Responding to Objections

The examiner need not say anything unless instructed to or encouraged to do so by the judge. However, the examiner may oppose an objection when necessary and may provide authority for the admissibility of the evidence or may make an offer of proof.

1.21 Presenting Contrary Evidence

Contrary evidence demonstrates that an objection should be sustained. An objecting advocate may have an opportunity to introduce contrary evidence before the judge rules on an objection that seeks to exclude evidence. An objection on the grounds of lack of competency may allow the objecting advocate to ask questions of the witness to support the objection. Judges may allow the examination to be interrupted and permit contrary evidence if the advocate appears able to establish the inadmissibility of the evidence. The objecting advocate may introduce contrary evidence by questioning the witness to lay grounds for the objection or, in unusual circumstances, through extrinsic evidence.

- *Questioning the Witness.* The most common way to introduce contrary evidence is through the questioning of the witness (voir dire), which allows the opposing advocate to question the other side's witness with leading questions to introduce contrary evidence and have the objection sustained.

- *Presenting Extrinsic Evidence.* Evidence from a source other than the witness on the stand, such as another witness or a document, may be admissible in very limited circumstances—to support a claim of privilege, for example.

D. EVIDENTIARY RULINGS

1.22 Discretion

Trial judges, arbitrators, and administrative law judges have broad discretion in making evidentiary rulings. The standard is whether there exists evidence sufficient to support a finding of the proposition sought to be proven.

1.23 The Ruling

Ordinarily, the judge or arbitrator rules immediately after an objection and says "sustained" (the objection is valid) or "overruled" (the objection is denied). Even if the question or answer is objectionable, many judges do not sustain an objection if an incorrect ground is stated, thus requiring the objecting advocate to identify and state the most correct ground.

1.24 Provisional Ruling

The judge or arbitrator may make a provisional ruling, which can be reconsidered later. The main reason for doing this is that the relevancy of evidence may be determined by evidence to be introduced later. When that later evidence is introduced, the judge will reevaluate the original ruling.

1.25 Inquiring About a Ruling

Examining advocates may ask the judge/arbitrator to explain the basis of the ruling. If the ruling is unclear, the advocate may ask for an explanation. For example, if an objection is sustained that there is a lack of foundation for the admissibility of evidence, the advocate can ask where the foundation is lacking or make an offer of proof demonstrating the foundation. Although judges or arbitrators do not often change their minds, they may be asked to reconsider a ruling.

1.26 Renewing an Objection

Opposing advocates may ask to argue in opposition to ruling; however, renewing an objection by objecting to the next related question may be more effective. Persistence should be coupled with respect.

1.27 Pursuing Objections

Objections to subsequent questions may be pursued if the original objection was overruled because it was premature. For example, if the question was not completed or the objection was to a preliminary foundation question, the objection should be restated after the next objectionable question.

1.28 Obtaining a Ruling

A judge or arbitrator may fail to make a ruling on an objection. Advocates have a right to a ruling and should insist on one.

E. MOTION IN LIMINE

1.29 What Is It?

A motion in limine (meaning at the threshold) seeks an advance ruling regarding the admissibility or inadmissibility of evidence. It may be made before a trial, arbitration, or administrative hearing. Motions in limine are used more frequently in trials, as arbitrations and administrative hearings are less formal and the rules of evidence are relaxed.

1.30 Why Make a Motion In Limine?

Motions in limine may be brought for several purposes:

- To prohibit the opponent from introducing or mentioning objectionable evidence

- To require the opponent to obtain a ruling on admissibility before evidence is offered

- To obtain a preliminary ruling by the court that evidence offered by the proponent is admissible

1.31 Motion In Limine Procedure

Motions in limine may be made either in writing or orally on the record, depending on the nature of the issue and the local rules. Motions in limine usually require that reasonable, advance notice be given to the opponent. The timing of the notice depends on the nature of the motion, the rules of the jurisdiction, and the evidence in question. A motion in limine should state the specific relief sought and the grounds supporting the motion.

1.32 In Limine Order

Judges, arbitrators, and administrative hearing judges may rule in one of several ways regarding an in limine motion. They may:

- Refuse to hear the motion because it is untimely

- Defer the ruling on the motion until later

- Deny the motion but permit the moving party to bring the motion again for reconsideration at a later time

- Grant the relief sought in the motion in limine

- Enter a conditional order requiring that only certain facts be introduced into evidence
- Grant a motion and preclude any introduction and reference either directly or indirectly to the inadmissible evidence

1.33 Preserving Error

A ruling on a motion in limine preserves that evidentiary issue as a ground for a new trial. In some jurisdictions, a party who loses a motion in limine may need to take further steps to preserve the evidentiary issue.

1.34 Violation of Order

Violating an in limine order may result in reversible error, and an intentional violation may subject an offending attorney to sanctions.

F. OBJECTION PROCEDURES

1.35 Offers of Proof

If an objection is sustained, the examiner must make an "offer of proof" to preserve the error for appellate review or to try to convince the judge to reconsider the ruling. The offer of proof describes the excluded evidence to demonstrate its admissibility and significance. There are three ways to make an offer of proof:

- *Summary Offer of Proof.* The testimony may be summarized by the attorney or the record. This is the most common method.
- *Question/Answer Format.* Witnesses may be questioned to demonstrate what the evidence will be.
- *Submission of Testimony.* A written statement of the anticipated testimony may be submitted for the record.

1.36 Reconsideration of Ruling

The offer of proof provides an opportunity for the advocate to explain why the evidence is admissible and also provides an opportunity for the judge or arbitrator to reconsider the original ruling.

1.37 Motion to Strike

A motion to strike is made after an objection has been made and sustained. A motion to strike clarifies the fact that the improper statement or inadmissible evidence is not to be considered by the fact finder. Nothing is stricken from the record. A motion to strike should be used if required to preserve the record or to satisfy a local rule.

1.38 Request for Curative Instruction in a Jury Trial

This instruction, requested by the attorney harmed by the improper question, objectionable evidence, or conduct, repairs the harm done. The judge instructs jurors to disregard what they heard or saw.

1.39 Limited Admissibility

Evidence that is admissible for one purpose, but not for another may be admitted.

A request may be made that evidence be admitted for a limited purpose, such as:

- Admit the evidence and limit its purpose by stating why it is being admitted.

- Admit the evidence without comment.

- Exclude evidence if unfairly prejudicial.

For example, a letter may be admitted to show that a response was written, but not to prove its contents, which may be inadmissible hearsay.

1.40 Objections to Court Questioning

An objection may be made to any question asked by a judge or arbitrator that violates a rule of evidence. All jurisdictions permit judges or arbitrators to ask questions of a witness. Most judges do not exercise this right in jury trials. It is more likely to occur in court trials, arbitrations, and administrative hearings.

1.41 Preserving the Evidentiary Error

A timely objection will put the issue on the record. All available grounds for an objection should be specifically stated and should include the evidentiary error that may be used in a motion for a new trial, new hearing, and on appeal.

1.42 Motion for Mistrial

Inadmissible evidence that has been improperly admitted may be a ground for a mistrial or a new hearing. The inadmissible evidence must be so unfairly prejudicial that a party is denied a fair hearing.

1.43 Prejudicial Error

Significant prejudicial errors may result in the outcome of a trial or hearing to be reversed; however, most evidentiary errors do not affect the outcome of the trial or hearing. If they do not substantially prejudice a party, they do not warrant a new trial or hearing.

1.44 Appellate Review

Judges have substantial discretion to determine what evidence to admit and what to exclude. Appellate courts seldom reverse cases on evidentiary rulings, although excluded evidence is more likely a basis for reversal than admitted evidence. Many judges admit questionable evidence and leave it up to the fact finder to decide how relevant or credible it is.

SECTION 2: EVIDENTIARY OBJECTIONS

A. OBJECTIONS TO DIRECT EXAMINATION QUESTIONS

2.01 Leading Questions

Leading questions are improper because they provide or suggest the answer—the advocate is testifying instead of the witness. A limited number of leading questions are permitted in direct examinations and are allowed in all cross-examinations (FRE 611(c)).

Responses to objection:

- Rephrase the question and ask a nonleading question
- Explain that the question falls within one of the permissible uses of leading questions on direct examination
- Explain that the trial or hearing will proceed more quickly through the use of a reasonable number of leading questions

2.02 Narrative Answer (FRE 611)

An objection may be made to a question that calls for a narrative or for an answer that turns into a narrative. An improper narrative allows the witness to tell a long, uncontrolled story. Because the answer is not controlled, an advocate cannot anticipate the testimony and object to improper testimony before it is heard by the fact finder. Tactically, it might be beneficial to let a witness ramble if the uncontrolled testimony makes the opponent's direct examination ineffective.

Responses to objection:

- Politely interrupt the witness and stop the rambling
- Ask a specific question to maintain control of the examination's direction
- Explain to the judge that these open-ended questions save time
- Explain that the narrative answers cover uncontroverted, preliminary, or insignificant matters and do not cover significant issues in the case
- Say to the witness, "I'll ask you some specific questions so you can give specific answers"

2.03 Nonresponsive/Volunteered Answer (FRE 611)

A nonresponsive answer occurs when a witness provides unrequested information. The response that goes beyond the question is objectionable.

Responses to objection:

- Interrupt the witness politely and stop the nonresponsive answer.

- Ask more specific questions that require the witness to give shorter answers.

2.04   Vague and Ambiguous Questions (FRE 611)

Questions should be clear. They must not be vague as to time, circumstance, and phrasing. Tactically there may be no advantage in objecting if the questions are so confusing that they make no sense and the direct examination is not effective.

Responses to objection:

- Rephrase the question to make it clearer

- Ask the witness if the question was understood

- If the objection is overruled, request that the reporter read back the question to show how clear the question was and how the opponent is attempting to interrupt a proper examination

2.05   Cumulative Evidence (FRE 403, 611)

Cumulative evidence is repetitious evidence. A series of witnesses testifying to the same thing or a series of exhibits providing identical information would be repetitive and unnecessary.

Responses to objection:

- Explain that the evidence is not repetitive, but adds important details to evidence already admitted

- Explain that the evidence is not improperly cumulative; rather, the corroborative evidence from additional sources is needed to buttress the facts being proved

- If the objection is sustained, continue the questioning and return to the evidence during a later stage of the witness's examination.

2.06   Misstatement of Evidence (FRE 611)

Misstatement or mischaracterization of evidence is objectionable because it inaccurately describes evidence.

Responses to objection:

- Point out that evidence has already been introduced that refers to the question or answer

- Explain that the characterization in the question or answer is a proper admissible opinion

- Explain that there is a source of evidence that will support the question or answer; request that the testimony be conditionally accepted subject to the introduction of the supportive evidence

2.07 Assuming Facts Not in Evidence (FRE 611)

This objection is used to object to questions that assume facts that have not been introduced in evidence.

Responses to objection:

- Revise the question and remove the questionable facts
- If the witness can describe the facts, allow the witness to testify to the facts

B. OBJECTIONS TO CROSS-EXAMINATION QUESTIONS

2.08 Repetitious Questions (FRE 403, 611)

If a question has been asked and answered, all similar questions are objectionable. The question doesn't have to be identical. This objection is also known as "asked and answered." It prevents the opponent from gaining undue advantage by repeating testimony.

Responses to objection:

- Explain that the points need to be emphasized on cross-examination
- Explain that the witness is attempting to be evasive, thus requiring similar and related questions to pin the witness down
- Move to the next line of questioning, then emphasize the point during final argument

2.09 Misleading or Confusing Questions (FRE 403)

A question must be reasonable, clear, and specific.

Responses to objection

- Rephrase the question so it is not misleading or confusing
- Ask if the witness understands the question

2.10 Multiple or Compound Questions (FRE 403, 611)

A multiple or compound question includes two or more questions within a single question. These types of questions are objectionable because answers are ambiguous.

Response to objection:

- Repeat one of the questions, ask the witness to answer that question, then ask the other

2.11 Mischaracterization of Evidence (FRE 611)

This objection addresses questions that include facts not in evidence or statements that improperly misstate or mischaracterize the evidence. These questions may be an attempt to trick the witness or may be argumentative.

Responses to objection:

- Introduce the evidence before asking this question

- Explain that the evidence has been introduced previously and refer the judge to that evidence

- Explain to the judge that such evidence will be introduced at a later stage and request that the judge conditionally accept this evidence subject to subsequent proof

- Argue that one of the purposes of cross-examination is to test the memory and credibility of a witness and that the witness can deny the asserted facts if the witness disagrees with the assertion

2.12 Argumentative Questions (FRE 611)

Any question that is essentially an argument is improper because it elicits no new information or harasses the witness. Often an argumentative question is delivered in a sarcastic or loud tone.

Responses to objection:

- Ask the question again, eliminating the objectionable comment

- Ask the question again, changing the tone so that the question does not sound argumentative

2.13 Improper Impeachment (FRE 613)

Improper impeachment is an attempt to incorrectly discredit a witness. A cross-examiner may attempt to impeach the witness on a collateral, unimportant, or irrelevant matter, or attempt to impeach the witness with a prior statement that is not materially inconsistent.

Responses to objection:

- Explain how the impeachment is not collateral or the prior statement is not materially inconsistent

- Ask additional cross-examination questions that establish the relevancy and importance of the impeachment

2.14 Beyond the Scope (FRE 611)

Cross-examination is restricted to the subject matter of the direct examination and matters relating to the witness's credibility. Since credibility is always an issue, the scope of cross-examination is quite broad. A cross-examiner may be permitted to raise new matters during cross. However, any questions that go beyond the permissible scope of an examination are objectionable. If the cross-examiner wishes to go beyond the permitted scope, the cross-examiner must usually call the witness on direct examination and ask questions.

Responses to objection:

- Point out testimony from direct examination that relates to the cross-examination question

- Explain that the questions relate to the credibility of the witness or another witness

- Explain that the judge has discretion to allow questions to be asked beyond the scope of direct examination

- Explain that if these questions are not permitted at this stage of the trial, the witness will be recalled at a later stage, and doing so will cause delay, create confusion, and inconvenience the witness.

C. OBJECTIONS BASED ON EXCLUSIONARY RULES OF EVIDENCE

The judge decides whether an evidence rule requires evidence to be excluded.

The exclusionary rules of evidence can be grouped into the following categories:

- Irrelevant and unfairly prejudicial evidence

- Privileged information

- Lack of personal knowledge and improper opinion

- Lack of foundation for documents and other exhibits

- Constitutional limitations or evidence in criminal cases

- Hearsay

2.15 Irrelevant Evidence (FRE 401–403)

Only relevant evidence is admissible (FRE 401, 402). Evidence is relevant if it is more than less likely to prove a point (FRE 401). Relevant evidence is admissible (FRE 402). However, relevant evidence may be excluded when the probative value is substantially outweighed by its prejudicial effect (FRE 403). Most relevancy objections involve circumstantial evidence that requires the drawing of a weak or remote interference. The advocate must have an explanation available for the admissibility of the evidence.

2.16   Immaterial Evidence (FRE 401–402)

Immaterial evidence is inadmissible because evidence must have some logical relationship to the case. It is not usually a distinct objection, but it falls under an irrelevancy objection. The concept of material and immaterial is related to the concept of "what's of consequence to a case," which includes issues contained in the pleadings and applicable substantive law.

2.17   Unfairly Prejudicial (FRE 403)

Unfairly prejudicial evidence is inadmissible even if it is relevant. All evidence is in some way prejudicial because it hurts one side or the other, but only unfairly prejudicial evidence is inadmissible. The prejudicial effect must substantially outweigh its probative value. For example, evidence that appeals primarily to passion and not the facts and law is not admissible.

2.17.1   Improper Character Evidence (FRE 404–405)

Character traits are usually inadmissible. They are not admissible to prove a person acted in conformity with those traits on a particular occasion. For example, evidence of a character trait of negligence is usually not admissible in a tort case.

2.17.2   Improper Habit Evidence (FRE 406)

Habits are generally not permitted to prove a person acted in a certain way. For example, evidence of intemperance is inadmissible because the fact finder may be unfairly inclined to find the party guilty or liable because of past conduct.

2.17.3   Subsequent Remedial Measures (FRE 407)

The term "subsequent remedial measures" refers to actions taken after an event which, if taken before the event, would have made the event less likely to occur. An example would be repairing a car's brakes after an accident caused by faulty brakes. Such evidence is not admissible. It is unfairly prejudicial and misleading because it implies a recognition of liability. On the other hand, such evidence is admissible when the issue to be proved involves controverted matters of ownership, control, feasibility of precautionary measures, or impeachment of a witness.

2.17.4   Offers of Compromise (FRE 408)

Evidence of offers to resolve a dispute is not admissible because the offer could be interpreted as an admission of liability. Evidence of a compromise offer may be admitted as an exception to the general rule to prove bias of a witness or to rebut a contention of undue delay.

2.17.5   Payment of Medical Expenses (FRE 409)

Offers to make payment for medical expenses may not be offered to prove liability for an injury.

2.17.6   Plea Bargains (FRE 410)

A person accused of a criminal offense may offer to plead guilty to a lesser offense and avoid trial. A person may also plead nolo contendere, in which she neither admits nor denies guilt. These offers may not be used as admissions of guilt and may not be used as evidence later. If a guilty plea is entered, but later withdrawn, it too is inadmissible.

2.17.7   Liability Insurance (FRE 411)

The existence or nonexistence of insurance coverage is not admissible regarding an issue of negligence or wrongful actions. It is only admissible if offered to prove agency, ownership, control, bias, or impeachment issues.

2.17.8   Religious Beliefs or Opinions (FRE 610)

Religious beliefs or opinions are not admissible evidence to show credibility.

2.18   Privileged Communication (FRE 501)

A privileged communication consists of a communication between persons having a confidential relationship. Protecting this privilege encourages open, honest, communication between certain persons. Statements made under the protection of a privilege are not admissible unless the privilege is appropriately waived.

2.18.1   Attorney/Client Privilege

For this privilege to attach, a professional relationship must exist between an attorney and a client who seeks legal advice, and a communication intended to be confidential must be made between the attorney (or agent of the attorney) and the client, who is the holder of the privilege.

2.18.2   Doctor/Patient Privilege

This privilege requires a professional relationship between a doctor and a patient who seeks medical assistance, and a communication regarding medical advice made between the doctor (or medical assistant) and the patient, who is the holder of the privilege.

2.18.3   Marital Communication Privilege

This limited privilege requires a valid marital relationship and confidential private communications between spouses made during the marriage.

2.18.4   Waiver of Privilege

Any privilege may be waived if:

- The holder or attorney, with the consent of the holder, knowingly and expressly waives the privilege

- Voluntary disclosure of the privileged information occurs during discovery or trial (*see* FRE 502)

- No objection is made to a question eliciting privileged communications

- A privileged matter is discussed in the presence of a third person

- An eavesdropper without using surreptitious means overhears a privileged communication

- The holder raises a claim or defense that places the privileged matter in issue

D. FOUNDATION OBJECTIONS

2.19   Lack of Personal Knowledge/Improper Opinion (FRE 601–602)

A witness may not testify to any matter unless that witness has personal knowledge of the matter or the matter is a proper subject for a lay person's opinion.

2.20   Lack of Foundation (FRE 901–903)

Foundation is preliminary information that must be established before specific evidence is admissible. Foundation objections prevent the introduction of the specific evidence or force the opposing advocate to provide the missing element. It may be strategically beneficial not to point out the missing element of foundation as the evidence will look more credible if the foundation can be supplied. It may be more effective not to object and to point out the missing elements during final argument.

2.21   Lack of Foundation for Expert Opinion (FRE 702–705)

Expert opinion is not admissible if the information is not scientific, technical, or otherwise based on specialized knowledge; the expert has insufficient expertise; or the opinion is unreliable.

2.22   Lack of Foundation for Lay Witness Opinion (FRE 701)

Lay witness opinions and conclusions are only admissible if they are rationally based on the perception of the witness and help the fact finder understand the facts of the case. Permissible lay opinions may be given on speed, distance, time, appearances, conditions, emotions, age, health, sobriety, value of personal property, and other rational perceptions.

2.23 Speculation (FRE 602, 703)

Questions that ask the witness to guess or engage in conjecture are objectionable forms of opinion testimony. Speculation on the part of a witness as to what could or should have happened is usually of little probative value.

E. DOCUMENT OBJECTIONS

2.24 Admissibility of Documents

Four evidence rules determine the admissibility of a document:

- Relevance
- Hearsay
- Original writing
- Authentication

Whenever a document is introduced, the opponent should scrutinize every part of it and object to any part that is inadmissible.

2.25 Original Writings (FRE 1001–1007)

This rule applies to writings, documents, e-mails, electronically stored information, recordings, and photographs. Originals and duplicate originals may be introduced to prove the contents unless the authenticity is questionable. Issues regarding electronic documents include the original native format of the document and any metadata that may exist.

The rule does not apply to oral testimony. The rule does provide that if the original or copies cannot be obtained, other evidence as to the contents is admissible. The modern rule is called the "original writings" rule, which is also traditionally called the "best evidence" rule.

There are three situations when oral testimony is reliable without the need for a document.

- *Signs, Titles, Labels, Tags.* Oral testimony about signs, titles, headings, labels, and tags is admissible because it involves only a few words on these items.

- *Independent Facts.* Facts that exist independently of a document and that are known to a witness may be established without requiring the document. For instance, a tenant can testify to the rent due date without producing the lease agreement.

- *Collateral Matter.* Oral testimony concerning a document is permissible if the issue being testified to is indirectly related and not significant to an important issue in the case.

2.26 Lack of Authentication (FRE 901–902)

Writings must be authenticated to be admissible—that is, they must be shown to be what they purport to be. A lack of authentication objection is similar to a lack of foundation objection.

2.27 Parol Evidence Rule

The parol evidence rule provides that a written agreement cannot be contradicted or modified orally. Exceptions include ambiguous writings, fraud, or incomplete writings.

F. CONSTITUTIONAL LIMITATIONS IN CRIMINAL CASES

Federal and state constitutional provisions establish limitations for admitting evidence in a criminal case. Evidence obtained in a way that violates the defendant's constitutional rights is inadmissible. The privilege against self-incrimination is an accepted privilege.

G. IMPROPER OBJECTIONS

Certain objections are improper, inapplicable, inappropriate, or not recognized in a jurisdiction.

They include:

- Objections on the grounds of irrelevant, immaterial, and incompetent (too general)
- Objections on the grounds of improper and unfair (too general)
- Objections on the grounds of self-serving (groundless)
- Objections on the grounds of prejudicial (must be unfairly prejudicial)

H. OBJECTION CHECKLIST

2.28 Common Legal Objections Checklist

COMMON LEGAL OBJECTIONS CHECKLIST

Title	Rule	Description
Relevancy	FRE 401–411	Irrelevant No probative value Unfairly prejudicial Improper character Improper habit Subsequent remedial measures

Title	Rule	Description
		Offers of compromise Plea bargains Payment of medical expenses Liability insurance
Privileges	FRE 501–502	Attorney/Client Physician/Patient Spousal testimony Marital communications Clergy/Penitent Trade/Business Secrets Informer identity Governmental information News sources
Competence	FRE 601–602	Incompetent Lack of personal knowledge Lack of memory
Inadmissible		Court order evidence not disclosed as required by discovery requests
Foundation	FRE 601–612	Lack of foundation
Lay Opinion	FRE 701	Impermissible opinion Impermissible conclusion Speculation
Expert Opinion	FRE 702–705	Unqualified witness Impermissible opinion
Authentication	FRE 901–902	Lack of Authenticity
Original Writing	FRE 1001–1007	Inauthentic copy Nongenuine original Not native format
Parol Evidence		Statutory or case law

2.29 Improper Form of Questions Checklist

IMPROPER FORM OF QUESTIONS CHECKLIST

Title	Rule	Description
Leading	FRE 611	Lawyer testifying
Narrative	FRE 611	No question before witness speaking
Nonresponsive	FRE 611	Volunteered
Repetitious	FRE 401, 611	Asked and answered
		Cumulative
Vague	FRE 401–403	Vague Confusing Misleading Unintelligible
Multiple Questions	FRE 611	Compound questions
Assuming Facts Not in Evidence	FRE 611, 701–704	No facts in evidence Inaccurate hypothetical
Mischaracterization of Testimony	FRE 611	Misstatement of evidence Inaccurate quotation of testimony Inaccurate/incomplete reading of exhibit
Argumentative	FRE 611	Badgering
Improper Impeachment	FRE 608	
Beyond Scope	FRE 608	Direct or cross

SECTION 3: HEARSAY

A. HEARSAY EVIDENCE

3.01 Introduction to Hearsay (FRE 801–904)

Hearsay occurs when a witness testifies to a statement made out of court. The statement may be one that is made by that witness or another person. Hearsay involves one or more defects that make it unreliable: the fact finder can't gauge the credibility or sincerity of the declarant when the statement was made, the out-of-court statement might not be repeated accurately, the declarant was not under oath when the statement was made, or it may not be possible to cross-examine the declarant.

Hearsay is inadmissible if it is unreliable. Most "hearsay" statements are permitted because they are sufficiently reliable, do not qualify as hearsay, or fall under an exception. The following sections explain the basis for admissible hearsay.

3.02 Hearsay Definition (FRE 801)

There are three essential factors to a hearsay statement:

- *The method of communication.* Hearsay statements may be oral, written, or asserted conduct.

- *The location when the statement was initially made.* Hearsay statements must be made out-of-court and repeated in court.

- *The purpose for which the statement is offered.* The out-of-court statement must be offered to prove the truth of what the statement says.

3.03 Admissible Out-of-Court Statements (FRE 802)

The following are admissible out-of-court statements:

3.03.1 Statements Not Offered for the Truth of the Matter Asserted

Statements not offered for the truth of the matter asserted are not hearsay and may be admissible. If the proponent offers the statement for a reason other than its truth, it will be admitted. For example, if the statement "I know it" is offered to prove the declarant could speak, it is admissible.

3.03.2 Nonassertive Conduct

Nonassertive conduct is conduct not intended by the actor to stand for the matter to be proved, and it is not hearsay. An example would be someone testifying "I saw people wearing heavy coats outside." The nonverbal conduct of the people is nonassertive because they did not intend their acts to stand for the proposition sought to be proved—it was cold outside.

3.03.3   Nonproposition Questions

Nonproposition questions are not hearsay because they do not assert a proposition. The question, "And then he said, 'Are you having fun yet?'" is admissible because it does not contain a proposition. "Are you having fun here at the fair?" may be inadmissible because it asserts the proposition that they are at the fair. This proposition permits most questions to be admitted, and many questions are part of an overall conversation. The responses to the question must be individually reviewed to determine if they are admissible as well.

3.03.4   Verbal Acts

Verbal acts or "operative words" are not considered hearsay because they are not offered for the truth, but for their legal significance. The most common examples are statements that constitute the words of an offer or acceptance creating a contract or defamatory words spoken to establish slander. This proposition permits conversations about the creation of a contract and its terms to be admissible.

3.03.5   Declarant Not a Person

A statement is hearsay only if made by a person. A result produced by an inanimate object or the conduct of an animal is not hearsay. A statement by a raven who says "nevermore" is not hearsay.

3.03.6   Party Admissions (FRE 801(d)(2))

Any statement made by an opposing party or the party's agent, employee, or representative is not hearsay and is admissible when offered against that same party. Anything an opposing party said or did that is relevant to the case will be admissible. This is a broad proposition that allows in all statements made by an opponent or a representative acting on behalf of an opponent. The statements do not need to be "admissions"—they can be any statement.

3.03.7   Prior Statements by Witnesses (FRE 801(d)(1))

Prior inconsistent statements made by witnesses under oath at a trial, hearing, deposition, or other proceeding are admissible as substantive evidence of the statements made. Other inconsistent statements may be used to impeach a witness. Prior consistent statements may be used to rebut an indirect or express charge against the witness of recent fabrications or improper influence or motive. These statements, if admissible, are usually offered on cross- or redirect examination.

3.03.8 Prior Identification (FRE 801(d)(1))

Prior identification of a person made by a witness after observing the person is admissible if the declarant testifies at trial and is subject to cross-examination. This proposition permits as evidence a description of a defendant given to the police by a victim or witness.

3.04 Hearsay Myths

Myths regarding hearsay arise from a misunderstanding of the application of the hearsay rules:

- All out-of-court statements are inadmissible. False. Many are admissible.

- A witness on the stand can testify to whatever the witness has said in the past. False. It is still a form of hearsay because it is a statement made out of court and repeated in court.

- If a witness can be cross-examined, all prior statements of the witness are admissible. False. They may still be hearsay and only admissible as an exception, such as a prior inconsistent statement offered to impeach or a prior consistent statement offered to rebut.

- If the proper foundation is laid to authenticate a relevant document, the document is admissible. False. It may be still be inadmissible hearsay. Foundation and relevancy are only two bases for the admissibility of a document; the contents need to be reviewed for inadmissible hearsay.

- Affidavits (statements made under oath) are admissible. Wrong. They are hearsay and may be admissible as any other document.

- Affidavits are admissible if the witness is unavailable. Really wrong. They are still hearsay and may only be admissible as a prior inconsistent or consistent statement.

- Res gestae ("the things done") makes much of hearsay admissible. Huh? The hearsay rules determine what is admissible.

- There is always a hearsay exception that makes the hearsay statement admissible. No. The rules only permit relevant and reliable hearsay.

B. HEARSAY EXCEPTIONS (FRE 803–804)

3.05 Scope

The Federal Rules of Evidence have codified twenty-nine separate exceptions, and many states recognize more. The exceptions recognize that many hearsay statements are reliable and trustworthy, whether or not the declarant is available to testify.

Two exceptions, whether the declarant is available or not, include specific types of **statements** and certain types of **records**. Other exceptions require the declarant to be an unavailable witness not able to testify at trial. Other exceptions may be available in unusual circumstances under the residual exception rule.

3.06   Statements

3.06.1   Present Sense Impressions (FRE 803(1))

Conditions describing or explaining an event or condition made while the declarant was perceiving the event or condition or immediately thereafter are admissible as present sense impressions. These spontaneous statements are deemed reliable because of the lack of time for reflection. This is a very common exception, which permits many statements to be admitted.

3.06.2   State of Mind or Body Exceptions (FRE 803(3))

Spontaneous statements by the declarant regarding the declarant's own mental, emotional, or physical condition are admissible. Statements about past conditions, however, are not admissible. This is also a very common exception, which permits many statements to be admitted.

3.06.3   Excited Utterances (FRE 803(2))

Statements made by the declarant while under stress or excitement that relate to a startling situation are admissible. The rationale for this exception is that spontaneous statements made under stress or during a startling event are reliable because a person with knowledge of the event does not have time to fabricate such statements.

3.06.4   Medical Treatment Statements (FRE 803(4))

Statements made by a person who describes medical history, past or present pains, or symptoms to a medical professional for purpose of diagnosis or treatment are admissible because persons seeking diagnosis have an incentive to be accurate.

3.06.5   Reputation Evidence (FRE 803(19)–(21))

Reputation evidence is admissible hearsay if it is a hearsay statement regarding reputation, or personal or family history, or general history or land boundaries or customs, or character among associates or in the community.

3.07 Records

3.07.1 Records, Generally

Several hearsay exceptions permit the admissibility of specific categories of records. These records are deemed reliable because the information they contain is usually entered and maintained in an accurate, trustworthy manner.

3.07.2 Business Records (FRE 803(6))

Records kept in the regular course of business are admissible (does not matter whether the organization is for-profit or not).

These include:

- Memoranda
- Reports
- E-mails
- Electronically stored information
- Data compilation
- Documents
- Other written, printed, or electronic records

Business records are admissible if:

- The entries are made at or near the time of the event or act
- A knowledgeable person has transmitted the information to a recorder
- The records are kept in a regular business activity
- The recording of the information is a regular practice
- A qualified witness testifies to these facts
- The records are reliable and trustworthy

3.07.3 Public Records (FRE 803(8))

Public records are reliable because public officials record the information pursuant to a public duty or law.

The following public records are admissible:

- Records that describe an agency's activities
- Records of matters observed and recorded pursuant to a duty imposed by law
- Factual findings resulting from authorized investigations
- Land records and property documents

3.07.4   Other Specific Records (FRE 803)

- Market reports and commercial data (FRE 803(17))
- Vital statistics (FRE 803(9))
- Religious organizations (FRE 803(11))
- Marriage/baptismal/and other certificates (FRE 803(12))
- Family records (FRE 803(13))
- Ancient documents of twenty years or more (FRE 803(16))
- Judgments of previous convictions (FRE 803(22))
- Judgments of personal, family, history, or boundary data (FRE 803(23))

3.07.5   Absence of Business or Public Records (FRE 803(7), (10))

The lack of an entry in a business or public record is admissible to prove an event did not occur. There must be a search for the missing entry, and it must be established that the event would have been entered had it happened.

3.07.6   Past Recollection Recorded (FRE 803(5))

Forgotten information that was recorded when the memory was fresh is admissible if:

- The witness cannot fully recall the event
- The witness has personal knowledge of the record
- The witness made the record or adopted it as correct at the time made
- The witness testifies that the report is accurate

3.07.7   Learned Treatises (FRE 803(10))

A learned treatise is a book, periodical, article, pamphlet, or magazine ordinarily the subject of expert opinion. A learned treatise is admissible when it is offered as a reliable authority on a matter and it is relied upon by an expert on direct examination or called to the attention of the expert on cross-examination.

3.8   Declarant Unavailable to Testify at Trial

3.08.1   Declarant Unavailable (FRE 803)

Some hearsay statements are only admissible if the declarant is unavailable. If the declarant is unavailable, hearsay statements regarding former testimony, statements against interest, statements of personal or family history, and dying declarations are admissible. Unavailability includes situations where the declarant is absent from the jurisdiction and unobtainable through subpoena, is too mentally or physically ill to attend, is unable to remember the subject matter of the statement, is exempted from testifying by a court ruling on the ground of privilege, or persists in refusing to testify despite a court order.

3.08.2 Former Testimony (FRE 804(b)(1))

In a civil trial, the testimony given by a witness at a deposition or other hearing may be admitted if the party against whom the testimony is offered had an opportunity to previously examine the witness.

3.08.3 Statements Against Interest (FRE 804(b)(3))

Statements made by a person that are contrary to that person's pecuniary or proprietary interests or subject the person to civil or criminal liability are admissible.

3.08.4 Statements of Personal or Family History (FRE 804(b)(4))

Statements regarding the personal or family history of the declarant are admissible as long as the person testifying was related to a person or intimately involved in a family and likely to have accurate information.

3.08.5 Dying Declarations (FRE 804(b)(2))

A declarant's words regarding the circumstances of the declarant's own death at the time that death is imminent are admissible if declarant believes death is imminent.

3.09 Multiple Hearsay (FRE 805)

A statement may contain more than one hearsay statement. This multiple form of hearsay is called "hearsay within hearsay." And it is common. Each statement must be individually analyzed to determine whether the statement falls within an exception or is defined as nonhearsay and is admissible.

3.10 Residual Hearsay Exceptions (FRE 807)

If a hearsay statement has not fallen into one or more of the above exceptions, the following exception serves as a "catch-all" for admissible hearsay:

- The statement is offered as evidence of a material fact,
- No other evidence exists that is more probative,
- Its admission will serve the interests of justice, and
- The offering party provides opposing counsel with prior notice of the introduction of such a statement.

All four conditions must be satisfied for admissibility. This exception is reserved for unusual evidentiary situations and is not often invoked successfully.

C. HEARSAY OBJECTION CHECKLIST

3.11 Hearsay Evidence Checklist

HEARSAY EVIDENCE CHECKLIST

Title	Rule	Description
Definition of Hearsay	FRE 801	Out of court statement? Assertive or nonassertive? Offered to prove truth of statement? Nonpropositions? Verbal acts?
Nonhearsay	FRE 801(d)	Party admissions Prior statements Prior identifications

3.12 Hearsay Exceptions Checklist

HEARSAY EXCEPTIONS CHECKLIST

Title	Rule	Description
Sense Impressions	FRE 803(1) FRE 803(2) FRE 803(3)	Present Sense Impression Excited Utterance State of Mind
Medical Diagnosis	FRE 803(4)	Medical Treatment Statements
Past Recollection Recorded	FRE 803(5)	
Records	FRE 803(6) FRE 803(8) FRE 803(9) FRE 803(7) & (10) FRE 803(17)	Business Records Public Records Vital Statistics Absent Entries Commercial Data

Title	Rule	Description
	FRE 803(14) & (15)	Property Records
	FRE 803(11) & (12)	Official Certificates
	FRE 803(13)	Family Records
	FRE 803(16)	Ancient Documents
Learned Treatises	FRE 803(18)	
Judgments	FRE 803(22)	Previous Convictions
	FRE 803(23)	Other Judgments
Reputation	FRE 803(21)	Character
	FRE 803(19)	Family
	FRE803(23)	General History
Declarant Not Available	FRE 804(b)(1)	Previous Testimony
	FRE 804(b)(2)	Dying Declaration
	FRE 804(b)(3)	Statement Against Interest
	FRE 804(b)(4)	Personal History
Reliable Hearsay	FRE 807	Material Fact
		No Other Probative Evidence
		Serve Interest of Justice

SECTION 4: EXHIBITS

A. SCOPE

4.01 Types of Exhibits

Exhibits help fact finders understand and remember evidence and some exhibits will be the only evidentiary proof available. Well-prepared and well-presented exhibits help the witnesses and the advocates communicate more effectively and help present an interesting, persuasive, and complete case. There are three major types of exhibits:

- Real evidence
- Demonstrative evidence
- Visual aids

4.01.1   Real Evidence

Real evidence consists of exhibits that are objects, writings, or electronically stored information and are "facts" in a case. Real evidence includes physical objects such as printed or electronic documents in a contract case or the gun used in a homicide. The existence of the exhibit may be the only way to prove a fact, may be corroborating proof, or may be part of a chain of evidence.

4.01.2   Demonstrative Evidence

Demonstrative evidence refers to those exhibits that are not a part of the "real" event. These exhibits are usually created after the event and have no intrinsic probative value. Demonstrative or illustrative evidence includes outlines, electronic or digital files, diagrams, charts, models, movable figures, computer graphics, video presentations, and anything else that augments verbal testimony. They are admissible if they help a witness testify or help the fact finder understand the evidence.

4.01.3   Visual Aids

Visual aids are created and used by advocates to effectively communicate information and to help the fact finder understand the presentation. They are usually not exhibits and are not offered as evidence. Examples include a chart, a PowerPoint presentation, models, computer graphics, a printed summary of test results explained by an expert, or a computerized program prepared as part of a final argument.

There are a variety of electronic hardware and software products that can produce visual aids, as well as demonstrative evidence, including computer programs, monitors, document cameras, LCD projectors, DVD and VCR machines, digital cameras, overhead and slide projectors, laptops, notebooks, and numerous electronic devices.

4.02   Electronic and Digital Evidence

Electronically stored information is routinely introduced in trials and arbitrations. This information is generated and contained in a large variety of electronic and computer devices. The rules of evidence apply to this type of evidence, which may be either real or demonstrative.

Common types of electronic and digital evidence include:

- E-mails
- Business and personal records
- Web site content
- Blog entries
- Chat room conversations

- Computer-generated animations and simulations
- Personal digital devices, such as cell phones and PDAs
- Digital cameras
- Global Positioning System devices
- Metadata in electronic documents
- Other internet information

Evidentiary issues regarding relevance and hearsay are governed by the rules of evidence applicable to handwritten and printed documents. Two evidentiary principles that may involve specialized issues are the rules governing authenticity and original writings (best evidence).

4.02.1   Authenticity

The digital nature of electronically stored information creates authenticity issues. The invisible to the eye and ethereal nature of electronic information makes it susceptible to authenticity challenges. Depending on the type of digital evidence, authentication can be established by:

- The testimony by a witness who can state that it is what it is. For example, Web site information, presented online or as a printed copy, can be authenticated by a witness who can state that he visited the site, is familiar with its contents, and can verify the accuracy of the contents of the site.

- An explanation of the system or process that produced the resulting information. For example, a description of the native format in which the document was originally composed and which reflects the current format should establish authenticity. This testimony may be offered by a custodian of the document or a technical expert.

- A description of distinctive characteristics unique or special to the information. This description may appear in or on the materials or may be established by a witness. Descriptions may include references to the internal content, the substance, or the appearance of the information. For example, a blog comment or a chat room conversation may include references to information only known to a party.

4.02.2   Original Writing/Best Evidence Rule

This evidence rule determines under what circumstances a party must introduce an original, a duplicate, or a copy of a document, writing, recording, or photograph. This rule was created to deal with written and printed information long before electronically stored information became a reality.

The rule allows duplicates of originals to be introduced unless the opposing party can raise a genuine issue regarding the authenticity of the original or can establish that the use of the duplicate is unfair. The rule also permits the use of oral testimony and other evidence to establish the substantive contents if there is no good reason to have the original or a duplicate introduced. These provisions can be used in lieu of having to establish the original of electronically stored information.

B. PREPARING EXHIBITS

4.03 Identifying Potential Exhibits

Real evidence is identified, located, gathered, and preserved during the investigation before the proceeding. Demonstrative evidence is obtained or created prior to and even during the proceeding.

4.04 Assessing the Use of Exhibits

Select exhibits that effectively communicate the case theory, present substantive information to the fact finder, emphasize important areas of evidence, refute the opponent's evidence, and persuade the fact finder of the truth of what happened. An advocate should consider whether the exhibit enhances the ability of the witness to testify more effectively, makes the evidence more memorable, lays a foundation, takes too long, outweighs any unfair impact with its probative value, is cost effective, appears unfair, or creates technical problems.

4.05 Planning a Professional Presentation

The advocate must be able to introduce and use exhibits in a professional manner. The advocate should prepare and rehearse ahead of time so that exhibits are handled properly and have a positive impact.

4.06 Selecting the Witness

Exhibits are usually introduced through a witness. This procedure requires that a witness be selected who is qualified to identify and lay a foundation for the admission of an exhibit.

4.07 Managing Exhibits

The advocate should have specific reference sheets itemizing the exhibits to be used, the necessary foundation for those exhibits, and the witnesses who will provide that necessary foundation.

4.08   Introducing and Using Exhibits

The introduction and use of exhibits requires:

- An understanding of evidentiary issues and problems
- The procedures applicable to the introduction
- The precise questions needed for the foundation
- Potential objections to the exhibits

C. EVIDENTIARY ISSUES

Real and demonstrative exhibits are subject to the rules of evidence like any other piece of evidence.

4.09   Is It Relevant or Unfairly Prejudicial?

An exhibit is relevant if it has any tendency to make more or less probable the existence of any fact that is of consequence to the determination of the action. Even relevant exhibits may be excluded if they are confusing, misleading, or unfairly prejudicial.

4.10   Levels of Foundation

- *Evidentiary Foundation.* Evidentiary foundation must be established before the exhibit can be admitted as evidence. The foundation for real evidence is established by a witness testifying that the tangible object or document is what it is claimed to be. The judge or arbitrator rules on whether sufficient foundation has been established for admissibility.

  The foundation for real evidence requires proof that the object or document is what it is claimed to be.

  There are two types:

  o Real evidence that is readily identifiable because it is unique, and

  o Real evidence that is fungible and lacks unique or readily identifiable characteristics.

- *Persuasive Foundation (FRE 901(b)(1)).* Persuasive foundation is additional evidence to convince a fact finder that the exhibit is important, real, accurate, complete, or true. The extent of this persuasive foundation evidence depends upon the type of exhibit introduced. The fact finder determines what weight to give the evidence.

4.11   Establishing a Chain of Custody

The witness must be able to identify the evidence by its own characteristics, or by the unique container in which a fungible object is kept, or by establishing a "chain of custody" that tracks the object from the relevant event to the courtroom. A chain of custody is not needed for exhibits that have unique identifying characteristics.

Objects that are not unique, that do not have distinctive characteristics, or that have not been marked in any identifiable way, may require a "chain of custody" foundation to make the exhibit admissible.

Objects that are not unique include:

- Liquids
- Narcotics
- Tobacco
- Dirt

A chain of custody accounts for the whereabouts of the exhibit during relevant times of the case.

There are two primary ways of establishing an unbroken chain of custody:

- It can be established that the exhibit at all times has been in the safe, continuing, and sole possession of one or more individuals. When more than one person has had custody of the exhibit, the exhibit must be tracked from one person to the next.

- It can be established that the exhibit bears a unique mark, was distinctively marked, or was sealed and placed in a safe or other tamper-proof container.

Electronically stored information may involve chain of custody issues. Digital evidence that appears on a computer screen, then is stored on a hard drive and backed up in server, and is printed in a hard copy and introduced in a case may require testimony of more than one witness to establish it is the same as the original.

4.12   Limiting an Exhibit's Purpose

The contents of some exhibits may be admissible for one purpose, but inadmissible for other purposes. FRE 105.

4.13   Redacting an Exhibit

When an objection to part of a document is sustained, the ruling will require that the inadmissible portions of the document be redacted (removed).

D. INTRODUCING EXHIBITS

4.14 What to Say

Many exhibits require the examiner to use precise legal terminology for their introduction and use. Advocates are allowed to provide a witness with the legal foundation words in the form of a leading question.

4.15 Steps for the Admissibility of Exhibits into Evidence

The introduction of exhibits requires several steps that the advocate should master and commit to memory.

The steps may vary but the following provides a general format:

- *Establishing Foundation for the Exhibit.* The testimony of the witness regarding the existence of the relevant exhibit is usually sufficient to establish this preliminary foundation.

- *Marking the Exhibit.* Exhibits are marked with a number or letter and are typically marked before the proceeding. The court reporter or clerk usually marks and records the exhibit.

- *Showing Exhibit to Opposing Advocate.* While not required in most jurisdictions, the exhibit should be provided to opposing advocate as a matter of courtesy to inform the opposing advocate of the nature of the exhibit. Doing so will also avoid an interruption by the opposing advocate, who may ask to see the exhibit before it is shown to the witness.

- *Approaching the Witness.* The advocate must approach a witness to give the witness the opportunity to see the exhibit. Some judges and arbitrators require the advocate to ask for permission to approach a witness, and many do not.

- *Examination and Recognition of the Exhibit by the Witness.* The advocate must make it clear for the record that an exhibit is being shown to the witness. The exhibit must be identified by its number or letter. The witness has the opportunity to examine the exhibit and testify how it is recognized.

- *Identification of the Exhibit by the Witness.* The witness may then testify how the exhibit can be recognized and what it is.

- *Offering the Exhibit into Evidence.* A declarative sentence can be used to offer the exhibit. The requirement of specific words may vary. However, once the exhibit is identified, a simple statement such as "I offer Plaintiff's Exhibit No. 1 into evidence" is usually sufficient.

- *Examination of the Exhibit by Opposing Advocate.* After the exhibit is offered, opposing counsel has the right to examine the exhibit and make an objection to its offer. Some jurisdictions require the exhibit be shown to the opponent at an earlier stage, and some advocates make it a matter of practice to allow the opponent to see the exhibit earlier even if not required.

- *Objection to the Admission of an Exhibit.* The advocate opposing the introduction of an exhibit should state the legal ground for the objection. In jury trials, argument concerning the introduction of the exhibit is usually made at the bench outside the hearing of jury. The objecting attorney may ask for permission to question the witness (voir dire) to provide the grounds for an objection to the exhibit.

- *Responding to Objections.* The advocate may need to respond to an objection by making an argument in opposition to the objection, by an offer of proof, or by asking additional questions to overcome an evidentiary deficiency.

- *Showing the Exhibit to the Fact Finder.* How the exhibit is shown depends on the type of exhibit, its importance, and the effect the exhibit will have. The exhibit may be shown to the fact finder; read, if it is a document; passed among the jurors; copied and distributed; enlarged; displayed on a monitor; or played with a video projector.

- *Using the Exhibits.* The advocate may use the exhibit by having the witness mark on it (diagram) or point out specific parts of the exhibit.

4.16 Using Stipulations

The advocates may stipulate to the foundation of an exhibit to avoid the need to ask detailed questions during the case. Stipulations can significantly reduce time and should be voluntarily entered into between counsel if there is no real dispute concerning the authenticity or accuracy of the exhibits.

Stipulations are helpful in introducing electronically stored information. If both parties have digital evidence to introduce, they may be more likely to agree to foundation and authenticity, presuming the information is accurate and complete.

4.17 Admitting Pleadings, Claims, Responses, Admissions, and Discovery Responses

Pleadings and discovery documents are a part of the case, but are not considered as evidence by the fact finder unless or until an advocate affirmatively offers such information as evidence during the case. They may need to be marked as an exhibit depending on the rules of the jurisdiction.

4.18   Abbreviating the Foundation

When there is a series of exhibits for which the foundations are similar, the advocate may abbreviate the process of laying foundation after the first few exhibits have been introduced.

4.19   Admitting Self-Authenticating Documents

Federal Rule of Evidence 902 and similar state rules make it unnecessary to introduce evidence to authenticate certain exhibits, including domestic documents, foreign public documents, certified copies of public documents, official publications issued by public authorities, newspapers and periodicals, trade inscriptions, acknowledged and notarized public documents, and commercial paper and related documents.

E.   EVIDENTIARY FOUNDATION FOR VARIOUS EXHIBITS

The necessary evidentiary foundation questions vary from exhibit to exhibit. Typically, responses are sought that establish the exhibit's existence, identity, authenticity, and accuracy.

4.20   Physical Objects and Properties
(including Products, Clothing, Appliances, and Weapons)

Elements of foundation:

- The exhibit is relevant to the case
- The witness recognizes and can identify the exhibit
- The witness can recall what the exhibit looked like at the previous relevant time
- The exhibit is now in the same or substantially the same condition as when the witness saw it at the previous relevant time

4.21   Documents
(including E-mails, Letters, Electronic Documents, Contracts, Leases, Digital Materials, and Other Signed or Printed Writings)

Elements of foundation:

- The document is relevant to the case
- The document contains a signature, was composed on a computer and printed or was handwritten, or bears some other identifying characteristics
- The electronic or handwritten signature, composition, or characteristic belongs to or identifies a person
- The witness saw the person sign, compose, or write the document; or

     o   The witness knows, is familiar with, or can recognize the content, signature, or handwriting; or

     o   The witness recognizes and can identify the contents of the document; or

     o   The witness is a party and admits signing, composing, or writing it, or identifies the contents of the document; or

     o   A handwriting expert states that the signature or writing is by a certain person; or

     o   A witness can testify to the process and system that was used to create, store, and produce the information; or

     o   The document can be identified by unique characteristics or distinctive information

- The document is authentic

- The document is an original or an admissible duplicate or other copy

- The document is now in exactly or substantially the same condition as when it was made and has not been altered

4.22　Business Correspondence (including Letters, Memos, Files, and Notes)

Business correspondence has similar foundational requirements as documents. Some types of correspondence may require additional foundation evidence to prove it was sent or received.

Elements of foundation:

- The correspondence was addressed to a certain person

- The witness saw or signed the original and a copy of the original

- The witness placed the correspondence in an accurately addressed delivery envelope; or the witness sent the message through an e-mail account; or the witness supervised a person who in the normal course of business processes such correspondence

- The envelope was placed in a mailbox or given to another carrier; or the document was sent by e-mail; or the witness supervised a person who in the normal course of business sends such correspondence

- The copy of the original is an accurate duplicate

- The original correspondence was received by the addressee or was never returned to sender; or an e-mail reply was received and receipt acknowledged

4.23 Electronic Business and Personal Correspondence (including E-mails, Text Messages, Blog Entries, Chat Room Comments)

Courts are developing foundational requirements for electronically stored information, including e-mails and similar digital documents.

Elements of foundation:

- The message was addressed to a certain person
- The message was sent electronically to that person
- The message was received by that person, or the system used to send the message operated properly, or the system receiving the e-mail verified the message was received
- The duplicate of the message introduced is an accurate copy

Other foundation elements may include:

- The receiver acknowledged receiving the e-mail
- The receiver sent back a reply
- The receiver forwarded a copy of the message
- The sender and receiver talked about the contents
- Metadata of the message establishes that it was received

4.24 Internet Information (including Web sites, Search Engine Data, Internet Archives)

Courts are also developing foundational requirements for electronically stored, created, and produced information on the Internet.

Elements of foundation:

- The party or witness is the owner of the Web site or is otherwise responsible for its contents
- The witness properly entered the Web-site URL (address) in a reputable search engine.
- The witness logged on and reviewed the information on the Web site
- The exhibit accurately reflects what the witness reviewed (the exhibit could be a printout, hard copy, monitor screen, or other display)

It is possible that the Web site information had been manipulated and is not authentic or accurate. The opposing party can offer evidence challenging the contents or claiming a hacker created the information. Courts, in determining these challenges, consider whether:

- The information is still on the Web site

- Other sources prove or disprove the offered Web site contents

- Others saw or relied on the Web site contents

- The information is consistent with the purposes of the Web site

- The information is otherwise published or republished

- Metadata proves the information was on the Web site

4.25 Business Records
(including E-mails, Electronic Documents, Memoranda, Reports, Writings, Printouts, or Data Compilations)

Records maintained in the ordinary course of business may be introduced through a witness who does not have personal knowledge of the recorded information, but does have personal knowledge concerning the business recording process. The introduction of this information is allowed by the foundation elements detailed in FRE 803(6) and similar state rules. The term "business" includes any business, hospital, institution, organization, association, profession, occupation, and calling of any kind including nonprofit agencies. The content of business records may include facts, acts, events, conditions, opinions, or diagnoses that are relevant to the case.

Elements of foundation:

- The report must have been "made at or near the time" of the occurrence that gave rise to the report

- The record was made by "a person with knowledge" of the information or was made "from information transmitted by" a person with knowledge

- The record was made in the regular practice of that business activity

- The record was kept "in the course of a regularly conducted business activity"

- The witness is the "custodian" of the documents or is in some other way a "qualified witness"

E-mails, electronic documents, and computer printouts qualify as business records. Questions regarding their creation, composition, retention, and distribution will need to be asked to establish the necessary foundation for admissibility.

4.26 Copies

Modern copying and printing equipment creates accurate copies of original documents and records. These "duplicate" originals are admissible. *See* FRE 1003. A copy may be routinely admitted unless it is of questionable authenticity or it would be unfair to admit a copy. *See* FRE 1003.

Elements of foundation:

- The copy is relevant
- An original did once exist
- The copy was made or produced from the original
- The copy is an authentic and accurate duplicate of the original

4.27 Electronic Recordings (including Audio and Video Recordings)

Elements of foundation:

- The electronic recording is relevant to the case
- The operator of the equipment was qualified to run the equipment
- The recording equipment was checked before its use and operated normally
- The witness heard or saw the event being electronically recorded
- After the event had been recorded, the witness reviewed the recording and determined that it had accurately and completely recorded the event
- The witness can recognize and identify the sounds or images on the recording
- The recording is in the exact same condition at the time as it was at the time of the recording

4.28 Test Results (including MRI Results, CT scans, X-ray Films, Similar Tests, and Laboratory Analysis)

Exhibits containing results from tests and other procedures require special foundation information.

Elements of foundation:

- The exhibit is relevant to the case
- The witness is qualified to operate the equipment
- There exists a procedure that regulates the testing or analysis process
- The witness personally conducted or supervised an operator who conducted the testing, developed the results, or completed the analysis
- The equipment was in normal operating condition
- The witness can recognize and identify the results or analysis
- The results or analysis are in the same condition as when they were completed

4.29 Digital Images, Photographs, and Electronically Produced Images (including Prints, DVDs, and Film)

The use of digital images and photographs is an effective way of making the facts of a case more real for the fact finder.

Elements of foundation:

- The image or images are relevant to the case

- The witness is familiar with the scene displayed in the image at the relevant time of the event

- The image fairly and accurately depicts the scene at the time of the event

There is no need to establish the type of camera or equipment used, focal lens, shutter speed, lens opening, other photography or imaging details, or even when the picture was taken, unless these facts are an issue in a case.

4.30 Demonstrative Evidence (including Visual Demonstrations, Diagrams, Charts, Models, Drawings, PowerPoint Presentations, and Similar Illustrative Aids)

Various types of demonstrative evidence may be useful during the presentation of a case.

Elements of foundation:

- The witness is familiar with the event, depiction, or presentation

- The witness recognizes the depiction or content or is familiar with the exhibit

- The demonstrative exhibit will help the witness explain evidence or will help the fact finder understand the evidence

- The demonstrative evidence is reasonably accurate and is not misleading or distorting

4.31 Computer-Generated Demonstrations

This specialized type of demonstrative evidence can also be very useful in proving or disproving issues in a case.

Elements of foundation:

- The witness is familiar with the scene or event

- The witness has reviewed the demonstration and is familiar with the exhibit

- The exhibit will help the witness explain the evidence or will help the fact finder understand the evidence

- The exhibit is reasonably accurate and does not distort the scene or event

The nature of the computer-generated graphic may require additional foundation:

- The witness has specialized computer training

- The witness is familiar with the underlying facts of the case

- The witness properly entered the relevant data into the hardware and software

- The results produced reflect a reasonable depiction of what happened

4.32   Summary Exhibits

Summaries of evidence may be introduced as an efficient and effective means to explain evidence to the fact finder. Summary exhibits may include an electronic file with evidentiary content, a chart detailing the testimony of one or more witnesses, or a summary description of documents. FRE 1006 and similar state rules permit summaries of writings to be introduced as evidence.

Elements of foundation:

- All the information summarized must be relevant

- The witness has knowledge concerning the information contained in the summary

- The witness has reviewed the exhibit and verified that it is an accurate summary of the evidence

4.33   Past Recollection Recorded

A witness who, at the time of the proceeding, does not have an independent recollection of an event may have previously made a record of that event, and that record may be introduced as an exhibit of real evidence. They may have composed an e-mail, created a blog entry, texted a friend, printed a diary, or written a note.

Elements of foundation:

- The witness has no present recollection of the relevant event

- The witness once had knowledge of the event

- The witness made a record of the event when the matter was fresh in the witness's memory

- The recorded recollection accurately reflects the knowledge of the witness

- The exhibit is in the same condition now as when it was made

4.34   Demonstrations

Live demonstrations or experiments are difficult and unpredictable. They may work well at rehearsal, but can fail too easily at the trial or hearing. A simple demonstration that can be easily performed may be conducted if appropriate. It may be more effective to use a videorecorded or graphically created demonstration.

Elements of foundation:

- The witness can perform or assist in the demonstration
- The demonstration will help the witness explain what happened
- The judge or arbitrator determines that the demonstration will help the fact finder understand what happened.

4.35   Judicial, Administrative, Arbitral Notice

At any time during a proceeding, a judge or arbitrator may take notice of facts that are accurate, verifiable by reliable sources, and indisputable. *See* FRE 201.

F.   THE USE OF TECHNOLOGY

Today's technology provides tools to the advocate that are far more sophisticated than chalk boards, flip charts, and simple diagrams. The introduction of evidence through electronic and digital devices can be very effective and impressive, but technology should not be a substitute for a well-told story. The use of new technological methods of communication should be used carefully and thoughtfully to enhance the presentation of testimony, not distract from it. The advocate must consider the design, cost, placement, backup, and limitations placed on the use of technology by the judge, room, and applicable rules.

4.36   Technological Exhibits and Visual Aids

In most cases simple and inexpensive visual aids and demonstrative exhibits are appropriate and effective.

In some cases an advocate may find the following useful:

- Computer-generated graphics
- Computer-generated reconstructions and working models
- Bar code readers for locating evidence and displaying it on television monitors
- Electronic marking pens and boards
- Digital designs and presentations
- Holographic images
- Virtual reality—an idea whose time has not yet come

G. OBJECTIONS TO THE INTRODUCTION OF EXHIBITS

4.37 How to Prepare for Objections

Anticipate and prepare for any possible objections to the introduction of an exhibit. When an objection is anticipated, foundation questions can be prepared along with arguments and short responsive briefs.

4.38 How to Respond to Objections

If an objection to the introduction of an item of real evidence is sustained, the offering advocate should make an offer of proof, offer the exhibit for a limited purpose, or offer the exhibit as demonstrative evidence.

4.39 Questioning by the Opponent

The opponent may question the witness after an exhibit has been offered to determine if there is a basis for an objection.

4.40 Common Objections

- Irrelevant (FRE 401–402)
- Unfairly prejudicial (FRE 403)
- Misleading and distorting (FRE 403)
- Waste of time (FRE 403)
- Does not assist or aid the fact finder (FRE 401)
- Cumulative or repetitious (FRE 403)
- Lack of foundation (FRE 901–903)
- Inadmissible hearsay (FRE 801–803)
- Violation of original writing rule (FRE 1002)
- Constitutional objections in criminal actions

APPENDIX D. FORMS *(FORMS ALSO AVAILABLE ON DISK)*

OBJECTIONS

EXHIBITS

File Number: _____
Client Name: _____
Contact Info: _____
_____
_____

Objection Planning Worksheet

A. **Evidentiary Questions to be Resolved by Motion in Limine**

Opponent's Evidence Sought to be Excluded

Reason/Argument

Authority

B. **Ruling on Motion in Limine**

C. **Objections to be Asserted Against Opponent's Evidence During Trial/Arbitration**

Evidence

Objections

Authority

D. **Anticipated Objections by Opponent**

Evidence

Potential Objections

Authority

File Number: _____
Client Name: _____
Contact Info: _____
_____
_____

Common Legal Objections Checklist

Title	Rule	Description
Relevancy	FRE 401–411	Irrelevant No Probative Value Prejudicial Unfairly Improper Character Improper Habit Subsequent Remedial Measures Offers of Compromise Plea Bargains Payment of Medical Expenses Liability Insurance
Privileges	FRE 501–502	Attorney/Client Physician/Patient Spousal Testimony Marital Communications Clergy/Penitent Trade/Business Secrets Informer Identity Governmental Information News Sources
Competence	FRE 601–602	Incompetent Lack of Personal Knowledge Lack of Memory
Inadmissible		Court order precludes evidence not disclosed as required by discovery requests
Foundation	FRE 601–612	Lack of Foundation

Title	Rule	Description
Lay Opinion	FRE 701	Impermissible Opinion Impermissible Conclusion Speculation
Expert Opinion	FRE 702–705	Unqualified Witness Impermissible Opinion
Authentication	FRE 901–902	Lack of Authenticity
Original Writing	FRE 1001–1007	Unauthentic Copy Nongenuine Original
Parol Evidence		Statutory or case law

File Number: _____
Client Name: _____
Contact Info: _____
_____
_____

Improper Form of Questions Checklist

Title	Rule	Description
Leading	FRE 611	Lawyer Testifying
Narrative	FRE 611	No Question before Witness
Nonresponsive	FRE 611	Volunteered
Repetitious	FRE 401 & 611	Asked and Answered
		Cumulative
Vague	FRE 401–403	Vague Confusing Misleading Unintelligible
Multiple Questions	FRE 611	Compound Questions
Assuming Facts Not in Evidence	FRE 611 & 701–704	No Facts in Evidence Inaccurate Hypothetical
Mischaracterization of Testimony	FRE 611	Misstatement of Evidence Inaccurate Quotation of Testimony Inaccurate/Incomplete Reading of Exhibit
Argumentative	FRE 611	Badgering
Improper Impeachment	FRE 608	
Beyond Scope	FRE 608	Direct or Cross

File Number: _____
Client Name: _____
Contact Info: _____
_____
_____

Hearsay Checklist

Title	Rule	Description
HEARSAY EVIDENCE		
Definition of Hearsay	FRE 801	Out of court statement? Assertive or nonassertive? Offered to prove truth of statement? Nonpropositions? Verbal acts?
Nonhearsay	FRE 801(d)	Party admissions Prior statements Prior identifications
HEARSAY EXCEPTIONS		
Sense Impressions	FRE 803(1) FRE 803(2) FRE 803(3)	Present Sense Impression Excited Utterance State of Mind
Medical Diagnosis	FRE 803(6)	Medical Treatment Statements
Past Recollection Recorded	FRE 803(5)	
Records	FRE 803(6) FRE 803(8) FRE 803(9) FRE 803(7) & (10) FRE 803(17) FRE 803(14) & (15) FRE 803(11) & (12) FRE 803(13) FRE 803(16)	Business Records Public Records Vital Statistics Absent Entries Commercial Data Property Records Official Certificates Family Records Ancient Documents

Title	Rule	Description
Learned Treatises	FRE 803(18)	
Judgments	FRE 803(22) FRE 803(23)	Previous Convictions Other Judgments
Reputation	FRE 803(21) FRE 803(19) FRE 803(23)	Character Family General History
Declarant Not Available	FRE 804(b)(1) FRE 804(b)(2) FRE 804(b)(3) FRE 804(b)(4)	Previous Testimony Dying Declaration Statement Against Interest Personal History
Reliable Hearsay	FRE 807	Material Fact No Other Probative Evidence Serve Interest of Justice

File Number: _____
Client Name: _____
Contact Info: _____
_____
_____

Exhibit Selection Worksheet

Tangible Objects

Clothing

Products

Appliances

Weapons

Others

Documents

Letters

Memos

Correspondence

Contracts

Leases

Bills

Checks

Others

Business Records

Computer Data

Test Results

       X-Rays _____   Laboratory Analysis _____   Other _____

Photographs

       Prints _____   Slides _____   Movies _____
       Other _____

Diagrams

       Charts _____   Maps _____   Graphs _____
       Drawings _____

Visual Aids

Computer Generated Information/Exhibits

Past Recollection Recorded

Exhibit Summaries

Demonstrations

Chain of Custody Problems

File Number: _____

Client Name: _____

Contact Info: _____

_____

_____

Exhibits Chart

Exhibit Identification Number

Description of Exhibit

Identified By (Witness)

Introduced By (Witness)

Offered Through (Witness)   Date _____   Time _____

Received/Denied   Date _____   Time _____

Offer of Proof Made   Date _____   Time _____

Exhibit Identification Number

Description of Exhibit

Identified By (Witness)

Introduced By (Witness)

Offered Through (Witness)   Date _____   Time _____

Received/Denied   Date _____   Time _____

Offer of Proof Made   Date _____   Time _____

Exhibit Identification Number

Description of Exhibit

Identified By (Witness)

Introduced By (Witness)

Offered Through (Witness)   Date _____   Time _____

Received/Denied   Date _____   Time _____

Offer of Proof Made   Date _____   Time _____

File Number: _____
Client Name: _____
Contact Info: _____
_____
_____

Exhibit Foundation Checklist

EXHIBIT:

Foundation Elements	Witness	What witness will say
•		
•		
•		
•		

EXHIBIT:

Foundation Elements	Witness	What witness will say
•		
•		
•		
•		

EXHIBIT:

Foundation Elements	Witness	What witness will say
•		
•		
•		
•		

EXHIBIT:

Foundation Elements	Witness	What witness will say
•		
•		
•		
•		

File Number: _____
Client Name: _____
Contact Info: _____
_____
_____

Exhibit Introduction Checklist

_____ Establish sufficient *foundation* for the witness to be able to *identify* the exhibit.

_____ Have the exhibit *marked* or pre-marked before the trial.

_____ Determine whether the judge required permission to be obtained to *approach* the witness.

_____ *Provide* opposing *counsel* with a copy of the exhibit or establish for the record that counsel already has a copy (also provide judge with a copy).

_____ Request that the witness *examine* the exhibit.

_____ Have the witness *identify* the exhibit.

_____ Lay the necessary foundation for the *introduction* of the exhibit.

   a.   Relevance

   b.   Authentication

   c.   Hearsay Analysis

   d.   Original Writings (if necessary)

_____ *Offer* the exhibit into evidence by referring to its exhibit number or letter.

_____ Respond to any *objections* made by opposing counsel regarding the exhibit.

_____ Publish (show) the exhibit to the *fact finder*.

CHAPTER FIVE

JURY TRIALS

SECTION 1: SELECTING THE JURY

A. SCOPE

1.01 Jury Selection

Voir dire, another name for jury selection, means to "speak the truth," and the primary purpose of jury selection is to identify and select jurors who can fairly listen to the evidence and reach a verdict. Additional goals are to discern the beliefs, perspectives, and values of jurors and to educate them about the case.

Jury selection could more correctly be called jury de-selection, because it is actually the attorneys' attempt to remove jurors who seem unfavorable to their side. Deciding who to remove is difficult because of limited time and information available. Federal Rules of Civil and Criminal Procedure and similar state rules give judges discretion in conducting jury selection. *See, e.g.,* FRCP 47(a) and FRCrimP 24(a).

1.02 Role of the Attorneys

The role of attorneys varies among jurisdictions. In all jurisdictions, attorneys may bring motions to strike jurors for cause and may exercise peremptory challenges to remove jurors. In some jurisdictions the attorney can only submit written questions that the judge asks the jury; in others, the attorney may ask extensive questions. In federal courts, the judges commonly ask the questions; in state courts, the lawyers typically do.

1.03 Client Participation

When deciding how much input the client should have in jury selection an advocate should consider the ability of the client to make informed decisions about jury selection, the underlying theory or theories that have been chosen for jury selection, the relationship with the client, the impression made on the jurors when a "team" attorney and client effort is demonstrated, and the ramifications of a disagreement with the client about a certain juror.

1.04 Role of the Judge

The role of the judge varies significantly depending on the jurisdiction and the judge. In jurisdictions where the judge asks all the questions, the judge may ask the questions they typically ask or use questions submitted by the attorneys. In jurisdictions where the attorneys ask the questions, the judge may also participate by asking some questions. The lawyers may ask the judge to inquire into sensitive and private matters in an effort to obtain more accurate information and keep from antagonizing members of the panel.

1.05 Familiarity with Procedures

An attorney should always be familiar with a judge's approach by either watching the judge in different cases or asking colleagues, clerks, or bailiffs. Specific procedures for jury selection should be discussed with the judge and opposing counsel. If they opt for the "usual way," do not presume to know what that is. It is necessary to ask.

B. JURY SELECTION PROCEDURE

Jury selection procedures are controlled by statutes, rules of procedure, local court practice, and the preferences of individual judges. This section briefly summarizes some of those procedures.

1.06 Jury Pool

Jurors are obtained from the community where the case is heard. The community is usually the same as the district in which the court sits. Jurors' names come from public records (voter registration cards, driver's licenses, utility records, property documents, etc.). The jury pool cannot exclude any class of people.

1.07 Juror Summons

The clerk of court or court administrator summons individuals selected to serve as jurors. A statute or court rule will list legitimate excuses for not appearing. Jurors complete their jury services after the set period (usually a few days or a week) has elapsed or after they reach a verdict.

1.08 Jury Orientation

The clerk conducts an orientation program, which may include a lecture, pamphlets, or a film or video describing the roles of jurors. After orientation jurors may leave and be contacted when needed or remain at the courthouse in a jury waiting room.

1.09 Preliminary Information about the Panel

Jurors typically complete an information sheet or questionnaire about themselves. On this form the jurors may provide information about family, occupation, education, hobbies, etc. A juror may be excused based on this information. If this preliminary information is not available, questions should be asked by the judge or attorneys to obtain it.

1.10 Jury Panel

The clerk selects a panel of prospective jurors from the jury pool. A bailiff or other court official escorts the panel to the courtroom where the case is to be tried.

1.11 Number of Prospective Jurors

The number of prospective jurors in a panel usually includes the number of jurors who will deliberate, plus one or more alternates, plus the number of individuals equal to peremptory challenges the attorneys may exercise, plus additional individuals to replace any juror who may be removed for cause. For example, for a civil jury of six, the initial panel may include fourteen or more prospective jurors.

1.12 Seating Prospective Jurors in the Courtroom

Typically, the court clerk randomly selects prospective jurors from the group in the courtroom by drawing names and having them take a seat in the jury box.

1.13 Jurors' Oath or Affirmation

The oath or affirmation is usually given by the clerk, and the jurors promise to answer all questions truthfully and completely.

1.14 Preliminary Remarks

The judge ordinarily makes introductory remarks to the prospective jurors. The comments usually cover information needed by the jurors to understand what is happening and an explanation of the case. The judge also typically asks preliminary informational questions of the prospective jurors.

1.15 Presence of Judge and Reporter

Some jurisdictions do not require a judge or reporter to be present during questioning by the attorneys. An attorney should insist on the judge being present and request a reporter if necessary to control the room or record the questions of the opposing counsel.

1.16 Attorney Movement

Attorneys are usually permitted to move in the courtroom during jury selection; however, the attorneys must be certain that they can be heard and that the movement is not intrusive or distracting.

1.17 Order of Questioning

It is important to know whether the plaintiff/prosecutor or defense attorney questions first so questions can be appropriately planned. The order is usually established by a rule. Often, the party who has the burden of proof goes first.

1.18 Discussion of Law

Generally, a discussion of the law by the attorneys is not permitted, although what is permitted varies among jurisdictions and judges.

1.19 Amount of Time Available

Some judges restrict the amount of time for questioning. However, if the judge does not set a time limit, reasonableness and common sense should be a guide.

1.20 Open Courtroom

The press and the public are rarely excluded during jury selection; however, it is unusual that anyone attends unless it is a high profile case.

1.21 Jury Selection Materials

Attorneys should prepare and provide questions for the judge to ask, along with a summary of the case theories and a list of witnesses and exhibits.

1.22 Recording Information during Jury Selection

Notes concerning prior responses should be recorded in an organized manner; however, counsel should not let notes become distracting, delay questioning, or limit effective communication. Counsel should also be aware if extensive note taking is making jurors suspicious or uneasy. Notes can be taken by hand or on a computer. Cocounsel, a paralegal, or the clerk can help record the responses to questions.

D. QUESTIONING THE JURY PANEL

FRCP 47(a) and FRCrimP 24(a) prescribe jury questioning in federal courts.

1.23 Questioning Exclusively by the Judge

Judges ask all jury selection questions in about one-fifth of the state courts and approximately two-thirds of the federal courts. Efficiency is optimized by the judge asking all of the questions, but the disadvantage is that the judge does not know the case as well as the attorneys. The attorneys can submit questions they want asked, which the judge has the discretion to accept or ignore. After the judge is finished questioning, the attorneys may be able to submit clarifying or additional questions to be asked by the judge.

1.24 Questioning by Judge and Attorneys

In most state courts and in some federal districts, the judge and attorneys share the questioning. The attorneys may obtain the relevant information as well as develop a rapport with the jurors.

1.25 Questions Directed to the Panel

Ordinarily, jurors are questioned as a panel, with general questions typically seeking "yes" or "no" responses directed to all of the prospective jurors in the presence of each other.

1.26 Questions Directed to Individual Jurors

Jurors may be individually asked questions, which require responses beyond a "yes" or "no" or to clarify or expand their previous response.

1.27 Questions Directed to Individual Jurors outside the Presence of the Panel

Jurors may be questioned individually outside the presence of the other panel members in major criminal cases and significant civil cases with very sensitive issues. Sometimes prospective jurors are questioned in isolation so that possible jurors may be more likely to reveal personal or embarrassing information or to avoid a juror's answers from influencing other jurors.

1.28 Introductory Remarks by Attorneys

In jurisdictions where the attorneys question the panel, the attorneys are usually allowed to make brief introductory remarks about the process or case.

1.29 Types of Questions

Attorneys can ask questions that are open-ended, close-ended, general to the panel, specific to the panel, general to an individual, or specific to an individual.

1.30 Selecting Questions

The type of questions depends on the applicable jury selection process, the approach of the judge, the preference of the lawyers, the responses of the jurors, the nature of the case, the time available for questions, and the purpose for asking the questions.

1.31 Concluding Questions

The concluding questions should elicit a positive and affirmative response that supports a verdict for the client.

F. THEORIES OF JURY SELECTION

Jurors will be guided by their values, beliefs, principles, norms, experiences, and standards in life. They will decide a case based on the facts and law similar to how they make other important decisions in life. This is the information the attorneys need to discover.

1.32   Impressions and Intuition

This approach relies on the intuition of the attorney or client to decide which jurors will be most appropriate to sit. It may be based upon the extensive or limited experience of a trial lawyer. Or it may be as simple as first impressions and perceptions.

1.33   Generalizations and Stereotypes

Some attorneys select jurors based on generalizations regarding types of people. This theory can be detrimental or helpful depending on the validity of the stereotype and its application to an individual juror. Some factors are inappropriate or disallowed. For example, it is improper to exclude prospective jurors based only on their religion.

1.34   Character and Personality Traits

Some attorneys identify favorable jurors based on traits like being open-minded, being a good listener, being a good communicator, and how honest and open a juror appears. If all else appears equal, they may favor these jurors.

1.36   Nonverbal Behavior

Positive or negative body language exhibited by the jurors may influence an attorney's decision. Care must be taken not to misinterpret or put too much emphasis on ambiguous body language.

1.36   Jury Profile

A jury profile describes the ideal and the unfavorable juror. Some attorneys try to match prospective jurors to this profile. Other lawyers find this approach speculative and too difficult to apply.

1.37   Social Science Data

This theory identifies demographic characteristics that favorably correlate with a case theory. This approach relies on the expertise of social scientists. Not many cases justify this expense, and many attorneys are reluctant to rely extensively upon the judgment of nonlawyers in selecting jurors.

1.38   Improper Bases

Jurors may not be excluded in either civil or criminal cases because of their race, gender, or other protected classifications. The parties have a right to have these individuals as jurors, and the prospective jurors have a constitutional right to be jurors.

G. OBJECTIVES OF JURY SELECTION

There are six objectives trial attorneys may try to achieve during jury selection process:

- Obtain information to make challenges for cause
- Obtain information to exercise peremptory challenges
- Educate the jury about the case, facts, clients, parties, witnesses, and the law
- Develop a rapport with the jurors
- Neutralize negative and build on positive juror attitudes, opinions, and beliefs
- Obtain commitments from the jurors

1.39 To Support a Challenge for Cause Motion

A juror's bias or prejudice determines whether grounds exist that would disqualify the juror and support a motion to challenge for cause. Areas of questioning include prior knowledge of the case, relationships or familiarity with the parties or attorneys, existing attitudes regarding issues in the case, and related areas. The attitudes of the jurors about the parties, witnesses, theories, weaknesses, and strengths may be explored to uncover any prejudice against a party or bias in favor of a party.

1.40 To Exercise a Peremptory Challenge

These questions seek to determine jurors' opinions, feelings, and attitudes that may cause a juror to favor or disfavor one side. Examples of areas to be explored include hobbies of jurors, how they spend their free time, literature they read, television or movies they watch, family background, where they grew up, and other relevant information.

1.41 To Educate the Jury

Attorneys can educate the jurors about relevant facets of the case. Questions may be asked in a way that explains the theories of the case. Questions may also be designed to anticipate and counter efforts by opposing counsel to educate the jury about the weaknesses in your case. However, there are limits to these types of questions, and they must be based on a need to obtain information useful in deciding whether to exercise a peremptory or cause strike.

1.42 To Develop Rapport with the Jurors

An attorney who engages the jurors in an effective conversation increases the likelihood that the jurors will perceive the attorney to be caring, sincere, and honest and may look favorably on that attorney's case. These impressions can be lasting and influence the jurors.

1.43 To Neutralize Negative and Build on Positive Jurors' Attitudes, Opinions, and Beliefs

Questions also may overcome negative opinions and build positive feelings. Negative and potentially harmful information may be revealed as a part of jury questions. The harmful effects may be neutralized by an honest approach, and positive attitudes towards witnesses and evidence may be used to counter negative information.

1.44 To Obtain Commitments

Attorneys may ask the jury to commit to issues like not holding weaknesses in the case against a client, being fair and impartial, or following the law as explained. Some judges will not allow attorneys to obtain these commitments.

H. QUESTIONS AND APPROACHES TO ACHIEVE OBJECTIVES

Judges exercise discretion when defining the scope of questions, and many jurisdictions limit jury selection questions to areas that explicitly establish bias or prejudice. Effective jury selection questioning should follow some common-sense communication guidelines. Attorneys should engage the jurors in conversation, be receptive and responsive, encourage the jurors to give complete, honest answers, listen carefully, observe nonverbal demeanor, and reward helpful answers.

1.45 Information about Jurors

Lawyers should collect and review as much information as possible about the prospective jurors in order to make the best possible decision concerning the removal of a juror for cause or through the use of a peremptory challenge. Observations of each juror should begin as soon as the jury enters the courtroom.

- *Information from observations of prospective jurors.* A lot may be learned from the jurors' conduct, physical comfort, and manner of speaking to others while they wait for the process to begin.

- *Information about prospective juror associations.* Attention should be paid to friendly and unfriendly associations as they may affect jury cohesiveness. Those who appear to be leaders may influence the other jurors.

- *Information about juror body language and appearances.* Observations of a juror's failure to make eye contact, alertness, a positive or negative attitude toward either side, ability to listen, and other body language cues may help make a decision about a juror.

- *Observations by a team member.* An associate or assistant not involved in the questioning may be able to make observations and assess the jurors' behavior in addition to recording information obtained from the jurors and may help in making the final decisions about jurors.

1.46   Juror Questionnaires and Investigations

The questionnaires the jurors complete and, if names and addresses of the potential jurors are available before trial, an independent, appropriate investigation may provide substantial preliminary information about each juror.

1.47   Information about Jury Duty

Trial attorneys need to review the jury orientation program to discover the information prospective jurors receive before they appear in the courtroom. This information may have an impact on the jurors' attitudes and approach to jury duty.

1.48   Obtaining Factual Information

If a question seeks factual information, the question should be phrased to generate a specific response. Some information is sensitive, and it may be uncomfortable for jurors to provide this information, especially about matters they consider private or confidential.

- *Obtaining information about relationships with parties, lawyers, and witnesses.* These questions are usually asked by the judge in the initial process of jury selection and may be supplemented by questions from the attorneys.

- *Obtaining information about opinions and attitudes.* Questions that seek specific information about a prospective juror's opinion or attitudes may be phrased as open-ended or leading questions.

- *Obtaining information to demonstrate a bias.* When a juror has indicated a bias, leading questions may be used to demonstrate that juror cannot set aside a bias and be fair.

- *Obtaining information about pretrial publicity.* The words people use to describe publicity about a particular case may reveal their attitudes.

1.49   Educating the Jury

Questions may be carefully crafted to inform the jurors about facets of the case. This education must be in question form and must always be phrased in a way to learn about a bias or prejudice.

The areas that may be addressed are:

- Facts
- Clients or parties
- Lay witnesses

- Expert witnesses
- Burden of proof
- Liability
- Defenses
- Elements of a case
- Types of evidence to be introduced
- Use of electronic and digital evidence
- Introduction of computer generated demonstrations
- Weaknesses and strengths in the case

1.50   Developing Rapport with the Jury

Jurors' initial perceptions of the lawyer and the client influence the ability of the attorney to persuade the jury as the trial progresses.

- *Observations of jurors.* The attorney must appear organized, comfortable, and confident in front of jurors from the very beginning.

- *Addressing the panel properly.* Jurors should be addressed by their last names along with the appropriate form of address or title for each juror.

- *The effect of body language and appearances.* The attorney's and client's physical appearance, clothing style, gestures, body language are some factors that may be used to enhance rapport with the jurors.

- *Questions that develop rapport.* Questions should be asked in a respectful way, and the attorney should display interest in the answer.

- *Recognizing jurors' discomfort or anxiety.* Recognition of a problem and a sincere approach will help develop a positive relationship. Over-solicitous behavior is insincere and ineffective.

- *Questions that permit the juror to clarify or expand responses.* When a juror is permitted to explain or expand an answer the juror may become less anxious or nervous and may clarify a previous response.

- *The style and tone of the questions.* Overly aggressive approaches and dumb questions should be avoided because jurors will react negatively. However, if they happen to occur, the attorney must recognize the problem, acknowledge the error, and change behavior.

- *Dealing with hostile jurors.* Dealing with a hostile juror is difficult and can be avoided by not asking more questions of the juror when it becomes clear that the juror will be removed later. However, an open and direct approach to a hostile juror may help to develop rapport with other jurors or may defuse hostility and turn negative jurors into positive jurors.

- *Avoid embarrassing jurors.* Carefully selecting words and questions and being sensitive to juror reactions can keep an attorney from embarrassing jurors.

- *Use humor.* Humor is helpful as long as it is appropriate and not unnecessarily artificial.

- *Allow the jurors a chance to talk.* Giving the jurors a chance to talk is critical, and attorneys should listen carefully and not interrupt a juror's answer.

- *Thank jurors.* Thanking jurors helps establish rapport. The remarks must be sincere and appropriate.

1.51 Neutralizing Negative and Building on Positive Attitudes, Opinions, and Beliefs

Attorneys should ask questions that uncover bias and prejudice, but these questions should also be used to neutralize negative attitudes and build positive attitudes.

1.52 Obtaining Commitments

Attorneys can attempt to obtain a promise from the jurors to not hold some fact or weakness against a client or a witness, unless the judge disallows those types of questions. Such a request should be phrased as a question seeking a "yes" or "no" response.

I. CHALLENGING JURORS

Attorneys may remove a juror based on two primary types of challenges—challenges for cause and peremptory challenges. A third and rare challenge, challenge to the array (the entire panel), challenges the lawfulness of the process used to select the pool of jurors.

1.53 Challenges for Cause

This challenge seeks to remove a juror from the panel for lack of qualifications, actual bias or prejudice, or an implied bias. Statutes, rules, or case law ordinarily establish the grounds supporting a challenge for cause.

- *Establishing bias or prejudice.* Establishing bias or prejudice is based on the juror's response. It must be shown the juror is so obviously sympathetic or prejudiced that it would be impossible for the juror to be fair.

- *Procedure for challenge.* An attorney must request the court to remove a juror for cause, stating the grounds for the challenge. The challenge is usually made outside the hearing of the jurors.

- *Number of challenges.* There is no limit to challenges for cause. However, courts are conservative in granting challenges because the grounds are difficult to establish and they delay the trial.

- *Strategies for exercising challenges.* A challenge for cause is usually made before peremptory challenges. An attorney should establish objective reasons, determine the judge's practice for granting challenges, and assess whether the type of case will support the granting of a challenge. If peremptory challenges are no longer available, a challenge for cause may be more likely to be granted. Attorneys should also compare the replacement jurors from the panel with the prospective jurors in the jury box.

- *Options for the challenging attorney*
  - o Convince the juror to state explicitly that the juror is biased
  - o Hope the judge will decide to excuse the juror without a challenge
  - o Anticipate that opposing counsel will challenge a juror for cause
  - o Challenge the juror for cause

- *Options for the opposing attorney*
  - o Oppose the challenge and argue that the juror is qualified
  - o Request the judge to ask rehabilitative questions
  - o Seek permission of the judge to ask rehabilitative questions
  - o Join in the challenge for cause

- *Rehabilitation procedures.* When a juror has demonstrated a lack of fairness, the attorney who wishes to retain the juror can ask rehabilitative questions designed to show that the juror can be fair and impartial. New information may be developed to rebut facts supporting a cause challenge.

- *Reversing apparent bias or prejudice.* The goal of the rehabilitating attorney is to establish reasons why the juror can be impartial and to obtain a commitment from the juror to be fair in spite of a potential problem raised by the other side.

- *Replacement jurors.* If a replacement juror was not in the courtroom during preliminary questions, these questions should be repeated. The process of questioning and challenging replacement jurors is the same process used for previous jurors.

1.54 Peremptory Challenges

These challenges permit the attorney to remove a limited number of prospective jurors from the panel without any reason or explanation to the court. However, members of constitutionally protected classes (e.g., race and gender) may not be removed. The number of peremptory challenges available to each party is controlled by statute or court rule and type of case. In civil cases, each side may have two challenges to a jury of six. For criminal cases, *see* FRCrimP 24(b).

The method of exercising peremptory challenges varies widely. However, three common ways to make peremptory challenges include:

- The plaintiff and defendant each strike an equal number of jurors at the conclusion of the questioning

- The plaintiff and defendant alternate striking jurors

- The plaintiff and defendant independently list the names of jurors to be removed after questioning, and the list is provided to the court

1.55 Opposing Peremptory Challenges

A juror may not be removed for an improper, unconstitutional basis. A party may successfully challenge the removal of a prospective juror if the removal is based on race, religion, gender, or other unconstitutional basis. The party seeking to remove the juror must demonstrate a proper independent basis for removal.

1.56 Alternate Jurors

One or more alternate jurors are selected to sit as an extra juror in case a juror is unable to complete a trial. This occurs most frequently in lengthy or complex trials. Alternate jurors are usually excused when the jury begins deliberations. However, the judge may allow them to deliberate with the other jurors.

J. MISCONDUCT AND OBJECTIONS

State and local rules of procedure, the applicable rules of professional responsibility, rules of decorum, and common sense establish standards for proper conduct by attorneys and jurors during jury selection.

1.57 Inadmissible Evidence

Any questions or behavior by counsel designed to introduce inadmissible evidence and prejudice the jury are improper.

1.58 Improper Questions

Questions designed to accomplish improper objectives may not be asked during jury selection, and the legitimacy of questions varies throughout jurisdictions. Questions that are unfairly prejudicial may constitute grounds for a mistrial.

1.59   Improper or Questionable Topics

Questions that touch on improper areas of inquiry must be avoided. However, there may be a good-faith basis for asking questions about an area that is sensitive. These questions should be carefully drafted and may require permission from the court before being asked.

1.60   Currying Favor

Communication with jurors before and during trial is forbidden except in the course of official proceedings. Trying to seek or gain favors by flattering the jurors is improper.

1.61   Misconduct by Jurors

Jurors commit misconduct if they answer jury selection questions falsely, violate court rules, or fail to follow directions of the judge. Trial attorneys have a duty to immediately report juror misconduct.

1.62   Misconduct by Attorneys

Attorneys must maintain a fair and impartial relationship with prospective and actual jurors before, during, and after trial. It is unethical to talk with jurors individually or in a group, contact any friends or relatives of jurors, or have a colleague or client contact a juror or her friends and relatives.

1.63   Objections

Counsel may object to the jury selection questions and conduct of opposing counsel, and when doing so counsel should consider the prejudicial impact of the questioning, the extent that opposing counsel is actually using jury selection for purposes other than to determine challenges for cause and peremptory challenges, and the tolerance level of the judge for prolonged questioning.

The following conduct is improper:

- *Arguing the case, the law, or the facts.* In most jurisdictions it is improper to present arguments in these areas during jury selection.

- *Improperly indoctrinating the jury.* In many jurisdictions, questions that are asked solely to indoctrinate the jurors are improper; however, what is considered indoctrination varies among attorneys and judges.

- *Referring to inadmissible evidence or topics.* References to inadmissible evidence or topics are not allowed.

- *Repeating questions.* Areas of jury selection already explored by the judge or opposing counsel may not be repeated. However, if there needs to be clarification or more detail, an area may be addressed. It is within the judge's discretion to permit additional questions.

- *Asking the jurors to prejudge the case.* Questions seeking commitments regarding an issue or evidence may be improper because they ask the jurors to make a judgment before they hear evidence.

- *Irrelevant questions.* Questions having no bearing on subjects within the appropriate scope of jury selection are not proper even if they are entertaining or educational.

- *Questions that improperly or incorrectly explain the law.* Jurors may be asked if they will follow the law. Most judges do not want the attorneys to go into detail about the law and will sustain an objection to misstatements about the law.

- *Questions that are unfair or embarrassing.* Sensitive or embarrassing questions that have a legitimate purpose are permissible. What is legitimate depends on the case and issues involved. Questions that serve no legitimate purpose and are embarrassing or seek inappropriate personal information are improper and may alienate the jurors.

SECTION 2: INSTRUCTING THE JURY

A. JURY INSTRUCTIONS

An essential part of the planning process involves identifying and preparing jury instructions and verdict forms. It is critical that instructions be selected early during trial preparation, even though they ordinarily need not be submitted to the court until the trial.

2.01   Right to Jury Instructions

A party usually has a right to an instruction if evidence has been introduced to support the instruction and if the instruction correctly states the applicable law. The trial lawyer wants the jury instructions to explain the elements of the law involved in the case, the legal issues underlying the claims or defenses, and any other material issues in a case.

2.02   Jury Instructions and Presentation of the Case

Instructions influence the presentation of a case and unify the various components of the trial. Jury instructions directly affect what is asked in jury selection, what is said in the opening statement, how evidence is presented, and what is said in final argument.

2.03 Source of Instructions

Instructions, also called charges, must be based on the law of the jurisdiction. Case law, statutes, rules, and other legal authorities provide the basis for the content of the instructions. Nearly all jurisdictions have jury instruction guides (JIGs) or "pattern instructions" that are generally recognized and accepted.

2.04 Overview of Instructions

There are several types of instructions:

- *Preliminary instructions.* These are instructions the judge gives the jury at the beginning of the case that explain to the jury their responsibilities during the trial and may also include an explanation of the law applicable to the case.

- *Periodic instructions.* These are instructions given periodically during the trial, particularly when the issues are complex or unusual.

- *Cautionary instructions.* These are instructions given before recesses and adjournments to remind jurors to conduct themselves properly.

- *Curative instructions and motion for curative instructions.* These are instructions given after an inappropriate event has occurred. The instruction is given to repair damage done by improper testimony, question or behavior.

  A motion for a curative instruction is a request for the judge to advise the jury to disregard some objectionable matter.

- *Final instructions.* These instructions fall into two categories—general and specific. General instructions apply to all cases and involve conduct such as the role of jurors, burden of proof, and credibility. Specific instructions include the legal theories and elements of the claims and defenses applicable to the specific case.

2.05 Verdict Forms

There are different types of verdict forms:

- *General verdict.* In this form, the jury simply finds for or against a party.

- *Special verdict.* The judge may submit a special verdict form when jurors are required to answer specific questions and make findings of fact on critical factual issues.

- *General verdict form with written interrogatories.* This form combines both a general verdict and special interrogatories. The answers to the interrogatories must be consistent with the general verdict.

2.06 Proposing a Verdict Form

The type of case and nature of the issues determine which verdict form should be used. In criminal cases, the general verdict form is usually used. In personal injury cases, special interrogatories are typically used. Procedural rules and case law establish guidelines for how verdict forms should be used.

B. HOW TO PLAN AND SUBMIT JURY INSTRUCTIONS

2.07 Legal Theories and Factual Summaries

The preparation of jury instructions begins early in the case. An instruction explains the law on a matter and provides, in effect, an outline of the elements of law that need to be proved.

The jury instructions must contain the legal elements reflected in the claims and defenses. The instructions must be consistent with the evidence. The instructions may have to be modified as legal issues are modified and as the evidence is presented.

2.08 Clear and Understandable Instructions

Instructions should be drafted to accurately reflect the law and explain legal issues and should use words that are understandable to the jurors and support the client's case theory. Instructions should not be biased in favor of one party.

2.09 Withstanding Challenges

Opposing counsel may challenge proposed instructions by objecting to the use of certain words, phrases, or instructions. To withstand a challenge, the instructions must correctly and completely explain the law.

2.10 Ethical Rules

Ethical rules prohibit an attorney from knowingly making a false statement of law to the court and from failing to disclose controlling legal authority adverse to the attorney's position.

2.11 A Complete Set of Instructions

The instructions must cover all legal and factual issues and must be complete and concise. Each instruction is a part of the entire set.

2.12 Submitting Instructions

Instructions must be submitted in accord with the applicable rules of procedure. Instructions must ordinarily be in writing. *See, e.g.*, FRCP 51 and FRCrimP 30. Some courts require a memorandum of law to be submitted in support of significant instructions. Instructions may be submitted in a variety of ways, depending on the preference of the judge and the type of instruction. General or less important instructions that appear in the JIG may be submitted by providing the judge with a written list of the respective numbers from the pattern JIGs. Or they may be provided to the court and opposing counsel as a printed or electronic document.

C. JURY INSTRUCTIONS AND THE VERDICT FORM

2.13 Jury Instruction Conference

After the attorneys have submitted their proposed instructions and verdict form to the judge, the judge decides what instructions are to be given and which verdict form is to be used. The judge bases this decision on the appropriateness of the proposed instructions, revisions of proposed instructions, and the inclusion of other instructions. The attorneys should be informed of the final instruction before final argument.

2.14 The Judge's Charge

The judge instructs the jury in open court before or after final arguments. Most commonly, the judge instructs after final argument. Many jurisdictions permit judges to comment on the evidence. The verdict form is explained to the jury and is to be completed by the jury. Many judges give a copy of the written instructions to the jury.

2.15 Objecting to Instructions and the Verdict Form

Errors made in jury instructions are a ground for the trial judge or appellate court to grant a new trial. The standard for a new trial and appellate reversal is whether an instruction was legally accurate and whether evidence supported the instruction. Minor errors may be harmless and may not support a new trial. An objection should be made at the time the improper instruction is given.

Examples of objections to proposed instructions include:

- No factual support in the record exists for the proposed instruction
- The proposed instruction misstates the law
- The proposed instruction fails to follow the pattern instruction approved in that jurisdiction
- The proposed instruction is cumulative
- The proposed instruction is argumentative
- The proposed instruction will confuse the jurors

2.16 Stipulations in Jury Trials

Counsel may stipulate to certain procedures. Before the case is submitted to the jury, the judge may request, or the attorneys may suggest, the following stipulations be agreed upon:

- The court, in the absence of counsel and the parties, may re-read and explain to the jury any instructions previously given or answer any relevant questions if the jurors request such information while they are deliberating

- The parties waive the right to have the clerk or court reporter present when the jury returns a verdict

- A sealed verdict may be returned

- The parties waive their right to be present when the jury returns the verdict and allow the judge to announce the verdict in open court on the record

- The parties waive their right to poll the jury

- A stay of entry of judgment for an agreed upon number of days shall be granted after a verdict

D. JURY DELIBERATION PROCEDURES

2.17 Deliberations

Jurors typically deliberate during normal court hours on weekdays until they reach a verdict. If they deliberate more than one day, they usually go home and return for continued deliberations the following day.

2.18 Sequestering the Jury

In major criminal cases and well-publicized civil cases, the jury may be sequestered during deliberations and stay at a hotel or motel instead of going home.

2.19 Copy of Jury Instructions

A copy of jury instructions is typically provided to the jurors during deliberations.

2.20 Exhibits

The trial judge has discretion to decide which exhibits received into evidence will be allowed in the jury room during deliberations. Real evidence is usually allowed in the jury room; demonstrative evidence may or may not be allowed.

2.21 Jurors' Notes

Although jurors are often allowed to take notes during the course of the trial, some judges do not allow the jurors to bring these notes into the deliberation room.

2.22 Questions by Jurors

Traditionally, jurors could not ask questions during a trial, but could ask limited questions during deliberations.

In most jurisdictions, jurors cannot question a witness. There are some judges who permit and even encourage jurors to submit witness questions to the judge, who will provide the questions to the lawyers, who in turn may ask the witness or have the judge do so. Some of these questions will be improper or inappropriate and will not be asked.

In all jurisdictions, jurors can ask some limited types of questions during deliberations. If a jury has questions regarding instructions, the foreperson can write a note to the judge asking the question or requesting to meet with the judge to have the question answered. The judge will prepare an answer, consult with the attorneys, and then announce the question and answer in open court.

2.23 Unanimous Jury Verdict

In criminal cases, a jury verdict must usually be unanimous. In civil cases, verdicts are typically unanimous, but many jurisdictions allow non-unanimous verdicts in some situations.

2.24 Hung Jury

If the required minimum number of jurors cannot agree on a verdict after a significant amount of time, the jury is said to be "hung," and the judge may discharge them and declare a mistrial.

E. COMPLEX CASES

2.25 Helping the Jurors

Effective methods that assist jurors understand the facts, issues, and law are particularly important in complex cases. A trial judge has broad discretion in developing approaches to assist jurors. Judges can instruct the jurors on effective ways to take notes and their proper use.

Suggestions that may assist the jurors are:

- Provide jurors with a loose-leaf notebook that contains the preliminary jury instructions and other instructions provided during the trial

- Include in the notebook uncontroverted facts in summary or detailed fashion

- Provide in the notebook a glossary that defines technical terms and other words

- Include in the notebook a witness list that briefly identifies each witness and includes photographs of the witnesses and copies of all exhibits or relevant parts of exhibits

- Provide jurors with a daily list of the witnesses who will testify that day

- Permit jurors to take notes during the trial; juror notebooks can be collected by the clerk each day and returned to the jurors the following day

- Add a copy of the final instructions before final argument, including special interrogatories to the notebooks

- Allow jurors to use their notebooks during deliberations

- Prepare juror instruction packets, which provide the jurors with a structure from which to deliberate

- The notebooks need not be retained by the court after the verdict because they are not a part of the record

F. RETURN OF THE VERDICT IN A JURY TRIAL

The foreperson informs the bailiff when a verdict has been reached. The bailiff then advises the clerk or the judge, who contacts trial counsel. Criminal defendants have a right to be present and almost always are present when the verdict is read. Civil parties may decide not to be present.

2.26 Polling the Jury

After the verdict has been read, and before the jurors have been dismissed, the attorney who has lost may request that the jurors be individually polled, which involves asking each juror individually if the juror voted for the verdict.

2.27 Discharging the Jury

After the verdict has been read and after the jurors are polled, the jurors are thanked and discharged.

2.28 Contacting Jurors

A trial attorney may or may not talk with the jurors after they have been discharged. In any event, they cannot inquire into the jury deliberations. Jurisdictions have different limitations on the scope of these conversations. Some jurisdictions only allow very limited contact or questioning such as allowing the jurors to comment on how the attorney could have done a better job.

2.29 Misconduct of the Jury

Misconduct is grounds for a new trial. It must be of such a substantial nature that a party has been adversely and prejudicially affected.

2.30 Impeaching a Verdict

Deliberations will not be interrupted, and a verdict will not be vacated, unless some extraneous prejudicial information or improper influence has affected the decision of the jurors. Most jurisdictions prohibit a juror from testifying about discussions during deliberations and about jurors' emotions or mental processes during deliberations. *See* FRE 606(b). Jurors may testify only in unusual circumstances where extraneous prejudicial information was improperly brought to the juror's attention or where outside influence was brought to bear on a juror. The ability to impeach a verdict is severely limited to insure the finality of verdicts.

2.31 Motion to Question the Jurors

A trial attorney who receives reliable information that prejudicial matter may have adversely affected jury deliberations may move the court for a hearing.

APPENDIX E. FORMS *(FORMS ALSO AVAILABLE ON DISK)*

JURY SELECTION

Form 5-A   Jury Selection Worksheet

Form 5-B   Jury Selection Chart

File Number: _____
Client Name: _____
Contact Info: _____
_____
_____

Jury Selection Worksheet

What kind of person would probably best identify with the client, the case, or witness in the case?

What kind of person would probably least likely identify with the client, the case, or witness in the case?

Specific questions/topics to be asked of the prospective jurors:

File Number: _____
Client Name: _____
Contact Info: _____
_____
_____

Jury Selection Chart

Name:

Address:

Approximate age/demeanor/dress:

Occupation/employer:

Education:

Marital status:

Spouse's occupation/employer:

Children:

Knowledge of case:

Know parties/witnesses:

Past claims/lawsuits:

Similar case experience:

Past jury duty:

Opinions about issues:

Attitudes toward case:

Will juror identify with client, case, witnesses?

Do we like juror?

Overall rating 0-10:

Peremptory challenge?

Cause challenge:

APPENDIX F

PLANNING GUIDE AND CHECKLIST

The planning guide and checklist is provided to help the preparation of legal substance and presentation. It provides the basis for the preparation of more detailed planning.

Section 1. General

A. Professional Responsibility
- Pervades all activities
- Role of attorney
  - o Fact finding
  - o Evaluating evidence
  - o Analyzing applicable law, legal elements, and precedent
  - o Developing legal theories
  - o Applying applicable law to specific facts
  - o Assessing strengths and weaknesses of client's case
  - o Assessing strengths and weaknesses of opponent's case
  - o Presenting options
  - o Evaluating and prioritizing options with client input
  - o Counseling client
  - o Negotiating an advantageous result for client
  - o Advocating zealously for client
  - o Drafting and reviewing documents
  - o Keeping client reasonably informed
  - o Advising client of legal rights, obligations, implications, and consequences
- Attorney-client privilege
- Confidentiality
  - o Model Rule of Professional Conduct 1.6: Confidentiality of Information
- Conflict of interest
  - o Model Rule of Professional Conduct 1.7: Conflict of Interest: Current Clients
  - o Model Rule of Professional Conduct 1.8: Conflict of Interest: Current Clients: Specific Rules
  - o Model Rule of Professional Conduct 1.9: Duties to Former Clients
  - o Model Rule of Professional Conduct 1.10: Imputation of Conflicts of Interest: General Rule
  - o Model Rule of Professional Conduct 1.11: Special Conflicts of Interest for Former and Current Government Officers and Employees
  - o Model Rule of Professional Conduct 1.12: Former Judge, Arbitrator, Mediator or Other Third-Party Neutral
- Authority to settle

       o Model Rule of Professional Conduct 1.2: Scope of Representation and Allocation of Authority Between Client and Lawyer
- 1.2(a) "A lawyer shall abide by a client's decision whether to settle a matter."

B. Client/Witness Interviews
- Preparation
    - o Confirm time and location with client/witness
    - o Have client/witness bring all relevant documents or other evidence
    - o Develop a basic understanding of client's/witness's situation
    - o Conduct preliminary research and investigation
- Rapport
    - o Know client's/witness's name and preferred form of address
    - o Make client/witness feel at ease
    - o Establish trust
- Efficient factual inquiry
    - o Elicit all facts, favorable and unfavorable
    - o Find out what client/witness needs and hopes to accomplish
    - o Focus on pertinent issues; avoid tangential, nonrelevant inquiry
- Anticipate and analyze pertinent legal issues
    - o Statutes of limitations
    - o Evaluate all possible causes of action and remedies
    - o Eliminate frivolous or marginal theories
- Assess client's case
    - o Be realistic
    - o Compare probable outcomes with client's expectations and needs
    - o Consider emotional and financial impact of contemplated action
    - o Estimate time required to effectively represent client
- Reject client if necessary
    - o Clearly explain reasons for rejection to client
    - o Inform client of applicable statutes of limitations and filing deadlines
    - o Encourage client to seek another opinion as soon as possible
    - o Refer client
    - o Confirm rejection by e-mail and letter, clearly stating reasons and deadlines
- Develop preliminary strategy with client
    - o Negotiation
    - o Mediation
    - o Arbitration
    - o Litigation

- Have client sign all necessary documents
  - o Representation agreement
  - o Information releases (school, medical, workplace)
  - o Waivers

C. Representation Agreements
  - Specifically tailored to the identity and needs of the individual client
  - Client is clearly identified
  - Scope of the representation is clearly defined
  - Clearly defining allocation of authority
  - Responsibility for attorney fees, costs, and expenses is adequately explained
  - Reasonable and customary fees, costs, and expenses are explained
  - Billing procedures are clearly stated
  - Attorney responsibilities are adequately defined
  - Client responsibilities are adequately defined
  - Appropriate termination provisions are included
  - Agreement overall complies with local Rules of Professional Conduct
  - Coherent grammar
  - Proofread
  - Client can easily understand agreement
  - Reviewed and signed by client

D. Fees
  - Abide by applicable Rules of Professional Conduct
    - o *See* Model Rule of Professional Conduct 1.5: Fees
    - o Give client a simple memorandum or copy of customary fee agreement including:
      - General nature of legal services
      - The basis
      - Rate or total amount of fees (reasonable and customary)
      - Whether and to what extent fees are subject to change
      - Whether and to what extent client is responsible for costs, expenses, or disbursements
      - The responsibilities of the attorney and client under the agreement
  - Contingency
    - o Must be in writing, stating method by which fee is determined and percentage
    - o Conforms to legal limitations
      - Ceiling on percent
      - Required alternative fee offering
    - o Clearly explained to client

- o Including how disbursements and costs affect contingency fee and client's recovery
- Straight time (hourly)
- Price per project
- Billable time
  - o Client and witness interviews
  - o Phone calls
  - o E-mail
  - o Consultation with other attorneys
  - o Research
  - o Prepare exhibits and schedule
  - o Legal assistant/law clerk time
  - o Drafting/reviewing documents
  - o Depositions
  - o Filing court documents
  - o Negotiation
  - o Mediation
  - o Arbitration
  - o Court time/appearances
- Billing procedures
  - o Accurate timekeeping
  - o Itemized statements
  - o Clear explanation of payment terms
  - o Regular billing cycle

E. Costs and Expenses
  - Filing and other court fees
  - Notary/service of process fees
  - Investigation costs
  - Expert witnesses
  - Fees and travel
  - Court reporters
  - Exhibits
  - Travel and mileage
  - Phone charges
  - Postage
  - Copies
  - Couriers/service fees

F. Sources of Law
-   Statutes
    o Specific to issues
    o Source of substantive law
    o Time limitations on claims—*see* local statutes for applicable law
-   Case Law
    o Source of substantive law
    o Interprets the elements of a claim
-   Other Sources
    o Treatises/hornbooks/textbooks
    o Practice guides/CLE materials
    o Digests and annotations
    o Looseleaf services
    o Specialized publications and periodicals/law review articles
    o Legal dictionaries and encyclopedias
    o Electronic services/CD-ROM
    o Consultation with others
    o Administrative materials
    o Briefs

G. Rules of Evidence and Procedure
-   The rules of evidence and procedure may vary—check with judge/arbitrator
-   For persuasive purposes, foundations for testimony and exhibits should be presented even if not required
-   Check local rules and practice
    o Elements of the claim
    o Sufficiency of evidence
    o Burden of proof
    o Order of evidence
    o Validity of claims
    o Limitation of remedies
    o Damages/Measure/Mitigation
    o Admissibility of potential evidence, testimony, and exhibits
       – Federal Rule of Evidence 105: Limited Admissibility
       – Federal Rule of Evidence 404: Character Evidence Not Admissible to Prove Conduct; Exceptions; Other Crimes
       – Federal Rule of Evidence 802: Hearsay Rule
       – Federal Rule of Evidence 804: Hearsay Exceptions; Declarant Unavailable
-   Relevancy of potential evidence, testimony and exhibits
    o Federal Rule of Evidence 104(a): Questions of Admissibility Generally
    o Federal Rule of Evidence 104(b): Relevancy Conditioned on Fact

- o Federal Rule of Evidence 401: Definition of "Relevant Evidence"
- o Federal Rule of Evidence 402: Relevant Evidence Generally Admissible; Irrelevant Evidence Inadmissible
- o Federal Rule of Evidence 403: Exclusion of Relevant Evidence on Grounds of Prejudice, Confusion, or Waste of Time
- Objections to potential evidence, testimony, and exhibits
  - o Mischaracterization of evidence
  - o Misstatement of facts
  - o Irrelevant question
  - o Misleading or confusing question
  - o Outside the scope of rebuttal argument
  - o Multiple or compound questions
  - o Leading question
  - o Improper impeachment
- Local Rules of General Practice/Civil Procedure
  - o Primary source of procedural law at trial level
  - o Venue-specific rules
- Litigation timing
- Pleading and motion requirements
  - o Federal Rule of Civil Procedure 4: Summons
  - o Federal Rule of Civil Procedure 4.1: Serving of Other Process
  - o Federal Rule of Civil Procedure 5: Serving and Filing Pleadings and Other Papers
  - o Federal Rule of Civil Procedure 7: Pleadings Allowed; Form of Motions and Other Papers
  - o Federal Rule of Civil Procedure 7.1: Disclosure Statement
  - o Federal Rule of Civil Procedure 8: General Rules of Pleading
  - o Federal Rule of Civil Procedure 10: Form of Pleadings
  - o Federal Rule of Civil Procedure 11: Signing Pleadings, Motions, and Other Papers; Representations to Court; Sanctions
  - o Federal Rule of Civil Procedure 15: Amended and Supplemental Pleadings
- Discovery options and limitations
  - o Federal Rule of Civil Procedure 16: Pretrial Conferences; Scheduling; Management
  - o Federal Rule of Civil Procedure 33: Interrogatories to Parties
  - o Federal Rule of Civil Procedure 34: Production of Documents, Electronically Stored Information, and Tangible Things, or Entering upon Land, for Inspection and Other Purposes
  - o Federal Rule of Civil Procedure 35: Physical and Mental Examinations
  - o Federal Rule of Civil Procedure 36: Requests for Admission

- o Federal Rule of Civil Procedure 37: Failure to Make Disclosures or Cooperate in Discovery; Sanctions
- Pretrial responsibilities
  - o Federal Rule of Civil Procedure 3: Commencing an Action
  - o Federal Rule of Civil Procedure 4: Summons
  - o Federal Rule of Civil Procedure 5: Serving and Filing Pleadings and Other Papers
  - o Federal Rule of Civil Procedure 7: Pleadings Allowed; Form of Motions and Other Papers
  - o Federal Rule of Civil Procedure 7.1: Disclosure Statement
  - o Federal Rule of Civil Procedure 8: General Rules of Pleading
  - o Federal Rule of Civil Procedure 10: Form of Pleadings
  - o Federal Rule of Civil Procedure 11: Signing Pleadings, Motions, and Other Papers; Representations to the Court; Sanctions
  - o Federal Rule of Civil Procedure 15: Amended and Supplemental Pleadings
  - o Federal Rule of Civil Procedure 16: Pretrial Conferences; Scheduling; Management

H. Practical Considerations
- Internal memos
  - o Used as a preliminary internal analysis of the strengths and weaknesses of the case
  - o Not to exceed reasonable page length
  - o Appropriate margin, font, and line-spacing adjustments
  - o Coherent overall, paragraph, and sentence structure
  - o Proofread and checked for misspelling
  - o Pertinent issues clearly identified
  - o Applicable procedural and substantive law identified
  - o Applicable law applied to specific case facts
  - o Neutral assessment as to how the pertinent issues may be resolved
  - o Appropriate substance and level of analysis for intended audience
  - o Easy to read and informative
- Demand for payment on policy (if insurance company is involved)
  - o Information disclosure
  - o Deadline for responses
  - o Negotiations
- Pleadings
  - o Summons and Complaint
    - – Short and plain statement showing pleader is entitled to the specific relief demanded
    - – Filed within statute of limitations

- Appropriate jurisdiction and venue, service of process
- Proper format, caption, acknowledgments, and signatures
- Clearly identifies the court and parties'/attorney's name and address
- States a valid cause of action, necessary elements
- Alleges facts sufficient to support prima facie claims
- Timely served on court and opposing party

o Answer and Counterclaim
  - Short and plain defenses to each claim
  - Admit/deny each allegation
  - Appropriate challenges to sufficiency of process and service of process
  - Must state if not enough information to admit/deny
  - Appropriate challenges to jurisdiction and venue
  - Appropriate challenges to stated claims
  - Proper format, caption, acknowledgments, and signatures
  - Answer raises applicable avoidance or affirmative defenses
  - Answer adequately responds to all allegations of the complaint
  - Counterclaim states a valid cause of action/necessary elements
  - Counterclaim alleges facts sufficient to support prima facie claims
  - Counterclaim clearly specifies and requests appropriate relief
  - Timely served on court and opposing party

o Reply to Counterclaim
  - Appropriate challenges to stated counterclaims
  - Proper format, caption, acknowledgments, and signatures
  - Raises applicable affirmative defenses
  - Adequately responds to all allegations of counterclaim
  - Timely served on court and opposing party

o Motions
  - Failure to state a claim upon which relief can be granted
  - Challenges to jurisdiction and venue
  - Challenges to sufficiency of process and service of process

o Pleading Deadlines

o Discovery Deadlines

o Pretrial motions
  - Dispositive
  - Nondispositive

o Pretrial settlement conference/hearing

Section 2. Negotiations

A. Negotiation Preparation
*   Preliminary Negotiation Preparation
    o   Initial client meeting—derive basic factual picture
    o   Alternate questions—open, follow-up, closed, leading, summary
    o   Convey expectations and recognition of full, relevant disclosure
    o   Anticipate and overcome etiquette barriers (e.g., talk of trauma, medical problems)
    o   Gather information—funnel, chronological order, quietly persist, prove, re-create events
    o   Review conflicts, nature/scope of representation
    o   Maintain normal client-attorney relations, if client mentally or physically disabled
    o   Decision making—lawyer-centered or collaborative
    o   Decide attorney role(s)—draftsman, agent, negotiator, advocate, spokesperson
    o   Obtain client objectives and prioritize
*   Strategy
    o   Style—working with client: directive or facilitating, broad v. narrow focus
    o   Goals—problem resolution considering any future relations
    o   Research facts and law
    o   Plan and prioritize arguments and evidentiary support
    o   Anticipate counterarguments
    o   Concessions
    o   Worst Alternative to a Negotiated Agreement (WATNA)
    o   Likely and Best Alternative to a Negotiated Agreement (LATNA, BATNA)
    o   Value of case, minimum/maximum ranges, remedies, aim high
    o   Liability, elements, special damages, insurance coverage, past verdicts
    o   Develop multiple, creative options
    o   Discuss nonlegal (psychological, social, economic, and moral) options, pros/cons
    o   Discuss legal options—best, likely, and worst consequences (percent probability of each)
    o   Set flexible time allowed for negotiation and deadline(s)
    o   Communicate logistical requirements, concerns
    o   Confer—who is permitted at negotiation?
    o   Confirm prior:
        –   authority to settle
        –   attendees
        –   agenda
        –   format

- method(s) of recordation
- publicity parameters
- confidentiality

o Inventory, classify, and compare both sides' needs, interests, and objectives

o Outline other's potential gains and losses

- Style Decision
  o Effective competitive negotiation style:
    - high opening demands
    - few concessions
    - positions related to interests
    - exaggeration
    - threats
    - aggression
  o Alternatively, effective cooperative negotiation style:
    - high opening demands
    - rational, logical persuasion
    - ours, theirs, and shared interests
    - objective criteria
    - fairness
    - trusting open exchanges
    - concessions to demonstrate good faith
    - realistic and analytical
- Negotiation Location and Arrangements
  o Make physical arrangements
  o Decide on beneficial psychological environment
  o Neutral site, or any reason to allow one party to host, advantages/disadvantages

B. The Negotiation
  - Pay attention to non-negotiation conversation
  - Establish rapport
    o Facilitate open communication to net valuable information
    o Avoid religion, politics, personal, or sensitive subjects
  - Nonverbal behaviors
    o Observe nonverbal signals
    o Gauge eye contact for honesty, confidence, effect of communication
    o Watch facial expression, posture, and gestures
    o Check for surprising nonverbals
  - Listen
    o To acquire previously undisclosed information
    o Recognize interests, needs, and fears

- o Evaluate counterpart's position
- o Actively listen, reflect, paraphrase, clarify interests and positions
- o Acknowledge hostility, blame, nondefensiveness (e.g., "I see you are upset, so what *do you feel* is a fair solution that we might accept?")
- Information Protection
  - o Judiciously use "blocking techniques" to protect sensitive information
  - o Ignore question
  - o Declare question off limits (e.g., attorney-client privilege)
  - o Answer a question with a question (evade by seeking clarification or elaboration)
  - o Under/overanswering (generally to a specific question or conversely)
  - o Answer honestly but incompletely
  - o Beneficially reframe
  - o Answer a different question than the one asked (e.g., "I understand you want to know . . .")
  - o Answer a recently asked question again
- Communication
  - o Convince opposing parties to change their resistance point by a cost-benefit summary
  - o Frame options in reference to negotiator's objectives, as gain to other
  - o Dissuade rejection, solely from "reactive devaluation" of other's offer
  - o Reasonable, analytical, realistic, and rational
- Communicating offers and concessions
  - o Briefly (to reduce counterpart's response time)
  - o Specifically address conflict areas
  - o Justify with objective reasons
  - o Clearly state solutions, remedies, damage figures
- Reacting to offers
  - o React immediately to an inadequate offer
  - o Avoid bidding against yourself—ask opposing side how much better the offer has to be
  - o React strongly to outrageous offers
  - o Remain silent as long as possible, until the other speaks
  - o State that offer appears acceptable, but final approval must be made by someone else
- Assessing negotiating competence and effectiveness
  - o Outcome measures of effectiveness
  - o Obtained profit-maximizing amount(s) and/or desired outcome in settlement
  - o Reached agreement considering all relevant information and arguments
  - o Compromised and conceded only what you had decided in advance

o New information was factored into your negotiation
o Used the probable trial outcome as a baseline for evaluation
o Accurately estimated the value of particular items to the other side
o Able to reconcile style, strategy, and acceptability of offers with your client
o Process handled cost-effectively in terms of time, energy, and money
o If applicable, preservation of relationship to facilitate compliance, long-term relations
- Post-Negotiation Self-Analysis
o Decided in advance on style and strategy, yet remained flexible
o Analyzed the other side's style and strategy and adopted accordingly
o Reassessed client's BATNA, WATNA after receiving any new information
o Accurately estimated the value of case with appropriate minimum/maximum range
o Set/accomplished goals
o Set the desired tone
o Controlled the agenda
o Received sufficient information clarification or elaboration
o Did not reveal too much
o Failed to reveal information that should have been revealed (misrepresentation /fraud)
o Kept in mind that it is always an option to walk out
o No agreement reached, was result appropriate in the context of this negotiation?
o In case of deadlock what might have been done to break the deadlock?
o Maximized a fair, reasonable settlement
o What could have been done differently in this negotiation and why?
- Visual Aids
o If an indexed settlement brochure was used, were visual aids and factual history included to bolster credence, confidence, and preparedness?
o Were visual aids used tactfully to persuade, influence, and increase understanding?
o Does the cover letter have conditions for the aid's use, provide for its return, and limit its evidentiary use?

Section 3. Mediation

A. Mediation Preparation
- Preliminary Mediation Preparation
o Initial contacts—derive basic factual picture
o Alternate questions—open, follow-up, closed, leading, summary
o Distinguish problem, positions, and interests (hidden agendas)

- o Decide style—evaluative or facilitating, broad v. narrow focus
- o Goals—problem resolution considering parties' future relationship, if any
- o Research facts and apply to pertinent law(s)
- o Plan and prioritize agenda
- o Anticipate arguments/counterarguments
- o Concessions either side may need to make and reciprocal expectations
- o Anticipate Worst Alternative to a Negotiated Agreement (WATNA)
- o Anticipate Likely and Best Alternative to a Negotiated Agreement (LATNA, BATNA)
- o Value the case, minimum/maximum ranges and creative remedies
- o Send mediator a brief
- o Expect, but do not be overly concerned over high opening demands
- o Develop many creative options
- o Set flexible time frame allowed for negotiation deadlines(s)
- o Communicate logistical requirements and concerns
- o Confer—who is permitted to attend
- o Confirm immediately prior to mediation: formal authority to settle, attendees
- Procedure
  - o Consensus on ground rules, enforcement, just and fair standards/guides
  - o Breaks, recesses, breakdowns
  - o Be concrete, but flexible
  - o Identify issues
  - o Relate positions to interests (security, recognition, control, belonging)
  - o Rational, logical persuasion
  - o Identify conflicting, shared, and compatible interests
  - o Ensure buy-in through all parties participation
  - o Acknowledge, but do not react to emotional outbursts
  - o Recast attacks on mediator as an attack on the problem
  - o Dovetail differing interests
  - o Insist on objective criteria
  - o Agreement on fair standards/procedures
  - o Expectations of fairness determined by party's perceptions
  - o Facilitate trusting, open exchanges
  - o Surrender something of value to the other side—give to get
  - o If impasse, focus on positions, emotions; data, value, or relationship conflicts—continue mediation to later date as last resort
  - o Keep caucusing as an option (straight talk to each side)
  - o Ask for concessions to demonstrate good faith—confront if none
- Mediation Location and Arrangements
  - o Make physical arrangements
  - o Decide on beneficial psychological environment

o Neutral site, or any reason to allow one party to host, advantages/disadvantages

B. The Mediation
- Pay attention to non-mediation conversation
  o Establish rapport
  o Facilitate open communication to net valuable information
  o Avoid religion, politics, food, dress, personal, or sensitive subjects
- Nonverbal behaviors
  o Observe nonverbal signals
  o Telltale mannerisms and furtive expressions (e.g., tension shown by fidgeting)
  o Gauge eye contact for honesty, confidence, effect of communication
  o Watch facial expression, posture, and gestures
  o Check for surprising nonverbals (e.g., intentional false signals, pounding desk)
  o In diverse context—careful interpretation
- Listen
  o To acquire previously undisclosed information
  o Recognize interests, needs, and fears
  o Evaluate counterpart's position by hearing others' points of view
  o Ask for preferences
  o Actively listen, reflect, paraphrase; clarify interests, positions, and arguments
  o Acknowledge hostility, blame, defensiveness (e.g., "I see you are upset")
  o Do not accept a stalemate (e.g., "So what do you feel is a fair solution that the other side might accept?")
  o Repeat opponent's proposals and concerns to clarify
- Information Protection
  o Watch for "blocking techniques" and probe for relevant hidden information
    - ignoring questions and moving to other's area of interest
    - declaring questions off limits (e.g., attorney-client privilege or other plausible reason)
    - answering a question with a question (evade by seeking clarification or elaboration)
    - under/overanswering (generally to a specific question or conversely)
    - answering honestly but incompletely
    - beneficially reframing to avoid revealing sensitive information
    - answering a different question than the one asked (e.g., "I understand you want to know . . .")
    - answering a recently asked question again
- Communication
  o Reasonable, analytical, realistic, and rational
  o Convince opposing side to change resistance by cost-benefit summary

- o Frame options as gain to other
- o Dissuade rejection from "reactive devaluation"
- Communicating offers and concessions
  - o Briefly stated (to decrease opposing party's reflection/response time)
  - o Specifically addressed to conflict areas
  - o Relay justification with objective reasons
  - o Clearly stated solutions, remedies, damage figures
  - o Cleanly end final "niggling" (just one more thing) by other
  - o Finalize bargaining
  - o In drafting agreement, obtain buy-in on the language used
- Closure
  - o Trade concessions
  - o Give up enough to settle, but not more
  - o If niggling, can agree by asking what they will give up in return
  - o Encourage movement toward closure
  - o Decide who drafts, what conditions to include, who monitors compliance
  - o Provisions for time extension, compliance standards, follow through
  - o Provide for future differences, back to mediation or arbitration?
  - o Any exceptions to confidentiality
  - o Draft formal settlement agreement and execute (sign)
  - o Drafting fees agreed upon

Section 4. Discovery

A. Discovery
  - Mandatory Disclosures
  - Interrogatories (only to opposing parties)
    - o Proper citation and form (adequately inform of information requested)
    - o Do not exceed total number allowed (twenty-five maximum absent court order or local rule)
    - o Appropriate set of reasonable instructions
    - o Appropriate definitions, if needed
    - o Reminder to opponent of duty to update answers
    - o Original questions, not copied from a book or set of forms
    - o Clear, precise, and direct questions
    - o Questions not vague, multiple, broad, or overly inclusive
    - o Focus on appropriate subject matter
    - o Comprehensive in overall scope, do not overlook important areas
    - o Narrow and clarify issues
    - o Not objectionable

- o Pin down witness statements, recollections, opinions, or contentions
- o Clarify or corroborate specific relevant facts
- o Identify undiscovered witnesses, persons, documents, or other evidence (tangible things)
- o Disprove the opponent's theory and damage/relief claims
- o Require answers that are nonevasive and complete
- o Can be used with other methods of discovery
- o Properly served on opposing party

B. Answers to Interrogatories (in writing under oath)
  - *See* Federal Rules of Civil Procedure
    - o Objections to interrogatories
    - o Failure to answer and evasive answers
    - o Proper citation and form
    - o Reasonable and rational interpretation of interrogatories
    - o Appropriate and reasonable objections with specificity, executed by attorney
    - o Appropriate, accurate, and complete answers to all interrogatories
    - o Phrase answers to present best position of client
  - Requests for production of documents
    - o Proper caption and form
    - o States time, place, and manner for production or inspection
    - o Defines documents in a broad sense, including all known media
    - o Reasonable number of requests
    - o Not objectionable, requiring reasonable compliance and disclosure
    - o Requests adequately defined, identified, or otherwise described
    - o Will produce all documents reasonably related to those requested
    - o Probes for additional sources of documents
    - o Properly served on opposing party
  - Responses to requests for production of documents
    - o Reasonable compliance with nonobjectionable requests
    - o Appropriate method of compliance
    - o Seek protective order if necessary
    - o Properly served on opposing party
  - Requests for admissions
    - o Proper caption and form
    - o Appropriate preface or instructions
    - o Appropriate definitions
    - o Short, simple, precise requests
    - o No unnecessary adjectives, adverbs, or other characterizations
    - o Singularly listed in separately numbered paragraphs
    - o Not objectionable

- o Call for unqualified responses
- o Require reasonable admittance or denial of request
- o Confirm key facts and contentions relating law to facts
- o Establish the genuineness of documents
- o Properly served on opposing party
- Responses to requests for admissions
  - o Proper caption and form
  - o Appropriate and reasonable objections
  - o Phrase answers to present best position of client
  - o Properly served on opposing party

C. Witness Depositions
- Prepare client before deposition
  - o Reduce witness's anxiety
  - o Address any new information that witness has learned
  - o Deposition procedures
  - o Different deposition styles
  - o Review documents with witness in preparation for deposition
  - o Brief witness on applicable substantive law
  - o Brief witness on privileged areas of the law
  - o Explain objectionable questions
  - o Explain that witness must respond to objectionable questions unless otherwise ordered not to respond
  - o Outline of direct and expected cross-examinations
  - o Demeanor and appearance to eventual fact finder
  - o Instruct witness not to bring anything regarding the case to the deposition
  - o Instruct witness what not to say
  - o Where and when to meet on the day of the deposition
  - o Federal Rules of Evidence that govern expert/lay person testimony
- Questioning of Witness
  - o Focus on learning witness's version of the facts
  - o Begin with open-ended questions
  - o Clarify information received
  - o Finish with closed questions suggesting answer to lock in testimony
  - o Continue a line of questioning until all information has been extracted/ exhausted
- Expert witness depositions
  - o Prepare the witness before the deposition
    - – Deposition procedures
    - – Outline of direct and expected cross-examinations
    - – Demeanor and appearance to eventual fact finder

- o Be ready to object when appropriate
- o Direct examination
    - – Identify time, place, and individuals present
    - – Qualify the witness as an expert
    - – Properly lay foundation for and introduce exhibits
    - – Elicit the basis for expert's opinion
    - – Define technical terms
    - – Establish the opinion to a reasonable degree of certainty
    - – Introduce any harmful information
- o Cross-examination
    - – Control the witness with leading questions
    - – Challenge the expert's qualifications
    - – Challenge the basis for the expert's opinions
    - – Challenge the expert's opinions
    - – Reinforce helpful information
- o Redirect
    - – Rehabilitate expert's qualifications and opinions
    - – Clarify ambiguities and misstatements
    - – Reinforce helpful information

D. Defending Depositions
- • Provide emotional comfort and support to client
- • Preserve the record for anticipatory judge and jury
- • Sit next to client
    - o Enables conferral with client
    - o Enables protection of client's interests
- • Be prepared to object when appropriate
    - o State objection for preservation
    - o Relevancy
    - o Prejudicial
    - o Hearsay
    - o Confusion of the issues
    - o Competency
    - o Question form
    - o Foundation
    - o Privilege
- • Cross-examination
    - o Clarify previous answers
    - o Clarify answers (particularly where answers are subject to more than one interpretation)

Section 5. Motions/Oral Argument

A. Briefs

- Follow rules as to format and composition
  - o Does not exceed page limits
  - o Does not use margin, font, or line spacing adjustments to meet page limit
  - o Coherent overall paragraph and sentence structure
  - o Proofread and checked for misspelling
  - o Pertinent issues clearly identified
  - o Applicable procedural and substantive law identified
  - o Applicable law applied to specific case facts
- Table of contents
  - o Clearly label all parts of brief
  - o Provide accurate page references
- Table of authorities
  - o Separate authority by category
  - o List all authorities used in alphabetical order
- Legal issues
  - o Phrase issues concisely in a way favorable to client
  - o Give the referees an answer to each issue
- Statement of the case
  - o State the procedural history of the case chronologically
  - o Provide citation to authorities, the transcript, and appendix
- Statement of facts
  - o Provide all facts necessary to support argument
  - o State facts in a neutral manner
  - o Present facts in a logical order
  - o Provide citation to the transcript and appendix
- Argument
  - o Use appropriate subheadings (point headings)
  - o Outline standard of review
  - o Address each issue separately and thoroughly
  - o Apply applicable law to specific facts
  - o Provide compelling reasons why client should prevail
- Conclusion
  - o Briefly recap reasons client should prevail
  - o Ask for appropriate relief
- Appendix
  - o Properly indexed and paginated
  - o Contains all necessary exhibits and record excerpts

B. Oral Argument
- Obey all court rules
- Proper appearance and demeanor
- Proper verbal pacing and body movement
- Properly manage allotted time
- Reserve time for rebuttal, if desired
- Be totally familiar with client's and opponent's case
- Be familiar with all authorities cited by either side
- Avoid using notes
- Attorney for plaintiff goes first
- Ask judge if she needs a recitation of the facts
- Recite facts if necessary
- Present argument in a coherent manner (attorney is to educate judge on the law)
- Concede losing arguments when appropriate
- Be prepared to answer questions from the judge
- Be honest with judge if you don't know an answer
- Ask for appropriate relief

Section 6. Trial (Court/Jury)/Arbitration

A. Trial (Court/Jury)/Arbitration
- By mutual agreement, preexisting contract, statute, or court order
- Analyze case
  - Client's strengths and weaknesses
  - Opponent's strengths and weaknesses
- Plan appropriate strategy
  - Become familiar with rules of arbitration
  - Informal or strict trial-like setting
  - Relaxed or strict evidentiary standards
  - Witness preparation
  - Opening statements and closing arguments
  - Witness examinations
  - Exhibits
- Select neutral time and location for arbitration
  - Court appointed or selected by parties' agreement
  - Experience
  - Bias
  - Acceptable time and location for all concerned
  - Appropriate scheduling and total time allocation

- o Division/payment of arbitration/trial fees and facility costs
- Witness preparation
  - o Explain arbitration/trial procedure
  - o Instruct witness to tell the truth (answer "yes" or "no," do not volunteer information)
  - o Outline of direct and expected cross-examinations
  - o Demeanor and appearance
    - – Clothing
    - – Body language
    - – Pace
    - – Tone
    - – Voice
  - o Time and place of proceeding
  - o Subpoena uncooperative witnesses, if allowed
  - o Trial/arbitration notebooks should contain:
    - – All pleadings, motions, discovery requests, and responses
    - – Applicable substantive and procedural law
    - – Trial briefs
    - – Evidentiary objections
    - – Witness statements or prior testimony
    - – Voir dire questions
    - – Outlines of direct and cross-examinations
    - – Outlines of opening and closing statements
    - – Jury instructions (when applicable)
- Statement of the case similar to trial brief, by attorneys
  - o Advocacy document designed to persuade fact finder of case
  - o Statement of the issues
  - o Statement of facts
  - o Applicable law
  - o Theory of the case
  - o Conclusion (relief requested)
  - o Exhibit list (may be separate documents)
  - o Witness list (may be separate documents)
- Joint statement of the case
  - o Often required by judge/arbitrator
  - o Establishes and narrows issues and areas of agreement and conflict
  - o Focuses the presentation
  - o May help with settlement
  - o Assists judge/arbitrator in deciding case
- Exhibits
  - o Marked as per judge's/arbitrator's procedure

- o Proper foundation
- o Accepted by judge/arbitrator
- Stipulations
  - o Negotiated between parties and accepted by judge/arbitrator
  - o Avoids argument over uncontested issues or facts
  - o Jury selection (where applicable)
- Jury Selection (procedure varies—check local court rules)
  - o Introduction (attorneys, parties, witnesses)
  - o Question jurors individually and as a panel
  - o Have a workable system for charting response (e.g., clerk labels response by juror number)
  - o Explain trial procedures
  - o Gather relevant information about jurors
  - o Educate jurors about client and theory of the case
  - o Detect favorable and unfavorable bias
  - o Challenges for cause
  - o Pass the panel for cause
  - o Peremptory challenges
- Opening statements
  - o Plaintiff/party with burden of proof goes first
  - o Appropriate appearance and demeanor
    - – Clothing
    - – Body language
    - – Pace
    - – Tone
    - – Voice
  - o Use appropriate visual aids
  - o Tell client's story
  - o Explain what will be proved
  - o Do not make promises that cannot be kept
  - o Ask for relief that client wants
  - o Avoid being argumentative
  - o Use proper verbal pacing, body motion, and eye contact
- Case-in-chief
  - o Plaintiff/party with burden of proof proceeds with its evidence first
    - – Call witnesses in strategic order
    - – Primacy and recency effects
    - – Logical order that will not be confusing
    - – Designed to provide maximum impact
  - o Direct examination
    - – Use appropriate demeanor

- Use effective structure
- Calm the nervous witness, if necessary
- Establish appropriate background information
- Establish credibility of witness
- Use appropriate leading questions (*See* FRE 611c)
- Avoid leading questions regarding important testimony
- Keep the scope of the examination focused
- Elicit all desired information from witness
- Use witness to identify and lay foundation for exhibits
- Have witness explain any harmful information

o Cross-examination
- Use appropriate demeanor
- Use effective structure
- Ask only leading questions
- Short questions
- Insist on one-word answers
- Be persistent
- Avoid arguing with the witness
- Do not ask a question if the answer is not known
- Impeach the credibility of the witness
- Undermine the witness's perception of events
- Point out inconsistencies with prior statements
- Point out inconsistencies with other witnesses testimony
- Emphasize information helpful to client

o Re-direct examination
- Limited to scope of cross-examination
- Rehabilitate the credibility of the witness
- Reestablish the witness's perception of events
- Explain any inconsistencies
- Clarify any ambiguities or misstatements
- Use sparingly, do not repeat what has been covered
- Making appropriate objections
- Listen carefully to opponent's examination
- Consider the tactical or strategic implications of objecting
- Object promptly and decisively
- Follow correct procedure
- Briefly state a valid evidentiary reason for the objection
- Be prepared to counter opposing arguments

- Expert Witnesses
  o Scope of expert examination

- Technical or other specialized knowledge of the expert will assist the fact finder in understanding evidence or in determining a fact that is in issue
  - o Who is the expert?
    - A person with specialized knowledge by education, training, experience, or skill may be qualified as an expert; professionals who have extensive formal education and training may be readily qualified, such as doctors, engineers and economists
  - o Areas of expertise
    - An area of knowledge that contains scientific, technical, or other specialized information may constitute an admissible area of expertise
  - o The law of expert testimony
    - Federal Rule of Evidence 702
    - Federal Rule of Evidence 705
    - *Daubert v. Merrell Dow Pharmaceuticals*, 509 U.S. 579 (1993)
    - *Frye v. United States*, 293 F. 1013 (D.C. Cir. 1923)
  - o Qualifying the expert
    - Expert has education, training, experience, or skill beyond general knowledge of the fact finder
    - Expert has sufficient information on which to testify in the particular case
    - Expert opinion is based on education, training, experience, and skill of the expert as applied to the information and not on unfounded speculation or conjecture

- Direct Examination (see also direct examination generally)
  - o Purpose
    - Provide fact finder with factual information
    - Apply expert knowledge to the facts and render an opinion
    - Explain scientific principles and theories
    - Explain test procedures and results
    - Explain real evidence introduced in the case
    - Interpret facts and render an opinion regarding the likelihood of an event
    - Explain the amount of recoverable damages in a civil case
    - Give an opinion that contradicts the conclusions of an expert for the opposing party
  - o Outline of expert direct examination
    - Subject matter of the opinion
    - Theories or principles that support the area of expertise and opinion
    - Sources of information relied upon by the expert
    - Standard tests or procedures used in a case
    - Other basis of the opinion of the expert
    - The opinion and conclusion
    - Explanation of the opinion and conclusion

- Identify sources of information
- Personal, firsthand information perceived prior to the trial or hearing
- Information obtained from experts, documents, records, files, witnesses, and other sources prior to or during the trial or hearing
- Evidence including testimony heard by or told to the expert during the case
- Hypothetical questions
- Cross-Examination (*see also* cross-examination generally)
  - Preparing and presenting an effective supporting and discrediting cross-examination of an expert witness that includes:
    - Categories/Factors of Expert Cross-Examination
    - Supportive Cross-Examination
- Obtain concessions
  - Criticize the other side's positions
    - Discrediting cross-examination
      - Disclose expert fees and financial interests
      - Establish bias or prejudice
      - Attack sources of information
      - Show unreliable or insufficient information
      - Dispute facts
      - Show lack of thoroughness
      - Show insufficient testing
      - Attack validity and reliability of test
      - Establish existence of other causes
      - Show inappropriate or insufficient expertise
      - Establish differences of opinion among experts
      - Establish subjective opinions
      - Introduce inconsistent prior statements
      - Discredit hypothetical questions
      - Expose other deficiencies
      - Expose unreliability of expertise
      - Use conflicting treatises
  - Responding to objections
    - Stop the testimony
    - Listen carefully to opponent's objection
    - Offer an appropriate response
    - Continue if objection is overruled
    - Try another approach if objection is sustained
  - Closing Arguments
    - Plaintiff/party with burden of proof goes last (in some jurisdictions, plaintiff argues first, then defendant, followed by plaintiff's rebuttal)

- Use proper verbal pacing, body motion/language, eye contact, tone, and voice
- Be persuasive and compelling
- Use appropriate visual aids
- Explain why the law supports the client's case
- Tell why the client should win
- Tell why the opposing client should lose
- Explain how the verdict form should be completed

o Jury instructions (where appropriate)

- Before or after closing arguments, or combination (in complex and long trials, instructions may be read during the trial)
- Listen carefully as judge instructs jury
- Ask to approach bench if judge misinstructs jury

Index

A

Absence of evidence or witnesses
    final arguments, ch2 §3.56
    opening statements, ch2 §2.47

Abuse of discretion
    appeals, standard of review, ch1 §4.30

Accuracy of record
    preparation for case, ch1 §3.62

Additur
    jury award in civil cases, ch1 §4.08

Administrative judges
    disqualification, ch1 §2.31
    forum selection, ch1 §2.23
    permitted actions, ch1 §3.48

Administrative notice
    evidence and witnesses, ch1 §3.41
    exhibits, evidentiary foundation, ch4 §4.35

Administrative proceedings
    enforcement of decisions, ch1 §4.13
    planning after case, ch1 §4.02
    scheduling of hearing, ch1 §2.27
    stages of case, ch1 §3.10

Admissions, ch1 §3.39
    exhibits, ch4 §4.17
    hearsay evidence, ch4 §3.03.6

Advisory juries
    forum selection, ch1 §2.20

Advocacy, ch1 §1.01 to 1.49
    approach to advocacy, ch1 §1.28 to 1.38
    approach to witness/bench, ch1 §3.20
    arrangement of room, ch1 §3.24
    case materials, ch1 §3.26
    characterization of advocate, ch1 §1.03
    constraints, ch1 §1.49
    convincing, ch1 §1.21 to 1.27. *See* Convincing
    counsel table, location of, ch1 §3.23
    discussions outside hearing of jury, ch1 §3.21
    enjoyment of advocacy, ch1 §1.04
    equipment available, ch1 §3.25
    familiarity, avoidance of, ch1 §3.17
    focus on decision maker, ch1 §1.28
    interruptions, avoidance of, ch1 §3.19

    matching to case, ch1 §1.30
    methods of advocacy, ch1 §1.02
    mistakes, ch1 §1.35
    names, use of appropriate, ch1 §3.18
    objective partisanship, ch1 §1.33
    ovations, ch1 §1.39 to 1.47. *See* Ovations
    personal nature, ch1 §1.32
    persuasiveness, ch1 §1.05 to 1.12. *See*
        Persuasiveness
    place for bench/sidebar conferences, ch1 §3.22
    preparation for case, ch1 §3.17 to 3.28
        approach to witness/bench, ch1 §3.20
        appropriateness of actions, ch1 §3.27
        arrangement of room, ch1 §3.24
        case materials, ch1 §3.26
        counsel table, location of, ch1 §3.23
        discussions outside hearing of jury, ch1 §3.21
        equipment available, ch1 §3.25
        familiarity, avoidance of, ch1 §3.17
        interruptions, avoidance of, ch1 §3.19
        names, use of appropriate, ch1 §3.18
        place for bench/sidebar conferences, ch1 §3.22
        requests, ch1 §3.28
    professional advocates, ch1 §1.01 to 1.04
    professional rules of conduct, ch1 §1.48. *See*
        Professional rules of conduct
    reasons to be advocate, ch1 §1.01
    requests, ch1 §3.28
    right approach to advocacy, ch1 §1.31
    storytelling, ch1 §1.13 to 1.20. *See* Storytelling
    trustworthiness, ch1 §1.34
    understanding
        clients, ch1 §1.38
        fact finder, ch1 §1.36
        witnesses, ch1 §1.37
    values of decision maker
        identification of, ch1 §1.29
        matching to case, ch1 §1.30

Affidavits
    hearsay evidence, ch4 §3.04
    motions, ch1 §3.56

Affirmation or oath
    cross-examination of witnesses, prior inconsistent
        statements, ch3 §2.65.1, 2.65.2
    direct examination of witnesses, competence, ch3
        §1.03
    selection of jury, ch5 §1.13

Alternate jurors
    selection of jury, ch5 §1.56

National Institute for Trial Advocacy

I

National Institute for Trial Advocacy

T